T0316930

The European Capital of Culture 2016 Effect

STUDIES IN EUROPEAN INTEGRATION, STATE AND SOCIETY

Edited by Magdalena Góra, Zdzisław Mach and Katarzyna Zielińska

VOLUME 9

Paweł Kubicki / Bożena Gierat-Bieroń / Joanna
Orzechowska-Wacławska

The European Capital of Culture 2016 Effect

How the ECOC Competition Changed Polish Cities

PETER LANG

Bibliographic Information published by the Deutsche Nationalbibliothek
The Deutsche Nationalbibliothek lists this publication in the Deutsche Nationalbibliografie; detailed bibliographic data is available online at http://dnb.d-nb.de.

Library of Congress Cataloging-in-Publication Data
A CIP catalog record for this book has been applied for at the Library of Congress.

This publication was financially supported by the Jagiellonian University in Kraków.

The Polish edition of the publication was financed by the Impart 2016 Festival Office as part of the research project 'ECOC Effect. In search of new urban narratives'. Translation into English financed from the funds of the 'Wrocław Culture Zone'.

Translated and Proofreaded by Ben Koschalka

First published in Polish: Zakład Wydawniczy Nomos, Kraków 2017

Printed by CPI books GmbH, Leck.

ISSN 2193-2352 · ISBN 978-3-631-81878-7 (Print)
E-ISBN 978-3-631-82415-3 (E-PDF) · E-ISBN 978-3-631-82416-0 (EPUB)
E-ISBN 978-3-631-82417-7 (MOBI) · DOI 10.3726/b17052

© Peter Lang GmbH
Internationaler Verlag der Wissenschaften
Berlin 2020
All rights reserved.

Peter Lang – Berlin · Bern · Bruxelles · New York · Oxford · Warszawa · Wien

All parts of this publication are protected by copyright. Any utilisation outside the strict limits of the copyright law, without the permission of the publisher, is forbidden and liable to prosecution. This applies in particular to reproductions, translations, microfilming, and storage and processing in electronic retrieval systems.

This publication has been peer reviewed.

www.peterlang.com

Contents

Introduction

The European Capital of Culture is one of the European Union's most important cultural programmes, its significance transcending a narrow understanding
of the cultural sphere. The scheme has been one of the foremost mechanisms
contributing to the urban revival of European cities and increasingly close
integration in many areas of social and cultural activity. For Polish cities, it has
had added importance. The bidding process for the ECOC 2016 began in 2007,
the first competition of its type in Poland. Although in 2000 Krakow held the
title of European Capital of Culture (or "City of Culture", as it was at the time), its
selection did not follow a bidding process, but a competitive selection procedure.
The ECOC competition, entered by 11 Polish cities, took place in an exceptionally favourable context. Poland had joined the European Union just a few years
earlier, its cities becoming part of a European network that led to an unprecedented cultural diffusion that helped to revive the space of Polish cities. At the
same time, they were also undergoing a sometimes very painful transformation
of their economic foundations, seeking to find a place in the new post-Fordist
reality. Among the driving forces for development in this new economic situation was culture.

What is particularly important, however, is that in Poland's case neither
cities nor their culture played a major role in shaping national cultural models.
Moreover, they experienced strong stereotypes of otherness, and were presented
as values that were not compatible with the Polish national identity. In the early
twenty-first century, in the introduction to an extensive anthology of texts on
urban art, Ewa Rewers wrote that "in this respect, Polish cities are deficient, their
urban character is unrecognised, and the consciousness of the city overlooked".[1]
The ECOC bidding process came at an opportune time, becoming an impetus
for discovering the urban nature of Polish cities and strengthening their identity.
In this case we can speak of a genuine "ECOC effect", on the one hand rousing
residents' interest in their cities, and on the other contributing to building social
capital, which made it possible to fill the "sociological vacuum"[2] that was one
of the most characteristic features of Polish cities after 1945. As a result, the

---

1   Ewa Rewers, "Wprowadzenie", in Ewa Rewers (ed.), *Miasto w sztuce – sztuka miasta*
    (Kraków: Universitas, 2010), 14.
2   Stefan Nowak, "System wartości społeczeństwa polskiego", in *Studia Socjologiczne*
    1979, no. 4.

competition became a generational event, and for some cities even a kind of origin myth – a starting point for new urban identities.

The study on the "ECOC effect" took place in 2016, with the main part – in-depth interviews – being conducted between February 2016 and August 2016. Seven of the 11 cities which participated in the bidding process – Gdańsk, Katowice, Lublin, Łódź, Poznań, Szczecin and Wrocław – were selected for the study. The research project was funded by the IMPART 2016 Festival Centre and implemented by a team of researchers from the Institute of European Studies of the Jagiellonian University in Krakow: Paweł Kubicki (head of project), Bożena Gierat-Bieroń, and Joanna Orzechowska-Wacławska. The objective of the study was to analyse and reconstruct the processes triggered by the competition in 2007–2011, and especially its long-term consequences. The key goal of the project was to determine whether the candidacy of Polish cities for the title of European Capital of Culture 2016 had resulted in any *change* – in the broadest terms – in these cities, and if so, which indicators should be used to describe and measure this change and what influence it had on the transformation of Polish cities in terms of identity, cultural policies, social activations and the creative aspirations of both artists and residents. According to the simplest dictionary definition, a *change* is "an act or process through which something becomes different",[3] as well as modification, correction, reorganisation or metamorphosis. Almost all the participants in the application process were convinced that *change* had been experienced, especially members of the teams writing programmes and preparing festivals. This was also demonstrated by commentaries as well as neutral observers of this unprecedented phenomenon. The objective of the research was therefore to test our intuitive judgements, before attempting to describe the nature of *change* and interpretations of it. The research led to the conclusions that the ECOC 2016 bidding process resulted in wide-ranging and multifaceted activation of official and independent forces triggering profound and anticipated transformation of Polish cities.

This book comprises six chapters, a summary and an appendix. The first, "The ECOC Programme and Urban Renewal", presents the idea of the programme and its history. The broader context in which the ECOC programme developed is analysed in detail. The focus in this case was processes known as urban revival, which to a great extent contributed to the development and popularity of the ECOC programme in Europe. This chapter also takes examples of

---

3 *Oxford English Dictionary*, https://en.oxforddictionaries.com/definition/change, accessed 31 July 2019.

European cities holding the title of European Capital of Culture to analyse good and bad practices in its implementation. Chapter 2, "Research Premises and Methodology", focuses entirely on methodological issues. It presents a description of the study and the research methodology, as well as discussing the research hypotheses and selection criteria used for both respondents and cities.

In the subsequent chapters, we present the results of the research. One of the major long-term consequences of the ECOC effect concerned the question of the identity of cities, and this was therefore our main focus in Chapter 3, "Identity and Urban Narratives". After joining the European Union, Polish cities became the beneficiaries of vast funds designated for improving infrastructure and quality of life. For various reasons, the previous allocation of these funds has not always translated to balanced development of cities. Whether Polish cities embark on the path to lasting development will to a large extent be determined by the strength of their identities. This is therefore why we consider this aspect to be the most significant one from the perspective of the ECOC effect. As a result of complex historical processes, Polish cities have lacked city narratives, attractive stories strengthening the emotional ties between residents and their cities. The ECOC competition became a genuine incubator of changes in this respect, "opening eyes" to cities' own resources as well as contributing to building of social capital. Chapter 4, "Cities' Cultural Policies in the Light of the ECOC Competition", focuses on analysing the changes that the bidding process triggered in the institutional sphere, the ways of managing cultural institutions and defining the role of culture in the development of contemporary cities. In Chapter 5, "Urban Networks. Coalitions of Cities", authors describe one of the most important and lasting effects of the ECOC, whereby certain cities entering the bidding process formed a *Coalition of Cities for Culture*. The process itself, which initially evoked a spirit of competition, contributed to the creation of a unique alliance of cities that survived the conclusion of the bidding and continues to promote integration and exchange of good practices. Chapter 6, "Infrastructure. New Cultural Institutions", explores the city-making role that newly established cultural institutions can play in Polish cities. This is particularly significant since in the last decade Polish cities have experienced a real investment boom in this respect. In addition, the ECOC competition stimulated the cultural aspirations of the cities' residents, as well as allowing new, participatory methods for management of such institutions to be developed. In this chapter, we use the reference points of the Spanish experiences, since it is these cities that became European symbols of how to effectively include culture in the processes of urban revival (Bilbao) as well as how misguided investments in the sphere of culture and creative industries can bring a city to the verge of bankruptcy (Valencia).

Lastly, the final chapter in the empirical section, Chapter 7, "Europeanness and the Europeanisation of Polish Cities", describes the process of implementation of the European values of professionalism of the cultural sector and international-isation of Polish cities, and illustrates the role that the ECOC competition played in this context.

The book closes with a Summary and an Appendix, which analyses the application forms submitted to the European Commission by the Polish cities that were included in the study: Gdańsk – "Freedom of Culture. Culture of Freedom", Katowice – "City of Gardens", Lublin – "City in Dialogue", Łódź – "(R)evolution of Imagination", Poznań – "Poznań Cultural Storm", Szczecin – "Power to Join", Wrocław – "Spaces for Beauty".

***

The authors of this report would like to thank all the individuals and institutions who contributed to its publication, especially the Impart 2016 Festival Office. The opportunity to participate in an enterprise that was so compelling from an academic point of view represented a great challenge. The European Capital of Culture bidding process proved to be a major impulse of multifaceted change. We feel honoured by the fact that it was a research team from the Institute of European Studies of the Jagiellonian University that was given the chance to ana-lyse the "ECOC effect" in Polish cities. All the interviews conducted within the study constituted a rich source of inspirations and reflections. The respondents' statements had a significant effect on the quality of the publications. We would like to thank all our respondents for the time they spared and our inspirational discussions on cities and urbanity in the context of the ECOC competition.

Paweł Kubicki, Bożena Gierat-Bieroń

1. The ECOC Programme and Urban Renewal

When analysing the role played by the competition for the 2016 European Capital of Culture, it is first necessary to examine the nature of the ECOC itself. The mid-1980s, when the European City of Culture programme was established,[4] marked the beginning of processes which, after the profound crisis of the 1970s, contributed to a revival of cities in the West. The crisis, manifested particularly in the economic and material sphere, also had major consequences for the identity of cities and their subjectivity. The process of deconstruction of local urban identities is a complex phenomenon, and at this time, we can only point to a few key variables that conditioned it.[5] One of the main ones was the development of modern nation states, combined with nationalisation of urban spaces and domination of symbols alluding to national ideas (monuments, street names etc.) at the cost of local symbolism. The next was the predominance of modernism as an ideology in urban planning, which considerably reduced or even rejected the historical heritage of cities created over a long duration. The modernist tendency to unify often destroyed specific local characteristics, in a sense the *genius loci*. In Europe, this process was heightened after the Second World War, when a frequent pretext for breaking with the historical heritage of cities was work to reconstruct them after wartime damage.

The end of the twentieth century brought significant changes in this respect. For various related reasons, the cities of the West were characterised by processes leading to urban renewal. According to Andrzej Majer, urban renewal is "the metaphorical name of the next stage and interpretation of a process that in fact deepens the qualitative renewal thanks to which cities, at various speeds, gain attractiveness. This is demonstrated by at least two discernible tendencies. The first is the revival in a demographic and economic sense of entire agglomerations, which previously systematically lost their population and economic base, and the second the distinct 'revival' (meaning the emergence

---

4　The scheme was initially known as "European City of Culture". For the purposes of this book, hereafter we use the name in operation since 2004, European Capital of Culture.
5　For more on this subject: Paweł Kubicki, *Wynajdywanie miejskości. Polska kwestia miejska z perspektywy długiego trwania* (Kraków: Nomos, 2016), 48–67.

of many positive changes) of central districts of cities".[6] The process of urban
revival was stimulated among others by public policies, generating favourable
conditions for the development of cities in the new post-Fordist economy. This
was also incorporated into EU policy, as expressed in the Leipzig Charter, one
of the most important documents designating the framework for development
of European cities in the twenty-first century. This document focuses in particular on improving the quality of the urban space in the context of the innovation economy. We read, for example that "the quality of public spaces, urban
man-made landscapes and architecture and urban development play an important role in the living conditions of urban populations. As soft locational factors,
they are important for attracting knowledge industry businesses, a qualified and
creative workforce and for tourism. Therefore, the interaction of architecture,
infrastructure planning and urban planning must be increased in order to create
attractive, user-oriented public spaces and achieve a high standard in terms of
the living environment, a 'Baukultur'".[7] Leaving aside a detailed analysis of urban
renewal, at this point we would just like to address the three factors connected
to this phenomenon, which made a fundamental contribution to promotion and
development of the ECOC programme.

Firstly, from the late twentieth century onwards, a post-Fordist economic
model began to develop. In the new socioeconomic reality, the so-called symbolic economy became the economic foundation of cities. According to Sharon
Zukin, this is based above all on cultural consumption of the values produced by
the city: art, fashion, music, tourism, a particular lifestyle (restaurants, clubs, and
cafés), etc.[8] So-called creative industries began to develop, with the city becoming
their "natural" space. According to Majer, the term "creative industries" itself
first appeared in in 1997 in the United Kingdom, where from the start it was
conceived in the most liberal terms, as an element of the wider cultural complex
in a knowledge-based economy. In the United States, it is most often associated
with the information technology industry, in Germany it is referred to as the
"culture economy" (*Kulturwirtschaft*), while in the Netherlands it is known as
the "copyright industry". In the UK, it has the broadest definition, identical to the
concept of "creative industry".[9] At the same time as the process of development of

6   Andrzej Majer, *Odrodzenie miast* (Łódź–Warszawa: Wydawnictwo Naukowe Scholar
    & Wydawnictwo Uniwersytetu Łódzkiego, 2014), 137.
7   *Leipzig Charter on Sustainable European Cities* 3, https://ec.europa.eu/regional_policy/
    archive/themes/urban/leipzig_charter.pdf (accessed 4 June 2019).
8   Sharon Zukin, *The Cultures of Cities* (Oxford: Blackwell, 1995), 1–49.
9   Majer, *Odrodzenie miast*, 92–110.

creative industries, the notion of the "creative city", first described by the British author Charles Landry, also gained in popularity.[10] Landry's ideas fell on fertile ground. The United Kingdom at the time was undergoing far-reaching changes, transforming its economy and culture towards the aforementioned creative industries. The "creative city" became an attractive narrative, legitimising the profound and frequently painful changes taking place in post-industrial cities. What was especially important, however, was the fact that the idea was also confirmed in reality, as an effective cure to the maladies of post-industrial cities. Even today, Glasgow and Liverpool (thanks to the ECOC programme) as well as Bilbao are cited as model examples of the success of transformation of an industrial city using culture and creative industries.[11]

An additional significant branch of the new economy was tourism, an area in which major changes also took place.[12] Once only accessible to narrow, privileged elites, tourism today is a mass phenomenon. It is becoming an important factor stimulating the contemporary economy, especially urban, due in part to the nature of modern tourism. According to Marek Kozak, following the period of the boom of 3S tourism ("sun, sand, sea"), we are currently observing a transition to a 3E variant ("education, excitement, entertainment").[13] For the contemporary tourist searching for original experiences, cities offer more attractions than isolated resorts, with their key assets including the aforementioned symbolic economy and urban heritage in the broadest terms. At present, following a period of marginalisation and sometimes even destruction, this heritage is experiencing a renaissance.[14]

Secondly, the new post-Westphalian order that is developing has a major impact on urban revival.[15] In the late twentieth century the nation state, which

---

10 Charles Landry, *The Creative City. A Tool Kit for Urban Innovators* (London: Routledge, 2008).

11 An analysis of the factors influencing the success of these cities will take place in the subsequent parts of this book.

12 John Urry, *The Tourist Gaze* (London: Sage, 1990).

13 Marek Kozak, "Metropolia jako produkt turystyczny", in Bohdan Jałowiecki (ed.), *Czy metropolia jest miastem* (Warszawa: Wydawnictwo Naukowe Scholar, 2009), 120.

14 Although we should stress that the tourism that is beginning to dominate in the space of cities also has a darker side, leading to the phenomenon of so-called "touristification". Examples in Europe are particularly Venice and Barcelona, while in the Polish context the problem is an increasing cause for concern in Krakow.

15 It is important to emphasise here, however, that conceptions from around the turn of the millennium forecasting the end of the idea of the nation state have not quite come true. The conclusions presented here, though, mostly refer to this same period, when the idea of the ECOC was being conceived.

for hundreds of years had demarcated the main frames of reference – political, cultural and economic – began to become less significant. Relations between state and city are fundamental to the further discussion. Nationalism, stimulating the development of nation states, enforced cultural homogenisation, centralisation that put curbs on autonomy, and domination of national economies. This resulted in the nationalisation of urban spaces and limitation of their subjectivity.[16]

Owing to a number of processes related to globalisation and supranational integration, cities have begun to become independent from the domination of the structures of nation states. In the now classic book *The Global City*, Saskia Sassen described the essence of the phenomenon, with global cities being the product of spatial dispersal and global integration, providing them with a new strategic role. According to Sassen, irrespective of their long tradition of functioning as international trade and banking centres, today they operate in four new ways. First, as strongly centralised command points in the organisation of the global economy. Second, as key locations for financial and specialist services companies. Third, as places of production, especially in innovative, leading production sectors. And fourth and finally, as markets for products and innovations produced.[17] The cities included in the global network of relationships have increasingly been loosening their ties with their regional and national supply base. Sassen argues that the development of global financial market stimulates the process of formation of a transnational urban system. The distinct orientation towards global markets occurring in such cities means that questions arise as to their affiliations with individual nation states, regions, and the wider economic and social structure. Cities that are strategic areas of the global economy partly break away from their region, and even state. The space created by the global network of cities, one characterised by new economic and political potentialities, is perhaps one of the most strategic spaces in the process of formation of transnational identities and communities.[18] These processes have stimulated development of so-called global cities, whose cultural organisation is linked to both local and transnational relations. According to Ulf Hannerz, four categories of people play a key role in such cities: transnational businesspeople, migrants from developing

---

16 For more on this subject see Kubicki, *Wynajdywanie miejskości*, 48–65.

17 Saskia Sassen, *The Global City* (Princeton–Oxford: Princeton University Press, 1991), 3–4.

18 Saskia Sassen, *Globalization and Its Discontents. Essays on the New Mobility of People and Money* (New York: The New Press, 1999), xxv–xxxiii.

countries, individuals specialising in the artistic sector, and tourists. The people in these categories are actively engaged in the transnational flow of culture, and characterised by a high level of mobility.[19] As a result, cities are increasing their autonomy in the cultural, economic, but also political dimension. Hannerz goes as far as to suggest that "the time for something resembling the medieval city may be here once more. The cities which in the late twentieth century we call world cities are beginning to lead lives rather distinct from those of their territorial states again".[20] The concept of new medievalism acquired a certain popularity in the late twentieth and early twenty-first centuries in the humanities as well as political and geopolitical science.[21] As a result of the processes it describes, the Westphalian order that shaped international relations in the modern era, in which the sole subject of international politics was sovereign nation states, is subject to major transformations. Some scholars, such as Benjamin Barber in his much-discussed book *If Mayors Ruled the World*, regard cities as the key actors determining the new international order.[22]

Third, urban revival is closely related to the renaissance of local identities. As a result of the transformations described above, memory and heritage of cities are starting to gain in importance. In this context, Michel Maffesoli wrote that "the great forces may confront one another in order to run the whole world or to create History; as to the city, it is content to assure its perdurability, to protect its territory, to organize itself around common myths. Myth versus History".[23] Modern nations needed history, a coherent story to legitimise the new entities. In creating a homogeneous history of the nation, it was first necessary to erase the pluralistic memory of cities and/or regions. The changing context means that it is no longer the abstract idea of nation that is an appealing level of identification, but a city or region understood as a "place", meaning "a special kind of object [. . .] a concretion of value, though not a valued thing that can be handled or carried

---

19 Ulf Hannerz, *Transnational Connections: Culture, People, Places* (London: Routledge, 1996), 129–132.

20 Ibid., 143.

21 An interesting collection of such conceptions is the publication *Miasta w nowym średniowieczu* ("Cities in the New Middle Ages"), edited by Grzegorz Lewicki: Grzegorz Lewicki (ed.), *Miasta w nowym średniowieczu*, Seria "Strategia miasta dla przyszłości wydawca" (Wrocław: Biuro festiwalowe IMPART 2016, 2016).

22 Benjamin Barber, *If Mayors Ruled the World: Dysfunctional Nations, Rising Cities* (New Haven: Yale University Press, 2013).

23 Michel Maffesoli, *The Time of the Tribes. The Decline of Individualism in Mass Society*, trans. Don Smith (London: Sage, 1996), 124.

about easily".[24] The local memory and heritage of a city have been restored in many ways. Krzysztof Kowalski notes that a moment of distinct opening to issues of heritage came in 1975, declared European Architectural Heritage Year, when the *European Charter of the Architectural Heritage* was signed in Amsterdam. Yet mass interest in heritage would only surface some time later, in the 1980s. This was also the time of emergence of a new way of experiencing, seeing, and attaching meaning to the "old stones" that filled the centres of European cities. An era of mass production of heritage dawned,[25] falling on the fertile ground of economic transformations. Culture and heritage were to be the basis for "creative industries" to grow, becoming an impetus for development, especially in the case of post-industrial cities, which in a time of painful deindustrialisation had to search for new development potential. The restoration of cities' memory and heritage also contributed to strengthening local identities and social capital. Jürg Sulzer emphasised the importance of collaboration between residents and the city as a place of memory and roots. Residents who identify with their city are more likely to participate actively in planning and shaping it. This in turn heightens the sense of belonging to a city as a place of residents. The city becomes a homeland, in the sense of *being at home* and the feeling of satisfaction. One forms an emotional connection with the district where one lives. The city as a (small) homeland is essential as a kind of counterbalance to a society in constant flux and adapting flexibly to the new global conditions. For a European city to develop in a future-oriented manner, it must be conceived as a homeland. And owing to their complicated history, European cities are perhaps predestined to offer their residents *urban homelands*.[26]

All three variables combined to ensure that the ECOC programme arrived in a receptive context, delineated by profound transformations of European cities in the economic, political and socio-cultural dimension. This was one of the reasons why the initiative was able to develop so dynamically, being treated as an important impulse stimulating the development of renascent cities. One response to the crisis and deterioration of urban heritage was the idea of establishing the European City (later Capital) of Culture, emerging at a point when Southern European countries (France, Greece, Italy) were warning of the terrible condition

---

24 Yi-Fu Tuan, *Space and Place* (Minnesota: University of Minnesota Press, 1987), 12.

25 Krzysztof Kowalski, *O istocie dziedzictwa europejskiego – rozważania* (Kraków: Międzynarodowe Centrum Kultury, 2013), 22.

26 Jürg Sulzer, "Miejskie ojczyzny – Ojczyzna Tożsamość Pamięć" in Jürg Sulzer, (ed.) *Stadtheimaten. Miejskie ojczyzny. Niemiecko – polskie punkty widzenia* (Berlin: Jovis Diskurs, 2012).

of monuments of Greek, Roman and Mediterranean culture. Ancient European cities, it turned out, were in ruin, with the national governments in question ill equipped to cover the costs of the complete renovation of the oldest sites.[27] A particularly notable case was Athens, the city in which European Community culture ministers met in 1983 and decided to set up the ECOC programme. The EEC's first initiatives in the field of culture concerned conservation of ancient monuments and sites. The large-scale revitalisation work restored the life not just of the sites in question, but also the adjacent urban areas, to which people returned to live in these spaces, as well as spending their free time there. This trend also entailed a change in thinking about heritage. According to Jacek Purchla, heritage means not only the form – to which previous thinking about protection of monuments has accustomed us – but also the function of historical sites.[28] Heritage therefore began to be important for producing attractive public places, urban recreational areas, places in which culture is connected to the contemporary need to experience, entertainment, and even consumption.

A further important factor that contributed to the beginning of work on the European Cities of Culture project was the process of popularisation of high culture observed in the continent – or, in other words, festivalisation and promotion of major artistic events. The French led the way in this respect. The Avignon Festival entered its golden age, encompassing not only theatre productions in closed rooms, but also "outside" art on the streets, inviting audiences to participate in the world of art. The Edinburgh Fringe grew in prominence, presenting alternative art on a large scale, with theatres, artists, street performers and mimes gave shows in natural settings. At the beginning of the 1980s, the towns and major cities of Europe began to live and breathe culture.

The intensification of the integration processes leading to the establishment of the European Union were also a significant factor in the foundation of the ECOC programme. Concerned that culture was not playing a significant role in these processes, and encouraged by UNESCO and the Council of Europe to promote the idea of patronage of culture, culture ministers in the European Community decided to initiate wider cooperation. The increasingly close integration process, which Europe entered in the late 1980s and early 1990s, called for new narratives

---

27 Tobias Theiler, *Political Symbolism and European Integration* (Manchester: Manchester University Press, 2005), and Evangelia Psychogiopoulou, *Integration of Cultural Consideration in European Union Law and Politics* (Boston: Martinus Nijhoff, 2008).
28 Jacek Purchla, "Dziedzictwo kulturowe", in Jerzy Hausner, Anna Karwińska, Purchla (eds), *Kultura a rozwój* (Warszawa: Narodowe Centrum Kultury, 2013).

to join it above the seemingly weakening idea of nation states. The return to the urban heritage of Europe was to provide such a narrative. "Europe is a civilisation of cities" became a common phrase used to describe the essence of the continent. And indeed, Europe as a sociocultural space emerged as a result of the cities, the development of which allowed the specific characteristics of European culture to form. Thanks to the growth of trading networks, universities, schools, companies and contacts, cities became centres of social life, as well as – importantly in the context of culture – intellectual and artistic hubs. It was from cities that the political and civilisational concepts of Europe derived, the market was formed, and financial conditions were dictated. In this context, the selection of Athens – the city-state that was the cradle of Western civilisation – as the first European City of Culture acquires symbolic importance.

Lastly, the revival of the Ministers of Culture meeting within the Council in the 1980s was a defiant response to the Anglo-Saxon model of artistic patronage. Margaret Thatcher's government in the United Kingdom had made it clear to people of culture that the time of grants had ended, and it was now necessary to "get friendly" with business.[29] There were fears about the domination of conservative tactics in Europe, which, apart from protection of national goods, had no plan for cultural revival. Over time, however, the Anglo-Saxon, neoliberal model of cultural management was becoming popular. Among the reasons for this was that in its initial phase, neoliberalism had made a significant contribution to urban renewal, with New York and London becoming symbols of this trend. Increasingly, however, culture was being used more for promotion and building a city's image than for strengthening its identity. The ECOC programme too began to evolve in the direction of festivalisation. This term was introduced to the academic discourse by Hartmut Häußermann and Walter Siebel, analysing urban development policies. Häußermann and Siebel wrote about the "policy of festivalisation" and "policy through festivals" in the context of the relations between organisation of large cultural and sporting events and the development of host cities.[30] In the first decade of the twenty-first century, the ECOC programme conceived in these terms was regarded as an effective instrument

---

29   Bożena Gierat-Bieroń, Marcin Galent, "Wielka Brytania", in Bożena Gierat-Bieroń, Krzysztof Kowalski (eds), *Europejskie modele polityki kulturalnej* (Kraków: Małopolska Szkoła Administracji Publicznej AEK, Instytut Europeistyki UJ, 2005).

30   Mateusz Błaszczak, "Zanim kurtyna pójdzie w górę. Reprodukcja miejskiego spektaklu w kontekście Europejskiej Stolicy Kultury Wrocław 2016", in Mateusz Błaszczak, Jacek Pluta (eds), *Uczestnicy. Konsumenci. Mieszkańcy. Wrocławianie i ich miasto w oglądzie socjologicznym* (Warszawa: Wydawnictwo Naukowe Scholar, 2015).

for promotion of cities. Less attention was now being given to finding a city's own resources or strengthening the local identity. As a result of this evaluation logic, tourists and "consumers" of culture were becoming more important than residents. One could say that the ECOC programme had escaped the control of the project founders, reaching areas that had not been part of the original premises of the programme. In the many years of its operation, the objectives and definitions had not changed, but the role of culture itself had. "It is hard to suggest today that these cities gain solely in terms of culture, i.e. they are known in artistic communities, recognised on the map of Europe, and play an important role in shaping culture. They also gain through culture. This means that culture is firstly confirmed and reinforced in them, and secondly – as a result of this reinforcement effect – the city evolves in a number of other areas".[31] These areas are infrastructure, urban planning, and environmental protection issues. The ECOC triggers a huge mechanism of transformations, shaping cities' material tissue as well as their sociocultural tissue. It is not only a city's functions and recognisability in Europe that have changed, but also the understanding of the role of the citizen in the process of shaping a contemporary metropolis.

---

31 Bożena Gierat-Bieroń, *Europejskie Miasto Kultury/Europejska Stolica Kultury 1985–2008* (Kraków: Instytut Dziedzictwa, NCK, 2009), 157. Another important publication describing the history of the ECOC is: Danuta Glondys, *Europejska Stolica Kultury. Miejsce kultury w polityce Unii Europejskiej* (Kraków: Attyka, 2010).

Paweł Kubicki

2. Research Premises and Methodology

The objective of the research project whose results we present in this book was to analyse the long-term changes triggered by the European Capital of Culture competition in Poland in 2007–2011, in both the sociocultural and the institutional sphere. The research premises were based upon the hypothesis that in Poland's case the process of candidacy for the title of European Capital of Culture took place in an exceptionally favourable context, stimulating major changes in many spheres of urban reality. We were able to identify three main variables that activated these changes.

The first variable entailed the transformation of cities' economic foundations. Polish cities, whose economy was determined by relationships formed in the industrial era, in the post-industrial period were forced to search for new development opportunities. In many industrial cities, the transformation period acquired the hallmarks of a painful rite of passage. Such cities found themselves in something of a void between the two periods. Industry, which had hitherto demarcated their economic foundations but also defined their identity, declined. In the post-transformation reality, industrial heritage became an unwanted legacy, perceived as anti-development ballast. Given Poland's peripheral situation, however, the economic domains characteristic of the post-Fordist economy were unable to develop fully. Only accession to the European Union, and especially the ECOC bidding process, created new opportunities for formation of a so-called symbolic economy[32]: services, creative industries in the broadest terms, tourism etc., with the potential to become new driving forces for the development of cities.

The second variable concerned the effects of joining the EU. The ECOC competition opened at a time of exceptional optimism resulting from integration with the structures of the West. Simplifying somewhat, in this context we can refer to a feeling of the end of history in the sense coined by Francis Fukuyama.[33] Furthermore, Polish cities were presented with new, previously unavailable development opportunities. Specifically, these entailed funds for developing culture and creative industries, both "hard" ones used for putting the necessary

---

32 Zukin, *The Cultures of Cities*.
33 Francis Fukuyama, *The End of History and the Last Man* (New York: Avon Books, 1992).

infrastructure in place, and "soft" ones that made it possible to implement a number of projects strengthening social and cultural capital. Membership of the EU, based on freedom of movement of people, goods, services and capital, also meant that Polish cities were incorporated in European exchange networks, and thanks to the unprecedented cultural diffusion that this engendered they were able to become spaces of social and cultural innovations.

The third variable referred to sociocultural change. On the one hand, Polish society is remarkably peasant-based.[34] On the other, though, the cultural models forming Polish national identity are founded on the values of noble culture. As a consequence, cities and their culture did not play a major role in the formation of Polish national identity. Only now is Polish society becoming an urban society, albeit not so much statistically as in social and cultural terms. Each sociocultural change demands new narratives providing new frames of reference for social actors. The ECOC bids arrived in this specific context, contributing significantly to the *invention* of the urban essence of Polish cities, as well as triggering a process of self-reflection providing new urban narratives leading to discovery and strengthening of local identities.

The methodology of our study, the techniques and research methods we employed and the sample selection were closely connected to the research problems that we set. The starting point was the assumption that the dynamic of the changes we described is affected first of all by the changing discourse, which we understand as a relationship in the sphere of government, regulating the form of speaking and thinking about a specific reality and determining "regimes of truth".[35] Discourse in these terms determines and specifies the framework and ways of perceiving reality, in this case urban reality. A key role in its formation is played by opinion leaders concentrating important symbolic resources. The initiatives they undertake result in the creation of a dominant interpretive discourse. According to Alain Touraine, this comprises a set of representations and ideas that constitute a mediating authority responsible above all for constructing an image of the whole of an individual's social life and experience, where at the intermediary level – that of ideological discourse – intellectual choices take place and conditions of communication are forged that impose the rules of the game, and afford some and not others the privilege of being listened to.[36] We identified

---

34 Jacek Wasilewski, "Społeczeństwo polskie, społeczeństwo chłopskie", in *Studia Socjologiczne* 1986, no. 3.
35 Michel Foucault, *The Archaeology of Knowledge*, trans. A. M. Sheridan (New York: Pantheon Books, 1972).
36 Alain Touraine, *Thinking Differently* (Cambridge–Malden, MA: Polity Press, 2009).

as opinion leaders the people and institutions playing a major role in the formation of new urban narratives, who become frames of reference for actions undertaken by other social actors. A key role was attributed to opinion leaders based on the assumption that in a situation of cultural change, their role is that of bearers of change, and their subjective power (alongside the subjectivity of various social groups) is the fundamental driving force of change.[37] Opinion leaders understood in this sense were recruited on the basis of two fundamental criteria, which can be defined as institutional and non-institutional.

In the first case, these are institutional actors responsible for shaping and implementing cultural policies in the various cities. We held interviews with: (a) respondents directly involved in the preparation of the ECOC applications, (b) respondents making up the bidding teams, (c) respondents responsible for cultural policies in the various cities, not necessarily involved in the ECOC bidding process; these were mostly local government officials responsible for the cultural sphere as well as employees of local government cultural institutions. In the second case, they were the leaders of local urban movements, local media journalists and bloggers. The division presented here should only be regarded in terms of Weberian ideal types permitting an analytical classification of the phenomena. In practice, the two categories often overlapped.

For the requirements of the project, we adopted a method of qualitative research using the techniques of in-depth narrative interviews, participant observations and secondary data analysis, in this case mainly involving the cities' bids. The in-depth narrative interviews employed during the study makes it possible to pick up the important topics in the course of the interview/discussion and ask additional questions. Such interviews allow the respondent to speak freely, referring to all the themes covered in the questionnaire. They also have the important merit of providing a comprehensive overview of the phenomenon in question by testing respondents' attitudes and behaviours in their natural environment, in this case in the specific city. Analysis of the institutional and sociocultural changes in the various cities entailed the need to emphasise the role of participant observation – a technique applied during stays in the research field. This made it possible to verify the information obtained from respondents during the interviews, as well as permitting a more critical approach to analysis of secondary sources. The information collected during problem-based in-depth interviews are often marked by the respondents' biographical experiences, including their worldview, emotional states, available knowledge and ability

---

37 Piotr Sztompka, *Socjologia. Analiza społeczeństwa* (Kraków: Znak, 2005).

to process it. By using participant observation as well as analysis of secondary data documents, it is possible to examine them critically. Participant observation also permits analysis of one of the key variables in the research project, i.e. testing actual (not declared) participation in the city's social and cultural life. By applying various research techniques and working as a team, we were able to triangulate the results as a control of the research material.

We selected for the study seven of the 11 candidate cities competing to be named the ECOC: Gdańsk, Katowice, Lublin, Łódź, Poznań, Szczecin and Wrocław. There was an important reason for the decision to conduct research in selected cities, and not all of those entering the competition. With the 11 cities differing in many aspects, a comparative method would be hard to employ, ultimately meaning that the findings from the study would be more descriptive. Selection of a specific number of cities enabled the use of a multidimensional comparative method, allowing us to observe and explain the significant regularities. For this reason too, four main variables were used to select the cities.

Firstly, the cities were chosen in a way that meant they could be divided into two quite arbitrary groups. On the one hand, such cities as Gdańsk, Poznań and Wrocław had, in the dominant post-transformation discourse, been presented as cities of success which had relatively painlessly passed through the period of system transformation, and, making use of their assets, become beneficiaries of this transformation and European integration. On the other hand, cities such as Lublin, Łódź, Katowice and Szczecin were depicted as peripheral towns, struggling with an economic and sociocultural crisis. The second variable concerned the origins of the ECOC applications. In this case, we were faced with either a bottom-up social movement, as in the case of Szczecin or Łódź, or an initiative coming from the local authorities, as in Poznań or Wrocław. The third variable was to do with the role of the local government and its support for the bid: from full support and making it a strategic priority for the city (e.g. Lublin, Katowice, Wrocław) to moderate backing, the minimum needed for the bidding procedures (e.g. Szczecin, Poznań). Finally, the fourth variable classified the cities into those whose ECOC application was presented as a success in the public discourse (e.g. Lublin, Katowice) and those where the competition was presented as a failure (e.g. Szczecin, Poznań).

The field research lasted from February to August 2016. A total of 60 in-depth interviews were carried out. The interviews quoted in the report have been coded as follows. The first two letters indicate the name of the city where the interview took place, and the digits are ordinal numbers. In this case, "GD" means Gdańsk, "KA" Katowice, "LU" Lublin, "ŁÓ" Łódź, "PO" Poznań, "WR" Wrocław, and "SZ" Szczecin. The interviews were conducted by Paweł Kubicki (40): GD01-04,

KA01-04, LU01-05, ŁÓ01-05, PO01-08, WR01-06, SZ01-08, and Bożena Gierat-Bieroń (20): GD05-08, KA05-08, LU06-08, ŁÓ06-08, and WR07-012.

The aim of the in-depth interview questionnaire was to observe two fundamental research problems: changes in the institutional dimension and changes in the sociocultural sphere. In terms of the institutional dimension, the questions mostly concerned issues of local cultural policies in the various cities. On the one hand, the questions were designed to analyse the impact of the ECOC candidacy process on the formation of local cultural policies, streamlining of the decision-making process, and increase in participatory practices. On the other, the questionnaire was also supposed to deliver views on the operation of newly established cultural institutions, as well as to analyse the role they play in the city-making process. Since the matter of changes in the sociocultural sphere is manifested in several dimensions, more space was given over to it in the questionnaire. The questions that were asked largely concerned the broad subject of the city's identity. Bearing in mind the specific nature of the Polish context, the questions mostly addressed the following issues: reconstruction of the social memory of the city, strengthening social capitals and creating new urban narratives influencing changes to the city's image, both among residents and externally. A separate set of questions referred to the issue of networking of cities, associated with the idea of the Coalition of Cities. This coalition (more on which in the text), a kind of alliance among the Polish cities competing for the title of European Capital of Culture, which decided to collaborate after completion of the bidding process, proved to be one of the most lasting effects of the ECOC. In this case, the questions were on the structure and scope of the actions of the nascent Coalition of Cities as well as the role it might play in future.

The comprehensive analysis of the phenomenon of the ECOC effect was complemented by the Appendix, comprising symbolic portraits of the Polish cities aspiring to the title of ECOC. This section includes an examination of the application forms of the Polish cities competing for the title. We were thus able to show the scale of the candidates' ambitions, the diversity and legitimacy of their proposed changes in urban policy, and the capacity of these projects to apply two important criteria of the EU application process: Europeanness, as well as the city and citizens. Examining the content of the application forms and careful interdisciplinary analysis of them established a substantive foundation for discussions with the respondents. Confronting the theory with the practice helped to quickly identify the main topics and recognise secondary phenomena, which in many cases played a significant role.

Paweł Kubicki

3. Identity and Urban Narratives

Given the context outlined in the first part, which determines the developmental framework of contemporary cities, identity of a city acquires particular significance, becoming a valuable resource that has an impact on its effective development. This context is conveyed well by the words of Józef Rykwert, who writes that "a city's success cannot be measured in terms of economic development and participation in markets, or even placement in the globalisation process, a phenomenon of our times from which there is no escape. This success depends on the internal strength of the tissue of the city as well as its accessibility to the social forces that shape the lives of its residents".[38] This tendency is particularly visible if we look at the number of publications on the question of identity of a place. In a survey of electronic databases, Maria Lewicka noted that as many as 60 % of all the articles concerning place were written between 2000 and 2010.[39]

In order to further analyse this question of identity, we first need to clarify the meaning of the term "identity of a city". A city is too complex an organism to have an unequivocal identity attributed to it. Ewa Rewers brought attention to this fact, writing that the concept of cultural identity viewed in a traditional sense, i.e. based upon traditional notions of culture, presenting individual cultures also as single, isolated islands, almost always collapses in confrontation with the identities of specific cities.[40] Additionally, a city is not an anthropomorphic entity characterised by some form of reflective self-consciousness. If we are therefore to continue to speak about a city's identity, we first need to focus on the social actors whose actions produce its sociocultural tissue. In order to do this, however, they first need frames of reference – in this case urban narratives that create a symbolic picture of the world and give meaning to such actions. Second, social capital making community activities possible is also essential. Third and finally, memory plays an important role, allowing residents to find roots in the

38 Józef Rykwert, *Pokusa miejsca. Przeszłość i przyszłość miast* (Kraków: International Cultural Centre, 2013), 26–27.

39 Maria Lewicka, *Psychologia miejsca* (Warszawa: Wydawnictwo Naukowe Scholar, 2012), 21.

40 Ewa Rewers, *Post-polis. Wstęp do filozofii Ponowoczesnego miasta* (Kraków: Universitas, 2005), 300.

city and to think of it as a phenomenon created by successive generations – both those that came before and those yet to come.

Identity in this sense is becoming a valuable resource with an impact on the so-called "sustainable" (lasting, balanced) development of cities. This model of development assumes respect for the environment and thinking about future generations, which is only possible in cities with a strong identity. If this is missing, then the best-case scenario is imitative modernisation, and the extreme situation is overexploitation, in which market forces lacking in public and social control are geared towards short-term profit, contributing to the destruction of local resources, especially those that are difficult to recreate: spatial order and the natural environment. After accession to the EU, Polish cities received an enormous injection of funds for improving infrastructure and quality of life. For various reasons, their previous exploitation has not always translated into sustainable development of cities. As a result, as we wrote in the introduction, the question of whether Polish cities will embark on the path of lasting development will to a great extent depend on the strength of their identity. This is also why we consider this aspect to be the most important one from the perspective of the ECOC effect. Complex historical processes have left Polish cities bereft of urban narratives and attractive stories to strengthen the emotional ties between the residents and their cities. Intensive local government activity in marketing and promotion does not fill this gap.

Furthermore, marketing slogans copied from fashionable handbooks have often been entirely detached from cities' local characteristics and heritage; the standard example of this being the aforementioned hackneyed idea of the creative city. In many cases, marketing and promotion have been equated with a city's development. Unfortunately, the buzzwords such as "city culture" or "city identity" utilised in such promotion strategies frequently have little in common with what the actual essence of this culture or identity is. Mihalis Kavaratzis and Greg Ashworth call such actions the "hijacking" of culture by image-based policies.[41] Excessive use of the "city's identity" for promotional activities can in fact result in erosion of the actual identity. Maria Hilber and Götz Datko wrote in this context that "a city's identity and urban marketing – this is a clash of at first glance two entirely different worlds: identity is about the spirit, about the idea, the soul of a city, and in marketing about a visual manifestation, a *product*

---

41 Mihalis Kavaratzis, Greg Ashworth, "Hijacking Culture: The Disconnection Between Place Culture and Place Brands", *The Town Planning Review* 2015, vol. 86, no. 2, 155–176.

to sell".[42] Local government officials – and not only in Poland – used the concept of "identity" mostly in terms of a product for sale. Cities' social and cultural policies were subordinated to the logic of marketing and thinking in terms of corporate rankings. It was believed that the façade of a city brand constructed from advertising slogans could conceal the true city with all its complexity and problems. Operations of this kind were not conducive to discovering local identities and mobilising residents to participate. On the contrary, they were more likely to contribute to alienation and to generate social conflicts.[43] Jerzy Hausner highlighted this problem in the context of development of cities, noting that the influence of culture on territorial development (e.g. of the voivodeship or city) should not be reduced to a question of promotion and external attractiveness, i.e. to a matter of attracting investors, tourist capital or new residents. It is much more important to discern its importance for a city to discover, exploit, valorise and increase its own resources. The main criterion of development is not the level or dynamic of the pillars of GDP growth, but quality of life in the broadest terms.[44] The relationship between marketing and the identity of a city began to change markedly from the time of the ECOC bidding process.

In Poland, the ECOC competition played an important role – for some cities, indeed, a crucial one – in shaping local identities and social capital. In this regard, we can speak of major and lasting changes that contributed significantly to strengthening urbanity. In order to fully grasp the role that the process played in building the identity of Polish cities it is necessary to reconstruct the broader context. Based on the simple premise that social change is the difference between the condition of a social system at one point in time and the condition of the same system at another point in time,[45] to analyse the sociocultural changes resulting from the ECOC bidding process it is necessary first to consider the position of urbanity in the Polish values system.

42 Maria L. Hilber, Götz Datko, "Jak sprzedaje się duszę miasta", in Sulzer, *Stadtheimaten*, 28.
43 Przemysław Filar, Paweł Kubicki, "Podsumowanie", in Przemysław Filar, Paweł Kubicki (eds), *Miasto w działaniu* (Warszawa: Instytut Obywatelski, 2012), 214–126.
44 Jerzy Hausner, "Kultura i polityka rozwoju", in Jerzy Hausner, Anna Karwińska, Jacek Purchla, *Kultura a rozwój*, 101–102.
45 Piotr Sztompka, *Socjologia zmian społecznych* (Kraków: Znak, 2006).

The foreignness of cities as longue-durée heritage[46]

The notion of the city as a foreign, outside entity is one of the most durable stereo-types functioning in Polish culture. The belief that cities and urbanity are alien values to the Polish cultural model has been shaped over centuries, but became particularly consolidated at the time of the Partitions. Two main factors contrib-uted to this trend. The first was the process of formation of a national identity within an ethnic model in which Polishness was almost exclusively described from the perspective of noble culture and peasant folklore, and the idea of the city was presented in terms of foreign values threatening the homogeneous ethnic culture. The second factor was the growth in colonial relations, which meant that urban culture (the centre) was treated as a threat to the periphery that the Polish lands became during the Partitions. This was the reason for the growing resentment towards the more modern, bourgeois West, as Poles took refuge in the Arcadian myths of noble country manors and idealised rural life.

The origins of the stereotype of the foreign character of the city and urbanity in Polish culture can be found in early medieval times. The granting of city rights on the basis of German law was typically colonial in nature, bringing standards of civilisation perceived as culturally alien and imposed from the outside. This impression led to the belief, as Norman Davies put it, that "Cities have never been particularly prominent in Polish civilization. Their origins in the Middle Ages had such strong German connections that for long historians considered them to be mere colonial excrescences on the essentially rural Polish scene".[47] The stereotype of the city as a "colonial excrescence" was preserved for centuries, with Poland's peculiar semi-peripheral location helping to strengthen the ste-reotype. In Western Europe, where peasants gained personal freedom relatively early, migration to the cities tended to be a local matter: it was the inhabitants of nearby villages who migrated to cities, in time becoming fully fledged citizens. Such migration looked different in the European peripheries.[48] This problem, characteristic of the first stages of urban colonisation, was reinforced further as a result of the actions of the local nobility. Concerned with developing an

---

46 A detailed analysis of this process was conducted in Paweł Kubicki's book *Wynajdywanie miejskości*, 168–224. This subchapter refers directly to the arguments made there.
47 Norman Davies, *God's Playground. A History of Poland*, vol. 1 (Oxford: Oxford University Press, 2005), 225.
48 Maria Bogucka, Henryk Samsonowicz, *Dzieje miast i mieszczaństwa w Polsce przedrozbiorowej* (Wrocław–Warszawa–Kraków–Gdańsk–Łódź: Ossolineum, 1986), 497.

agriculture-based economy, in the late fourteenth century they brought about the introduction of so-called second serfdom. One of the consequences of this state of affairs was a restriction of migration movements to the cities from the immediate ethnic hinterland. As a result, Polish cities developed thanks to the influx of residents recruited mostly from groups which seemed ethnically and religiously foreign in comparison to the indigenous nobility and peasantry. This particularly applied to the most important group in the cities, the bourgeoisie, who had to compete for their position and privileges with the ethnically homogeneous nobility. In this case, the class conflict concerning competition for the key economic and political resources also overlapped with and intensified the ethnic and/or religious conflict. The nobility, united by the so-called Sarmatian ideology, forced burghers into the deep peripheries, in the political, economic, and sociocultural dimension. Historians have summarised the resulting situation as follows: "Feudalisation of large cities and agrarianisation of small and medium towns – these are the characteristic features of the urbanisation of the Polish Republic in the sixteenth and seventeenth centuries".[49]

The belief that cities and the urban way of life were outside, foreign phenomena was further reinforced by the experience of the Partitions,[50] which resulted in increased resentment to the bourgeois West. The values identified with the bourgeois culture of Western Europe were treated as alien and a threat to the native ethnic culture, the designate of which became the noble manor and village. The main reason for this was that the vast majority of the Polish intelligentsia shaping the public discourse of the period came from the pauperised nobility. As a result of social, political and economic transformations, they were forced to migrate to the cities. Yet this was a unique type of migration that Józef Chałasiński described as follows: "the Polish intelligentsia was formed from the Polish nobility in the process of its economic, social and political degradation. The emigration of the landed nobility to the cities was not an acquisitive type of emigration; it was not an acquisitive expansion, but an escape from social and cultural bankruptcy".[51] As a result of this type of migration process, the intelligentsia of noble origin felt like outsiders in the cities, which they viewed as a short-term, unwanted haven. The reaction to this situation was an escape to a

49 Jerzy Jedlicki, *Jakiej cywilizacji Polacy potrzebują. Studia z dziejów idei i wyobraźni XIX wieku* (Warszawa: W.A.B., 2002), 37–38.

50 Józef Chałasiński, *Przeszłość i przyszłość inteligencji polskiej* (Warszawa: Świat Książki, 1997), 58.

51 Elżbieta Rybicka, *Modernizowanie miasta. Zarys problematyki urbanistycznej w nowoczesnej literaturze polskiej* (Kraków: Universitas, 2003), 41.

sentimental paradise lost – the Polish noble manors. So the Polish intelligentsia looked at the cities from a rural perspective. Elżbieta Rybicka analyses Polish literature on cities, noting that in the eighteenth and nineteenth centuries urban issues essentially did not arise on their own terms. The city was perceived mainly from the perspective of the countryside, and this was what imposed the point of view and axiological characterisation in which the urban sphere of values did not function independently, but as a subordinated and negatively valorised element of the opposition. The city vs. country dichotomy of course meant not only spatial opposition, but also the conflict of two diametrically opposed styles of values: foreignness and own-ness, civilisation and nature, modernisation and tradition.[52] The literature of the period made a particular contribution to forming negative stereotypes referring to bourgeois professions, usually describing them in derisive fashion. This is significant because the nineteenth century represented the triumph of the bourgeois novel, in which the main character became the city and its residents. Such novels shaped the collective imaginary, creating urban narratives and myths and thereby providing frames of reference for the developing collective identities. In this period: "bourgeois Europe began to acquire a taste for the charm of urban life, aided by the romantic frisson of emotion emanating from the pages of Sue's *The Mysteries of Paris*, Flaubert's realistic morality plays, or especially popular novel-sagas in the style of Galsworthy. The sentimental vulnerability and sensitivity to social injustice of Dickens or the moral message of *Père Goriot* were now slightly outdated, and the huge behemoth-city finally seemed to have become domesticated".[53] It was an entirely different story with Poland. There were scant eulogies to the city in nineteenth-century literature, with certain exceptions (Bolesław Prus's *The Doll*). Moreover, it was literature and poetry that made a fundamental contribution to establishing the foreign nature of the city in the Polish national discourse. Later years did little to change this situation.

A crucial development in the identity of cities in Poland, however, would come with the Second World War and its consequences. Polish society suffered enormous losses during the war, and it was particularly the population of cities and towns that was affected. Poland, which for centuries had endured a

---

52 Andrzej Majer, *Socjologia i przestrzeń miejska* (Warszawa: Wydawnictwo Naukowe PWN, 2010), 131.

53 In 1947 the Wartime Losses Office estimated that of the 6 million Polish citizens who died in 1939–1945, residents of cities comprised 78.9 %, i.e. 4.76 million. See Tomasz Szarota, *Osadnictwo miejskie na Dolnym Śląsku w latach 1945–1948* (Wrocław–Warszawa–Kraków: Zakład Narodowy im. Ossolińskich, 1969), 78.

deficit in urban population, was struck by hit hard by the catastrophic events. Andrzej Leder goes as far as to describe the effects of the Second World War as revolutionary, writing that "the consequence of two key moments of Polish revolution – the slaughter of the Jewish bourgeoisie during the German Nazi occupation and Stalinist communism's destruction of the dominant position of the clerical, military and intellectual elites of noble origin – was production of a vast space for promotion violently occupied by those who were willing to accept Soviet political domination".[54] The mere fact that they lived in a city did not turn the new settlers into urban citizens helping to create the city's identity. Owing to the singular process of migration to the cities resulting from industrialisation and the simultaneous lack of urban foundations, towards the end of the communist period Jan Turowski noted in reference to the Polish urban question that the country was "a country of accelerated industrialisation and delayed urbanisation".[55] The rural migrants arriving en masse in industrial cities seldom identified with the city as a whole, and the result was the phenomenon of ruralisation, meaning "the process of transferring rural values and lifestyles to the urban space as an outcome of mass migration from the countryside to the cities coupled with a lack/weakness of social institutions precluding socialisation to the urban lifestyle and values of urban culture".[56] Added to this came the factor of the cultural foreignness of cities, which was especially strong in urban areas previously inhabited by a German and Jewish population, where the "unwanted cities" syndrome lingered for a long time.[57]

The next factor that influenced the question of cities' identity after the Second World War concerned their reconstruction and urban planning principles. On the one hand, the reconstruction itself – or construction from scratch in the case of the new town of Nowa Huta – strengthened identification with the cities. Yet this applied only to those groups that were directly involved in this rebuilding. On the other hand, the post-reconstruction of cities was guided by ideological premises. One of the main objectives of the new authorities was to erase the bourgeois, multicultural memory of the cities, and the shining light of modernism provided a perfect fit. As Maria Lewicka notes, modernism as an ideology

---

54 Andrzej Leder, *Prześniona rewolucja. Ćwiczenia z logiki historycznej* (Warszawa: Wydawnictwo Krytyki Politycznej, 2014), 36.

55 Jan Turowski, "Model urbanizacji a problemy rozwoju małych miast", in *Studia Socjologiczne* 1988, no. 3, s. 200–2011.

56 Kubicki, *Wynajdywanie miejskości*, 206.

57 Zdzisław Mach, *Niechciane miasta. Migracja i tożsamość społeczna* (Kraków: Universitas, 1998).

of urban planning turned its back on the city's tradition and history, and in places with totalitarian designs, as in the countries of the Soviet bloc, meticulously removed any historical relics that might recall the bourgeois nature of the pre-war city.[58] Cities with an amputated memory did not create attractive narratives on which to build local identities. On the contrary, they made the alienation and foreignness of the city even stronger. They also lost what was the foundation of the development of urban identities – diversity and pluralism. According to Zygmunt Bauman, the planners of modern cities assumed (usually tacitly) that human behaviours mirror their surroundings. If streets and houses are arranged in a regular pattern, the desires and actions of residents will also be regular. So, by simply cleansing the city of everything accidental and unplanned, one could prevent the people from acting in an unruly, whimsical and unpredictable fashion. For the prophets of utopia, therefore, urban planning meant declaring war on external, alien influences – and in particular, the lack of specificity and definition that rendered other people – fellow residents of the city – foreign. The outsider was an enemy of uniformity and monotony, indispensable conditions of order, and the leitmotif of the urban utopia (that of the perfect society, achieved through perfect planning of cities) was eradication of all outside influences, including outsiders themselves.[59] The anonymity and monoculturalism of cities was created in the name of functionality, one of the leading principles of modernism. Bohdan Jałowiecki and Marek S. Szczepański noted in this context that modernism as functionality reduced the city to the concept of a rational machine concentrating two types of housing: individual houses for a small number of wealthy families and gigantic housing blocks, so-called living machines, for the masses. The city machines had to function effectively, which was why for the sake of functionality it was necessary to demolish the old, dysfunctional districts, leaving behind only the most important monuments of the past.[60]

As a result of the factors described above, the new residents of cities sought legitimation for their new identities mostly in the crystallising idea of the nation state and family ties, rather than in the cities where they lived. Consequently, Polish cities were home not to an integrated urban society, but to a so-called

---

58 Lewicka, *Psychologia miejsca*, 428.

59 Zygmunt Bauman, "Wśród nas, nieznajomych – czyli o obcych w (po)nowoczesnym mieście", in *Pisanie miasta Czytanie miasta*, Anna Zeidler-Janiszewska (ed.) (Poznań: Studia Kulturoznawcze, vol. 9, 1997).

60 Bohdan Jałowiecki, Marek S. Szczepański, *Miasto i przestrzeń w perspektywie socjologicznej* (Warszawa: Wydawnictwo Naukowe Scholar, 2002), 139–143.

sociological vacuum.[61] In this vacuum, the only levels of identification were family in a narrow sense and the nation, understood as an imagined symbolic community; the city, meanwhile, remained an alien or at best indifferent space. The sociological vacuum did not vanish with the transformation of the political and economic system in 1989. In fact, a number of factors led to its continued growth. The syndrome of trauma from a major change and its consequences have been well documented.[62] At this point, let us concentrate on one mechanism that is important for the further discussion. The lack of emotional ties with cities, coupled with the noble-peasant cultural model, initiated a process of mass sub-urbanisation. The nascent Polish middle class, from which a native bourgeoisie could potentially emerge as the avant-garde of civic attitudes, found itself outside of the cities. This is significant because as a result of such processes there was increasing acceptance of the privatisation of public spaces, mass development of gated communities and shopping malls, which did not help to strengthen the social capital and identity of cities in the slightest.

The ECOC competition as a generational experience

In order to describe the role that the ECOC competition played in shaping cities' identity, we should first examine the nature of the teams responsible for compiling the bids. The way these teams were organised and located in the structure was largely determined by the ECOC effect. Each of the cities appointed the team to put their bid together from outside of official structures such as the municipal council or local government cultural institutions. In general, task forces were appointed immediately with the objective of preparing the application. An exception was Poznań, where compiling the bid was entrusted to an external public relations company. This structural situation of the ECOC teams was particularly significant in stimulating changes in the sociocultural sphere.

As a result of moving the teams preparing the ECOC applications outside of official structures, in some respects, their attachment to the structure can be described as the sphere of "communitas", in the sense of the term defined by Victor Turner. According to Turner, such examples of communitas are characterised by constituting a kind of interstice in the system in which experiments concerning norms and values are permissible, since the pressure of the main structures is

61   Stefan Nowak, "System wartości społeczeństwa polskiego", in *Studia Socjologiczne* 1979, no. 4.
62   See: Piotr Sztompka, *Trauma wielkiej zmiany. Społeczne skutki transformacji* (Warszawa: Instytut Studiów Politycznych PAN, 2000).

weaker and all deviations from the mainstream are treated as "play",[63] unthreatening to the overarching structure. This characteristic of the ECOC teams is illustrated by these quotations from respondents:

> The strength of the ECOC lay in the people from the ECOC office – fresh, young graduates of various degree programmes who saw the sense in it and were able to make something out of nothing, and that was the greatest value of the ECOC initiatives. (KA04)
> There was a moment when we were prepared for a qualitative leap, so those efforts set that leap off, and that all took place at the time when I was writing the application, when the budgets for culture increased and lots of people got involved. So the main stage, or even success of the ECOC came before 2016. (LU06)

The communitas, subject to less pressure from the dominant structures, constitutes a space in which cultural change can take place, since it is in these "interstices" that the new discourse and new narratives essential for such change are formed. Turner described this sphere, writing: "when we consider cultural institutions we have to look in the interstices, niches, intervals, and on the peripheries of the social structure to find even a grudging cultural recognition of this primordial human modality of relationship. On the other hand, in times of drastic and sustained social change, it is communitas which often appears to be central and structure which constitutes the 'square' or 'straight' periphery".[64] In the case of Polish cities, cultural change was taking place at the same time as the ECOC bidding process. An array of processes, such as EU accession, transformation of the economic foundations towards a post-Fordist economy, forming of a new bourgeoisie and development of urban movements, evoked major changes in the sociocultural space of Polish cities.[65] The problem, however, is that historical events had resulted in a dearth of narratives that could be used to legitimise this change. In this case, the ECOC applications became a major impetus for change. The huge social mobilisation that the competition brought about demonstrated to both residents and decision makers what an important role for a city's development could be played by its identity and culture:

> I remember the mayor's press conference after it turned out that we'd lost, the mayor was sad when he arrived, but said that thanks to our efforts he had realised how important culture is. He's a good economist, a good steward. (LU01)

---

63 Victor Turner, *Dramas, Fields, and Metaphors: Symbolic Action in Human Society* (Ithaca–London: Cornell University Press, 1974), 268.
64 Ibid.
65 Paweł Kubicki, "Nowi mieszczanie – nowi aktorzy na miejskiej scenie", in *Przegląd Socjologiczny* 2011, vol. LX/2-3 2011.

Therefore, as we shall see in the next section, the sphere of urban culture operating in the margins had the opportunity to shift towards the centre, with a significant effect on shaping the public discourse. The new urban narratives created
in the communitas niches were able to become frames of reference for the city
residents, thereby intensifying the processes of the cities' identity formation.
The location of the bid teams in the sphere of communitas was also important
in terms of the nature of the social ties created during the ECOC competition.
The bidding process released the social connections characteristic of generational experience, in the sense of a generation as a community of people who
have gone through the same, important historical occurrences, experienced the
same situations, and reacted to the same events.[66] The common generational
experience for the majority of respondents became the process of discovering
the identity of their cities and forming a sense of subjectivity in relation to urban
policies. This process is illustrated by the below response:

> As new communities were formed, that also led to processes of identity being declared, that
> these communities of young people knew how to define themselves, what to call themselves,
> what they wanted (. . .). I was surprised – and this was the most important thing in my
> view – that this city operating slightly on the edge, which doesn't really exist in Polish cul-
> ture, and not at all in European culture, that suddenly the artistic communities of the city
> were starting to demonstrate such dynamism and potential. (LU04)

The social ties established as a result of the generational experience have the
characteristic of being able to join together various social actors and various
communities that in other conditions would not have the opportunity to collaborate. This process was observed in all of the cities we studied. Quotations from
the responses from Gdańsk and Katowice serve as good examples:

> It was this moment of starting up a kind of common movement, that this was an emotional
> issue, for many artists, cultural organisers or politicians in the city. (GD02)
> It was an explosion of activity of very diverse people. There were members of NGOs, students,
> PhD candidates, various other organisations, entities, institutions. Everybody reacted very
> strongly and joined in. There was an eruption of something that had been slumbering very
> deep. Suddenly it turned out it was possible. Suddenly you could do everything everywhere!
> All spaces were available. . . So the sense of the initiatives was tremendous. (KA07)

For a long time, the various milieus dealing with diverse forms of culture –
clerical, institutional, activist, alternative and fringe – operated alongside one
another, since there was no shared space to unite them. This lack of contacts
encouraged the formation and consolidation of mutual stereotypes. The

---

66 Piotr Sztompka, *Socjologia. Analiza społeczeństwa* (Kraków: Znak, 2005).

individual groups concentrated more on reinforcing symbolic boundaries than building bridges permitting collaboration. By freeing generational ties, the ECOC completion made a substantial contribution to the blurring of symbolic boundaries and stereotypes, as well as to "opening up entry thresholds". Among the major problems with an impact on innovativeness and creativity, especially in the sphere of institutionalised culture, are so-called gatekeepers – who block the inflow of new, nonconformist (creative) individuals. Owing to the situation of the ECOC teams in the communitas sphere as well as to the nature of the generational ties, the role of traditional gatekeepers was considerably reduced. As a result, the ECOC teams attracted creative individuals from areas of life that for various reasons had hitherto been outside of the institutional circulation of urban culture. By appealing to dynamic and creative people, these teams proved to be open and creative institutions, enabling new urban narratives to be formed. This question will be discussed in detail in the next section. Just as an example, let us illustrate it with a few characteristic statements from respondents:

> There was this team of researchers there, kind of half-public, half-institutional, and it wasn't quite clear whether they were full-time or contractors, and they formed a kind of core. They processed an incredible number of ideas that came in from the public, it was a few hundred ideas. They combined it into one whole, and in my opinion that was the most interesting thing, behind that there was real energy of people. That was an absolutely unifying idea. (LU03)
> But in a certain sense it was a sort of turning point, because there'd never been anything like that in Szczecin, there was no institution based on the activity of people who are not employed professionally in cultural institutions, but here you could really come and have a chat and put these micro grants into practice. (SZ03)
> Gdańsk really went for a big kind of diversity, this idea of freedom that was manifested among other things in its being open to alternative forms of culture – that was how I interpreted it at the time. Also bringing culture out onto the streets, coming out of institutions, more to the people. (GD01)

As a result, the ECOC teams were extremely dynamic, with none of the rigid bureaucratic structures or hierarchies characteristic of traditional institutions. Many of the respondents highlighted this fact:

> We participants learnt a lot from it. When we came to work at the ECOC office, not many people at the time had much experience of working in culture, and straightaway we were in at the deep end and straightaway we had to take a lot of responsibility for the projects we were implementing, which none of us had experienced before, and that was super interesting. (KA03)
> Off the back of the movements formed around the applications, there needed to be working groups set up, open to various communities, because that was a requirement of the application rules. Some of the active people from the community were in the groups and there was

an exchange between the communities, between those involved in the official structures and those doing their work outside of them. (PO02)

Urban narratives

Owing to their semiotic characteristics, cities are often described as texts. Mikhail Bakhtin even argued that a city is an apocryphal text, since like a novel, it has a common social basis, and like a novel it is extremely polyphonic.[67] Cities provided the backdrop for literature, and from the mid-nineteenth century, they also began to be leading protagonists. Roger Caillois wrote that "just as the countryside, a mountain peak and a desert are natural scenery for poetry, the city with its suburbs, huge shops, human swarm and *thousands of uncertain existences* that were so interesting to Baudelaire prove to be the favourite place of the novel. The novel has just one theme: the life of a person in a big city".[68] Literature in which the city and its inhabitants became the main character shaped the collective imagination, creating urban narratives and myths. All big cities received their own, classic literature. Analysing the European literature of the modern era, Katarzyna Szalewska notes that "one of the fundamental experiences of modernism is the experience of being-in-a-city. One need not search long to find its representation – it suffices to cite the canon of texts written at the time. Paris, Vienna, Prague, London and New York became the protagonists of modernity, with their heroic histories recorded by loyal chroniclers – Apollinaire, Musil, Whitman, Kafka and many others – not limited to the role of building brick of the literary space, but turning into a mirror of anthropological diagnoses".[69] A unique role here was played by the urban crime story, a literary genre very closely linked to the topography of the city. As readers follow the characters' fortunes, they become immersed in the urban labyrinth and learn its symbolism. The crime novel is a typical product of the modern city, as Marcin Czerwiński highlighted, writing that "a crime puzzle becomes a typical situation only in the framework of big-city culture, and a kind of moralistic epic – the detective

---

67 Michaił Bachtin (Mikhail Bakhtin), *Problemy literatury i estetyki*, trans. Wincenty Grajewski (Warszawa: PWN, 1982)

68 Roger Caillois, *Siła powieści*, trans. Tomasz Swoboda (Gdańsk: Wydawnictwo UG, 2008), 23–24.

69 Katarzyna Szalewska, *Pejzaż tekstowy. Czytanie miasta jako forma doświadczenia przeszłości we współczesnym eseju polskim* (Kraków: Universitas, 2012), 7.

novel – can only grow on this soil".[70] Walter Benjamin even pointed to a mutual symbiosis between the development of modern flâneurism and that of the detective novel.[71] The writer Marek Krajewski provides a model example of how crime novels contribute to the formation of urban narratives. His detective novel *Death in Breslau*, published in 1999, was the first in an extremely popular series of stories about Eberhard Mock, a police detective in pre-war Breslau (today's Wrocław). Krajewski's novels reconstruct in minute detail the topography and atmosphere of the 1930s city, and their popularity shows that literature discovering the past of the lost city was much needed. A major factor in the success enjoyed by this series was its references to the legacy of Breslau. Modern-day Wrocław residents were able to become metaphorical "tourists in their own city", armed with something akin to guidebooks leading them through the history of a city that was no longer there.[72]

Urban literature created by distinguished writers played a major role in shaping the collective imaginations of successive generations. Today, the collective imagination is formed by various media alongside literature, including films, broadcast media, blogs, urban art, but also marketing and advertising. Regardless of the medium used, the key point is the process of shaping urban narratives, which Nicolas Beucker described as follows: "creating texts in the context of the city structure building a sense of its identity entails a direct, empathetic message aimed at the resident of the city as a critical and creative interpreter and actor".[73]

To analyse the identity of a city, we first need to examine the process of formation of understood urban narratives. Such narratives have traditionally been city origin myths. Practically every city that played an important part in the formation of Western civilisation possesses such myths. In the case of historical cities, whose beginnings are "lost in the mists of time", such as Rome, or, in the Polish context, Krakow,[74] such myths were formed in a longue-durée process, permanently determining the semiotic layer of these cities. In the cities under investigation here, the only one with such characteristics was Poznań, which reproduced its sociocultural fabric in, for Poland, relatively stable conditions.

---

70 Marcin Czerwiński, *Życie po miejsku* (Warszawa: Państwowy Instytut Wydawniczy, 1975), 168.

71 Walter Benjamin, *Pasaże* (Kraków: Wydawnictwo Literackie, 2005), 461–501.

72 For more on this subject, see Kubicki, *Wynajdywanie miejskości*, 308–336.

73 Nicholas Beucker, "Budowanie tożsamości miasta poprzez zastosowanie metod projektowych opartych na empatii", in Jurg Sulzer, *Stadtheimaten*, 62.

74 For more on this subject, see Paweł Kubicki, *Miasto w sieci znaczeń. Kraków i jego tożsamości* (Kraków: Księgarnia Akademicka, 2010).

For the respondents from Poznań, the city's identity was something certain and self-evident, inherited from their ancestors and not subject to any particular reflection. As an illustration, we can cite one of many similar statements referring to the city's identity, in which the respondents said that:

> It's determined mostly by the ideas of work at the foundations and positivism. Even during the Poznań protests in June 1956, in spite of all the tragedy, the demonstrators were very careful not to tread on the lawns. That says a great deal about our identity – we are very well organised, very sensitive about our shared space. The identity is marked by the figures who occupy the main places in squares, parks, pedestals, such as Hipolit Cegielski and Karol Marcinkowski. They're not great artists, but social activists who made people's lives better. An element of the identity is the Greater Poland uprising, the only victorious one. (PO01)

It is a different story in cities where the generational continuity was broken. Indeed, this was the experience of most Polish cities after the Second World War. In the cities we studied, experiences of migration[75] were also particularly significant for their identity. The iconic example of a post-migration city is New York, about which Rem Koolhaas wrote that: "In the middle of the 19th century – more than 200 years into the experiment which is Manhattan – a sudden self-consciousness about its uniqueness erupts. The need to mythologize its past and rewrite a history that can serve its future becomes urgent".[76] A Polish example is Wrocław, where the 1997 flood become something of an origin myth for the city.[77] In a certain sense, Gdańsk also fits the bill, with extensive literature on the city's complicated and yet exceedingly rich history – suffice it to mention the work of the Nobel Prize winner Günter Grass – as well as the Solidarity myth, with another Nobel laureate, Lech Wałęsa, to the fore. For a long time, other cities were lacking an event that they could use as an origin myth. The ECOC competition offered just such an opportunity, as an experience that could, to quote Koolhaas, bring about an "eruption" in self-consciousness, showing the cities' residents how exceptional they were. This also made to necessary to mythologise

---

75 Gdańsk, Szczecin and Wrocław are cities where there has been an almost 100 % population transfer, while Lublin, Łódź and Katowice too, albeit on a smaller scale, were fundamentally affected by the question of transfer of population after the Second World War.

76 Rem Koolhaas, *Delirious New York* (New York: The Monacelli Press, 1994), 13.

77 Paweł Kubicki, "Nowi mieszczanie – nowa generacja. Wrocław – miasto odzyskane", in Joanna Zając (ed.), *Pokolenie – kategoria historyczna czy współczesna? Obraz przemian pokoleniowych w sztuce i społeczeństwie XX i XXI wieku* (Kraków: Księgarnia Akademicka, 2010).

these cities' histories, to relay them in an empathetic, attractive form – creating new urban narratives. In practice, the specific features of the cities in question meant that this process followed various tracks. In this chapter, we shall present only the most important patterns observed during the research.

The ECOC competition contributed to the formation of urban narratives in two dimensions. The first concerned the formal bids, which triggered a process of self-reflection on the city. The second was based on bottom-up social energy, whose activation increased interest in cities, as residents began to discover the urban character of their cities. The second dimension is illustrated well by a statement recorded during the study:

> For example, my mum, who's never been interested in history, tells me that she's going again for a guided tour of the city, a tour of a city she's lived in her whole life, and she had to sign up a month earlier, because there were no spaces left. (LU01)

The application form guidelines meant that cities entering the ECOC competition first had to open up a process of reflecting on their own identity. Simplifying somewhat, this process involved searching for the local *genius loci*, discovering their own resources and restoring the city's memory. Most respondents remembered the bid applications as documents that forced the cities into self-reflection regarding two main variables.[78] The first was restoring memory and overcoming the "unwanted cities" syndrome. The second entailed dealing with the syndrome of post-transformation cities and peripheral complexes.

As we described in the chapter on the alienation of Polish cities, for a long time they struggled with the consequences of mass post-war migrations and erasure of multicultural memory. In fact, apart from the aforementioned Poznań, the only city with a relatively stable identity formed during a longue-durée process, in the other cities the intensive identity-forming process has only taken place in recent years. For this reason too, the applications focused particularly on the question of local identity and discovering local resources. This is illustrated well by the response from Wrocław quoted below. As we have seen, like Szczecin and Gdańsk, this city was characterised by an almost 100 % population transfer after the Second World War. The question of the discovery and shaping of the city's identity was therefore a rather common experience during the ECOC competition.

---

78 A detailed analysis of the bids from the various cities analysing this process can be found in the Appendix, and particularly in the section "Cities in the Process of Change: Redefinition of Identity, Reassessment of the Functions of a City, Metamorphosis of Image".

There's something like "Wrocław-ness". Since everyone is from somewhere else, there's no one identity to speak of because everyone had their own: those from the Eastern Borderlands, those from the Poznań region or those from central Poland. Wrocław-ness is the awareness that we haven't been here long, that we need to get to know one another, tolerate each other, be open to others. That builds us. Although Wrocław is a hotbed of nationalism, we look for Wrocław-ness in a city that once didn't belong to us. Perhaps that also entitles us to a large dose of self-deprecation or the sense that we have the right to experiment. (WR07)
The starting point was that it's the biggest city where history has exchanged the population 100 %. We had to start from that, and we wondered how to tackle it, what this community's achievements are, the value of its historical and material achievements. An important component of our thinking is the patriotic element. The discussion about Wrocław's Polishness and Germanness was closed a long time ago when we entered the EU. We have the sense that now we're creating the Polish history of Wrocław, giving us the Pan Tadeusz Museum, for instance, in two weeks we're opening the Zajezdnia History Centre. We wondered what formed residents' identity. Everything was situated in a place where the important history of Wrocław took place, and this was where the examples for constructing identity stemmed from. (WR09)

The question of restoring city's social memory is particularly important in this context. A city is a phenomenon formed in a longue-durée process, which is why its social memory plays such an important role in shaping urban identities. Lewicka noted that, just as "place identity" has a dual meaning, describing the characteristic of both place and person, "place memory" too is a characteristic of both. In the former case, the place "remembers" through its urban layout, often unchanged for centuries, historical buildings or the conscious actions of the city's inhabitants and authorities (street names, monuments), and thus thanks to its "places of memory". In the latter case, it is the residents who remember, equipped as they are with knowledge – sometimes better or more pertinent, sometimes less so – of the history of the place where they live. These two types of memory are tightly interlocked.[79] In historical cities with a well-preserved urban layout, memory works "harder". According to Rewers, "By generating and preserving myths, creating orders and hierarchies of values, the city tells us not only what was and is important for the people of a given time, but also how they perceived the world and their place in it [. . .]. The unquestioned historicism of a city, expressed in its memory and tradition, the capacity to maintain a narrative in the past tense, supplements the experience of its presence here and now".[80] Yet the Second World War meant that in most Polish cities the continuity of the historical urban fabric was broken, in both urban and sociocultural

---

79 Lewicka, *Psychologia miejsca*, 427.
80 Rewers, *Post-polis*, 304–305.

terms. Additionally, as a result of changes in borders, mass repatriations and resettlements, and traumatic wartime experiences, the memory of post-German cities (Gdańsk, Szczecin, Wrocław), post-Jewish districts (Łódź, Lublin), and cultural borderlands (Katowice) was subject to intensive processes of forgetting.

Memory is closely related to a specific place, unlike history, which, as Pierre Nora has shown, concerns an abstract idea of the nation. In Nora's view, social memory is living, evolving, present in the dialectic of remembering and forgetting, evaluated in various ways, and capable of enduring through a lull, suddenly being roused after a lengthy period of inactivity. History, meanwhile, means reconstruction, which is always problematic and incomplete. Collective memory is always a present phenomenon connected to the here and now, whereas history is a representation of the past. Memory is rooted in a place and has a more local character. History, on the other hand, acquires the hallmarks of an ideology, an abstract idea that can be realised in various places.[81] History belongs to the nation, and memory to a place (city). This was why in the period of domination of nation states, cities were subjected to intensive processes of nationalisation at the cost of local memory based on multicultural heritage. A distinct change in this respect began to appear in the late twentieth and early twenty-first centuries, as local memory assumed greater significance. As John Gillis notes, we are witnessing a post-national period in the exploitation of memory for building collective identities, in a situation of advancing processes of desacralisation of the nation state and democratisation of memory. In this new context, on the one hand, international and global identities have gained increased importance, while on the other hand, movements reconstructing regional and local identities have become active. As states and nations have lost their monopoly of control of the memory of individuals and communities, it is individuals and local communities that have begun to create alternative, individualised versions of memory.[82] At present, therefore, we can observe a true renaissance in local social memory, which requires its designate, what Nora called *lieux de mémoire*. As Krzysztof Kowalski argues, these sites of memory can be extremely formalised and institutionalised (museums, collections, archives, cemeteries, official ceremonies), but they can also include places with an individual and exclusively

81 Jacek Nowak, *Społeczne reguły pamiętania. Antropologia pamięci zbiorowej* (Kraków: Nomos, 2011), 34–53.

82 John Gillis (ed.), *Commemorations: The Politics of National Identity* (Princeton: Princeton University Press, 1994).

personal dimension. They are connected by the idea of remembering and the role they play in the entirety of the identity process.[83]

The process of restoring memory in Polish cities began sooner, before bidding for the ECOC opened. Yet the competition proved to be a significant catalyst stimulating the dynamic of this process. At the same time, a new Polish bourgeoisie was forming, characterised among other features by the search for new frames of reference and new urban narratives, created on the basis of the heritage of the cities in question.[84] In addition, the described changes to cities' economic foundations meant that multiculturalism began to be perceived as a valuable resource. Cities compete with each other to attract creative capital, and must therefore forge images as open and tolerant places. In this case, allusion to the multicultural heritage of a city creates a clear message that diversity is respected in such a place. This is particularly significant as the creative milieu demands tolerance and recognition of non-standard behaviours. Richard Florida made the case for this argument in his book *The Rise of the Creative Class*, which was as popular as it was controversial. Florida showed how important the "power of place" is for a modern economy. Certain cities are attractive as a result of quality of life, diversity and tolerance, which enables them to lure the most creative human capital.[85] Consequently, multiculturalism and tolerance become goods that can be exchanged for a real improvement in lifestyle and increase in income, becoming a condition of the effective development of a city in the contemporary knowledge- and culture-based economy. The return to the multicultural memory of cities is therefore largely conditioned by rational calculation of the balance of profits and losses. Inhabitants of cities are increasingly aware of the fact that openness and tolerance are an essential condition for a city to develop efficiently in its own economy.[86]

Even if many of the local governments' actions in this respect have resulted from rational calculation, restoring memory of the multicultural past has led to increased interest in otherness. This fact is confirmed by research conducted by a team led by Wojciech Burszta from the time of the ECOC competition. In the conclusions to their report, the authors wrote that "the main indicator of the identity of a place and the people who live there is becoming the concept

---

83 Krzysztof Kowalski, *O istocie dziedzictwa europejskiego – rozważania* (Kraków: Międzynarodowe Centrum Kultury, 2013), 51.
84 Kubicki, "Nowi mieszczanie – nowi aktorzy".
85 Richard Florida, *The Rise of the Creative Class* (New York: Basic Books, 2012), 183–202.
86 Paweł Kubicki, "Pomiędzy pamięcią a historią. Polskie miasta wobec wielokulturowego dziedzictwa", in *Pogranicze. Studia Społeczne* 2012, vol. XX.

of difference. Yet otherness is not perceived negatively. The respondents who emphasise the role of multiculturalism seem to be firm opponents of a mono-cultural vision of identity [. . .]. Associating with *the other* is becoming a positive challenge".[87] According to our respondents, a city's multicultural memory was a valuable resource, as one of many similar statements reveals:

> *Lublin is a place where multiculturalism is brought to mind in an interesting and original way, but in the sense of Polish Jews. A number of projects have appeared within which the former heritage is recreated. This takes place under the apparently modern façade of building a cultural of memory, which is what the Grodzka Gate centre does – these the-atre institutions were among the first to start putting on plays related to the Holocaust, with the crimes of Poles on Jews, with Polish-Jewish relations. So there were three main ideas here: theatre, multiculturalism as East-West, and multiculturalism as memory of the Jewish past; and these ideas overlapped in the application.* (LU04)

It is important to emphasise, however, that for the average residents of a city, the multicultural memory, which local governments and urban activists have been involved in restoring for years, is at best a matter of indifference, and frequently also an unprocessed trauma:

> *I think that it's the same as everywhere in Poland, that these bad things are chosen, espe-cially now with the politics of history being so crazy. We conduct a lot of these public projects with residents and we come up against situations when they make it clear that they don't want to talk about who lived here – what matters is what they left and that I'm here now. Here and now. And that's all I care about. But observing activities throughout Poland, I don't think that's anything unusual. But as for city policy, those roots are certainly referred to. The Dialogue Centre was founded, which above all is targeted at recovering the post-Jewish memory, but they also consider it their mission very much to discuss other cultures – they have an intercultural dialogue going on. And I know that there's strong pres-sure from the top, from Madam Mayor, for these cultural centres to sustain this image of multiculturalism.* (ŁÓ01)
> *Everyone can see that this history is very important for the city. The magnitude of this his-tory is really felt here. But if we go into details, you can see that the residents of Wrocław have a problem with knowing the history. Studies shows that they have a problem with putting events in order etc. The tendency is to say generally that it was a German, Jewish city, that it had beautiful architecture. So if we talk about identity, then it is strong, but kind of hazy. If you go to other cities, you don't get the same sense that the history is so impor-tant, here you have to find something out about the city the whole time. I often hear from students that there are a lot of things they don't know and would like to find out. Often that*

---

87 Wojciech J. Burszta, Piotr Majewski, "Tożsamość kulturowa", in *Kultura miejska w Polsce z perspektywy interdyscyplinarnych badań jakościowych* (Warszawa: Narodowe Centrum Kultury, 2010), 38.

doesn't lead to anything, but there is the need. And another question is whether the history has an effect on any civic engagement? Probably not, if the identity is so general, hazy, based on legends about the city, and heard vaguely. (WR03)

Whereas the process of restoration of cities' multicultural memory began much sooner, one result of the ECOC bidding process was an appreciation of the heritage of cities that did not necessarily fit into marketing templates. This particularly applied to Łódź and its memory as a working city, suppressed after 1989.

There's some root cause in the ECOC. Now you can see the interest in the past, especially that of the workers. (ŁÓ04)

The fact that something more is happening restores the memory of the 1905 revolution, because after '89 there was such a thick separation line from the workers' history. And on the one hand there's regret that we don't have streets named after the great manufacturers who built the city, got involved in charitable activity, and built the hospitals, whether for the Christian or the Jewish population. On the other hand, there's no disguising the fact that the working conditions in those factories were terrible. So there are two camps, and now another movement is appearing to appreciate the workers too. It's not black and white, of course, but I think we're on the right path to creating that kind of identity by alluding to this industrial and multicultural heritage, which reverberates most in the architecture that has survived, because the social structure is completely different. This multiculturalism of Łódź that we're working on, we have the Łódź of Four Cultures festival, the Dialogue Centre, we have a Protestant community here, an Orthodox Christian one, Jewish, but that's the amazing difference to the world as it once was. So this multicultural identity of the city, in this old version, is very hard to reproduce. (ŁÓ05)

As a result of these processes, it was possible for the various cities to discover and appreciate their own resources. The ECOC bidding process enabled them to unearth their assets, often obscured by complexes and stereotypes amassing over years. The character of the Polish public discourse, shaped above all from a Warsaw-centric perspective, meant that for many Polish cities it was possible to observe a typical example of so-called misrecognition. Charles Taylor described such situations in reference to the process of identity construction, noting that when the symbolic resources of one of the partners in social interactions are too high (in this case Warsaw), and the other one lacks them almost entirely, the weaker partner has a degrading or contemptible image of themselves.[88] From the Warsaw-centric perspective, location, industrial heritage etc. were presented as a burden hampering the development of cities in the post-Fordist, globalised economy. The processes unleased during the ECOC competition allowed the

---

88 Charles Taylor, *Sources of the Self: The Making of the Modern Identity* (Cambridge, MA: Harvard University Press, 1989).

"misrecognition" syndrome to be overcome. Characteristically, in the process of the research it was observed that the process of discovering one's own resources was most intensive in those cities which, prior to the ECOC competition, had grappled with peripheral complexes and/or the stigma of cities in crisis, undergoing the painful period of system transformation associated mainly with the decline of industry and all its consequences. In Lublin, Łódź and Katowice, the question of a change in the city's image was, in the eyes of residents, one of the most common themes cited during the interviews. Below we present a set of characteristic statements from these cities regarding this issue.

In the case of Katowice, it is evident that the bidding process became a turning point allowing the city to overcome the stigma of "misrecognition" and appreciate its own resources.

Before entering the competition, Katowice was a city with a lot of complexes, where hardly anyone was proud to be from Katowice. (KA03)

The outcome of the competition for me is that Katowice isn't a boring, sad city any more, as it was in the time when I was a student. I envy today's students that they can study in a city like this, which didn't exist just a few years ago. There definitely wasn't such a good and diverse range of culture on offer, kind of niche, low-budget, smaller theatres opened, there are film reviews, lots of debates, meetings, TEDx, that didn't use to exist. When I compared Katowice before 2010 and today, it's like comparing an old Polski Fiat with a Mercedes. It's a leap, and I'd dare to suggest that it was a civilisational leap. For me, the biggest success of Katowice in the bid was the fact that the residents twigged that there wouldn't be some Santa Claus arriving and organising a great life here, that until we found great leaders, people who'd get involved in culture in its broadest sense, there'd be nothing. And in my opinion that was what caught on the most, that people began to see for themselves that Katowice is quite a cool city. Certainly the very good marketing tactics in social media, using very good places, made a big difference, it opened people's eyes. For example, lots of people live here but have never been to the Nikiszowiec district. And lots of the ECOC bidding activity took place there, and Nikiszowiec was a big hit. And I could give a few more such examples. A city was shown inhabited by people living their life, like any other city. And people said, it's true, you can do cool things here, and up to now we were cooped up, and thought it was just grey, drab and dull. And that's the biggest change of the ECOC – a change in awareness. (KA02)

There's a persistent stereotype about Katowice that it's a dirty, boring city, that there's nothing to come here for, and all these activities connected to the ECOC showed that that's not the case. And there's really a lot happening now. (KA04)

Everything going on with the ECOC, all the papers wrote about it, there were lots of activities, promises etc., the residents saw that and I think a large number of Katowicans said to themselves: hey, my city isn't that crappy, it's not the city that everyone once thought it was, where if you came in a white shirt, after an hour you needed to wash it because of the air. We might not be the centre of the world, but we don't have anything to be ashamed of, we have a cool theatre, cool events, one of the coolest festivals, OFF Festival, we have the

NOSPR [National Polish Radio Symphony Orchestra], back then before its new building. I think the Katowicans realised that Katowice could be sexy, Katowice became KATO, more youthful, more fun. That coincided with Uszok [the mayor at the time] finally starting to rebuild the public spaces. The market square is what it is, go and have a look, you'll laugh, but it was worse, so it's better now. Everyone knew the NOSPR was being built, and a new Silesian Museum at the mine. People saw that Katowice can be cool, that it wasn't pretend, it was happening. (KA01)

Łódź, proclaimed the "Polish Manchester" at the peak of its development, during the transformation period began to be known as the "Polish Detroit". Yet the latter comparison was not a source of pride. Detroit became a symbol of the decline of an industrial city, the infamous capital of unemployment, crime, poverty and hopelessness,[89] and a similar stereotype was imposed on Łódź. But here too, the ECOC competition allowed it to be overcome:

From my point of view, the ECOC application was the first moment when Łódź was shown from a different, better side. This city has problems with identity – anybody will tell you that – but also with the sense of its own value. It looks different now, but still it's a great city, with a large amount of poverty and a lot of unemployment. And suddenly this endeavour and this belief that it might succeed was an element of local pride in your place of residence. That was mostly built up through open-air events, "picnics", it was a genuine widespread movement, lots of great events were going on, lots of people were involved. And as a result some places began to exist in public awareness, for example the Księży Młyn complex at the time was very much out of the way, and many people who lived in Łódź had never been there, and these picnics allowed them to get to know cool places. Also picnics in Bałuty, a district with the same dodgy reputation as Praga in Warsaw, and when the local lads were playing football at the picnic with activists that was very appealing. In my opinion that was a real interest, there was a load of positive energy in it, building pride in the place where you live. (ŁÓ03)

I'm convinced that our candidacy for the ECOC was strongest at the moment when we started to talk about "Łódź-ness", i.e. identity. Before that, there hadn't been such a strong and lively debate on the links between our history, identity, and what was to come. For the first time we were thinking about a vision of the city. It was a very visionary project, we couldn't do it without referring to our roots. That link of the past to the future ensured that we were responsible for the city, that it was in our hands. Creating culture together in Łódź meant that we started to think about what we are like, who we are and what next. That was a moment when Łódź was an unwanted city, and thanks to the candidacy a lot of people fulfilled themselves, set up companies, etc. Before that, many people had been ashamed of our workers' identity, and we tried to create this local patriotism and turn it into pride. We didn't hide the history of our city and its workers' legacy, we referred to certain symbols and traditions. (ŁÓ07)

---

89 Charlie LeDuff, *Detroit: An American Autopsy* (New York: Penguin, 2013).

With the ECOC, we were clearly struck by a redefinition of the identity of Łódź [. . .] this ECOC programme, although it wasn't very specific, it communicated well, it reached residents, hit upon a certain need to activate them, to revise the city space, that it's attractive, that people can take part in simple activities, such as wearing badges, or congregating for a joint photograph forming the ŁESK [Łódź ECOC] logo. And in my opinion this filled that gap: we don't know who we are, nobody offers us a narrative of who we're supposed to be, and nobody offers us what we can do, and that was given by ŁESK. And that roused Łódź, when it comes to urban movements. In the framework of that communication we were able to meet and to do something. I thought they didn't have any particular value or generate a symbolic surplus, but the very fact that we are in a community shows that we're reproducing a social structure. The engagement was incredible, although they didn't really know what to engage in, the need to engage was the key issue [. . .]. ŁESK also created the need for a story about the city, although I'm not so convinced that it created that story. Although there were a few strong slogans. But the fact that we saw that the city space is cool, that there are a lot of us, that we're able to arrange ourselves into the letters of the logo, that was cool, and the fact that we were able to do the same after a year, although by then it was a completely autotelic, community gesture, not a promotional one. It was ŁESK that changed the way ordinary people looked at the city, people who hadn't previously taken advantage of the culture on offer to the same degree as the middle class. (ŁÓ06)

It was a forgotten city, I wouldn't agree that it was a dead city. It was a city of women. When they closed the shipyards [in Gdańsk], the men protested, they managed to secure their rights. Here there were weaver women. They didn't protest. After the factories closed, they got on with it and got to work. There were no protests, there was no flood like in Wrocław. And the city was practically unscathed in the war. There was a passive attitude here. People felt that Łódź was an abandoned city, left to its own devices. It was too near to Warsaw, it was even administered from there. Identity is a process. Łódź lost its industry and therefore lost its character: working, textiles. It was Łódź that emphasised the approach that if we have to do something, we get working and do it. Don't wait, just get started. Grassroots activities. It's true that the ECOC efforts didn't come from the authorities at all, but from grassroots institutions. Today, people can decide on their own affairs, get involved in those initiatives. They come out with their own ideas, don't wait, and that translates into those creative initiatives. That's the point, that we can build something ourselves. (ŁÓ08)

Lublin played a very important role in Polish urban history. One of the country's most important centres of urban civilisation, it was also traditionally an important academic and artistic centre. During the transformation period, however, it became strongly stigmatised as a city of "Poland B", consigned to stagnation and to surrendering its best human resources to cities "on the right (left) side of the Vistula". In this case too, the ECOC bidding processes changed the way the city was regarded entirely. The specific local character of the city was turned into an asset, rather than a source of complexes:

The application made us aware of and allowed us to put into some order what we have here. That we have a long theatrical tradition, Lublin's multicultural tradition, that it didn't come from nowhere. I think it's mostly those things. [. . .] And the work on the project presenting Lublin in Wrocław makes me very aware of that, because on the one hand we're reaching for what was put together in the application, what we gave a name to, put into order, and how that translates into how we operate in terms of culture. And that's the Easternness, the multiculturalism, the slightly slower way of life than in other cities, greater openness [. . .], it's a city in the provinces, but that's a very large asset, how it translates into life, in many different aspects [. . .]. People gained an awareness of what's going on in Lublin, they started to come out of their home and stopped moaning in front of the TV that there was nothing happening [. . .]. It became a city you're not ashamed to live in any more. If you live in Lublin you have everything you need, you have great cultural events, if you feel like going out, you have somewhere to go. The standard of life in Lublin has improved, starting from the infrastructure and other things like that, and in general. Lublin has started to be a city in many respects. (LU02)

There's Easternness as regionality and this urbanity – Lublin-ness. As for the Lublin-ness, the main component I sense is the fact that we're not a metropolis, but provincial, in a certain respect. On the other hand, it's a clear centre, that's existed for centuries, you can sense the heritage there, it's an average-size identity. What that means, for example, is that you can walk everywhere, you have a constant community of people you can meet, the city is focused around one axis. (LU06)

That proved that if you're capable of creating something like that and disseminate the fact that the residents themselves are interested in their city, that's interesting because the city, like other similar ones, is partially an immigrant city. There's no industry here to absorb the many university graduates, they pass through. But also those who arrived in the city from the wheat-and-beet local area, as we used to jokingly call it, for them it's discovering the city. Once they got flats in certain districts and didn't know what was happening here in the old centre, because how were they supposed to know, but these big events have shown that those people are very much interested in the city and it's a really big success. And this success meant that these young cultural managers want to do more and more events about the city and its traditions. (LU04)

The urban narratives that are being created need mechanisms to help them to enter public discourse. This is a complex problem demanding detailed analysis, since, as was noted at the beginning, many transmission channels can be identified today. Here, though, we would like to concentrate on two, which were directly related to the ECOC bidding process. The first is the official city promotion and development strategies. During the study, we observed characteristic patterns in this area. The ECOC competition became a mechanism shaping new urban narratives, on condition that it was connected to the cities' official promotion and development strategies. As a result, it was possible to institutionalise the ideas that emerged in the communitas sphere, in which the ECOC teams were working. They were therefore able to gain a wider reception and to mould the public discourse. As an example, below we quote respondents from cities where the work on the applications coincided with an institutional search for new narratives[90]:

> Katowice started to look for its identity, and that coincided with a new promotion strategy for the city, because it was happening in parallel with the ECOC, the strategy. There was a new promotion strategy with the slogan "Katowice for a change", which in my opinion is quite clever, because we turn the page and look at the city from a completely different angle. And thanks to the ECOC, the Katowicans started to look at the city in a different way, that it's actually not bad. (KA01)

> I took the slogan "City of Gardens" in two ways. On the one hand, more on the outside, to surprise people: what gardens, in the mines? To break the ice. On the other hand, it was a kind of allusion to the traditional lifestyle here, the house garden, where the gardens on estates have great significance. And that made sense and was in keeping with the truth too, because Katowice is a very green city, as Silesian towns are in general. (KA01)

> Lublin's strategy emerged, and in my opinion it's dripping with the ECOC vision, participation, the academic character and those motifs are repeated there. I don't remember the application that well, what structure it had, but those motifs are repeated. And also the people working there were more or less the same people. As for development of culture, it's implemented very consistently, it's developing, it has its funding and its flagship events at quite a decent level. (LU03)

> "City of freedom" – more than anything the application was kind of prophetic. The question is how much is it worth talking about freedom and summarising it and raising the city to the status of a symbol of freedom. . . Gdańsk is associated with that. The application itself, and the endeavours that accompanied it, developed questions of freedom very strongly, bringing it both into the cultural sphere and into others. From today's perspective, I think that you need to talk about freedom in a continual way and continue to implement it. It's not a given value once and for all. While the people of Gdańsk identify with freedom. . ., I think that the wind off the sea in Gdańsk has always been there, and I hope it will stay. It's certainly a very important element. I don't know how much the city[91] is doing with that aspect. Definitely in the symbolic sphere. Talking about freedom and democracy is part of everyday life in Gdańsk – in terms both of history and of everyday life. Gdańsk is clearly a city of debates and meetings. (GD07)

In the cities where the narratives elaborated for the ECOC did not reflect the official promotional strategies, they were therefore not given an institutional

---

90 A detailed analysis of the new urban narratives created for the purposes of the bids can be found in the Appendix, where the applications of the individual cities are discussed.

91 It is worth noting here that our respondents – following a pattern that can be observed in spoken Polish today – would quite often use the word "city" to mean "city authorities" or "municipal authorities". It is therefore not uncommon to hear that "the city [meaning city authorities] is doing/thinking/acting/prohibiting. . . etc."

framework to establish themselves in, and were not present in the public discourse. The experiences of Poznań and Szczecin were examples of this tendency:

> At the time (during the bidding process), the Poznań know-how brand was being heavily promoted, the slogan was ridiculed, it didn't fit our identity. But it was heavily promoted, and the idea of the ECOC wasn't really. (PO05)

In Szczecin, the team responsible for preparing the ECOC bid was working almost in opposition to the structures of the city council and the official cultural institutions. This meant that the narratives they created did not receive any institutional backing, and failed to break through to the wider public discourse.

> The two issues clashed, but the European issue couldn't break through, although there was lots of energy and artists involved. Before that the city had created the Floating Gardens brand, and the Szczecin 2016 brand couldn't break through. Szczecin 2016 was never mentioned in the official publications, everything was covered by that campaign. That was the official council policy. The mayor somehow became more interested in our application when it was necessary to go to Warsaw and present it to the European Commission, and it happened to be an election year and he thought he could benefit from it. (SZ03)
> But it wasn't possible to include in the Floating Gardens promotion strategy the idea that Szczecin could also be the European Capital of Culture. And maybe that was the reason that the ECOC candidacy didn't quite fit the city line. [. . .] It was lacking in the Floating Gardens, because the emphasis there was on sport and recreation, that was very interesting for the powers that be, they're interested in these big sporting events. (SZ05)

A further pattern could be observed in the official city promotion and development strategies. Since the cities often had weak traditions and had remained on the peripheries of the main European processes, certain activities revealed a typical mechanism characteristic of imitative modernisation – mimicking the models flowing from the cultural centre. One of the main slogans of the Polish transformation was "catching up with Europe", which in practice often entailed unreflective copying of Western trends and lack of consideration of how they might fit the local scene and be an impetus for development. A typical example of this approach was the attitude to the industrial legacy and workers' culture. The power of the stereotype of the city of workers as something opposed to modernisation, created in the post-transformation discourse, was so great that in cities with strong working traditions this heritage was visibly pushed away, replaced by fashionable marketing slogans. Indeed, the idea of the creative city[92] and creative class[93] during the ECOC competition was most popular in traditional workers'

---

92 Charles Landry, *The Creative City. A Tool Kit for Urban Innovators* (London: Routledge, 2008).
93 Florida, *The Rise of the Creative Class*.

cities: Katowice and Łódź. In both cities, there were evident tendencies during the bidding process to reject this working-class heritage, perceived as a burden in the new post-Fordist reality, in favour of the trendy idea of the creative city. In Katowice's case, the process itself unleashed large amounts of social capital and social energy that made it possible to redefine the image of the city; yet residents clearly reacted coolly to the intensive promotion of the idea of a creative city rather than the mining tradition:

> *I think the city authorities had the idea maybe even to forcibly hide the city's industrial origins [. . .]. I heard from the promotion department numerous times that now we were breaking the stereotype of the industrial city, which for me is rubbish, because we were and will continue to be an industrial city, even if we spend billions on promotion and become who knows what kind of garden city, we'll always be an industrial city [. . .]. We'll always be an industrial city, and I don't think it's a burden, but quite the opposite, these cities grew from this tradition, and were shaped by this tradition. (KA02)*

In this context, respondents often recalled the story of one finale of the Great Orchestra of Christmas Charity appeal, planned to be held in Katowice. The event did not take place in the end, and the city's new marketing strategy had a role to play, as the promotion of the idea of the creative city forced out its mining traditions:

> *When the heavy industry began to collapse, the mayor and his entourage decided that we couldn't be an industrial city any more [. . .]. At a certain point, Katowice was very ashamed of its industrial character. There was a situation, five or six years ago, when [charity founder Jerzy] Owsiak wanted to do the launch of the Great Orchestra of Christmas Charity finale in Katowice, and had the idea that he'd drive out of the mine, so we drive out of the mine and finish up in the clouds, but Katowice refused, saying that they didn't want that kind of collaboration if he was going to say that he was in the mine in Katowice. (KA01)*
> *There was this event, I don't remember which year exactly. Owsiak wanted to start his Orchestra with an event that he'd be driving out of the mine, and the city council said no, because Katowice isn't a mining city and it didn't fit the promotion policy. And so Owsiak didn't come out of the mine. (KA04)*

The situation in Łódź was somewhat different. The city's application[94] highlighted its industrial heritage, but understood in particular in material terms. In this case, shifting the emphasis to the material industrial heritage made sense, since including this issue in the bid made it possible to focus on the intensive and unthinking process of destruction of the city's post-industrial legacy that was

---

94 In particular, the thematic axis "(R)econstructions", which emphasised the value of the city's post-industrial heritage. For more on this subject see the Appendix, in which Łódź's application is analysed.

taking place at the time. And yet the application, and later also the city's official promotion strategy, concentrated on shaping the idea of the creative city, ignoring Łódź's working-class culture almost entirely. This was perceived only in terms of imitative actions, and not as consolidation of the local *genius loci*. This theme cropped up frequently in the respondents' statements.

I'm very critical with regard to the Łódź application, if we're not talking about the whole event, the process of applying, but just the application, it was based on the idea of creative industries. That was a time when Florida was being translated, or about to be translated, the city authorities bought those ideas wholesale, and I'm not sure if that wasn't to our detriment, because they bought it in an empty, superficial way. And when you read the application in full, you can see incoherence there. The people working on the application were aware of Łódź's problems, the challenges it faced, and on the other hand there was the concept of creative industries, which aren't able to solve these problems. That was almost pasted onto it, but in the application it was presented as the main theme [. . .]. In my circles, those creative strategies were known as "building soap bubbles on shit". (ŁÓ02)

But an important point of the application was the creative industries, which we backed, and now, with the benefit of hindsight, it didn't quite work out, it didn't happen as it was described in the bid, it didn't become the driving force for the Łódź economy [. . .]. Incidentally, the city is itself slowly abandoning the "Łódź creates" idea, because even the author of that philosophy thinks it was a bit utopian. A utopia that slightly builds the caste system of society, assuming that everyone has to be creative. And, as with the working roots, that's something you can't get past. (ŁÓ01)

Another city where the narratives created during the ECOC bidding process overlooked the working-class traditions was Gdańsk. In this case, though, it was not the idea of the creative city that was the culprit. Gdańsk made the legacy of Solidarity the axis of its application and bid for the ECOC.[95] Yet this heritage was reduced above all to the idea of freedom, disregarding almost entirely the workers' traditions of the Solidarity social movement. As in the cities described above, in Gdańsk too, the competition sparked social energy and interest in the city, yet the omission of the workers' heritage was the subject of criticism. For the respondents from Gdańsk, this was particularly significant because at the same time as the ECOC application, the process of destruction of the city's industrial heritage was taking place, making room for new investments:

I should also mention the negative changes, because it was very painful for me that, just as the marvellous overpasses were built around Gdańsk overnight, the shipyards were also

---

95 A detailed analysis of the application can be found in the Appendix in the sections "Gdańsk: 'Freedom of Culture. Culture of Freedom'" and "Gdańsk – an axiological discourse on freedom".

destroyed overnight, and it's a terrible paradox that it's such an important place, symbolic for the identity of the city, and it was just abandoned and spoiled. (GD02)
There was the idea [in the application] of basing it on the legacy of Solidarity, and that was obvious, but also good, because it could have been effective. But it turned out that it contradicted the other initiatives of the city, especially spatial ones. Just then the shipyards had been destroyed by directing highways through them, and in fact the people evaluating the project even said that. (GD02)

These examples show that the new urban narratives being created, in order to become frames of reference for urban identities, need to delve into the cities' local resources and individual character. Fashionable advertising slogans cannot create a city's identity if they are not linked to its heritage. Moreover, the further marketing strategies deviate from the local character, the more they contribute to weakening the local identities. It is important to note, however, that our research conducted several years after the conclusion of the ECOC competition demonstrated that the people now responsible for shaping the local cultural policies are fully aware of this. The bidding process became something of a testing ground for practices used to forge city identities. This question had never previously been discussed so widely, and neither had there been good examples and experiences. This valuable capital in the form of a practical lesson – how to stimulate the processes shaping urban identities – is paying dividends today, as cities are clearly breaking through the discourse of imitative modernisation to discover and appreciate their own resources.

The second mechanism that gave the new urban narratives developed in the course of the ECOC competition a place in the wider public discourse was the changing role of culture and art in the urban space. In this case, the bidding process was truly revolutionary, contributing to introducing reflectiveness to the cultural sphere in the cities. Their previous lack of reflection meant that the culture in local government could in some respects be compared to autopoietic systems,[96] characterised by being closed to the external surroundings and lacking the need for self-reflection. Cultural institutions in this sense tended to be geared towards creating and reproducing symbolic boundaries separating the world of "high" culture from the urban world of the profane, everyday experiences and interactions. As a result, such institutions often functioned as isolated islands, making only a small contribution to the formation of local identities and not stimulating community initiatives. One of the tangible effects of the bidding was that it helped to break the discourse in which the role of culture in a city was seen

---

96 Niklas Luhmann, *Social Systems* (Stanford: Stanford University Press, 1996).

mostly in the context of the "high", ceremonial sphere. The traditional debate on culture tended to introduce a stereotypical division into so-called high culture (elite, ceremonial) and low culture (plebeian, everyday). At the discourse level, this is conveyed well by a colloquial phrase often used to describe participation, "to get some culture" (or literally, "de-philistining"), which shows that participating in a cultural event often became a kind of cleansing ritual that aspiring city residents ought to indulge in from time to time in order to confirm their social status.

Studies carried out to date on the cultural competencies of Poles and participation in culture confirm its elite nature, and consequently also its alienation from the everyday lives of residents of cities. According to the sociologist Marek Krajewski (not the author referred to earlier), culture for Poles is mainly associated with the sacred and exceptional sphere, not accessible to all and setting a certain ideal of social life.[97] This way of thinking about culture had far-reaching consequences, stimulating the process of institutional culture closing itself, or alienating itself even, from the urban environment. Culture financed from public funds, understandably, must be subject to evaluation. Yet the problem with this is that, as Tomasz Szlendak emphasises, only participation in ventures proposed in buildings with an institutional red plaque on the façade had the chance to capture the researchers' attention. Until recently, cultural statistics have been "glued" (with a very strong adhesive of values) to an elite, enlightened vision of culture divided into its high and low variants – the result being that certain forms of participation were simply excluded from these statistics. According to Szlendak, research on participation in culture defined in these terms tended – at least until halfway through the first decade of the twenty-first century – to disregard everything that people "practise" in non-commercial circulations, at home and visiting friends. It overlooked certain things that the respondents themselves regarded as cultural activity, for example the entire non-institutional sphere or "unofficially" practised pop-culture. By defining participation in these terms, official statistics on culture ignored active forms of contact with cultural products, ignored amateur production, and ignored non-organised, grassroots and spontaneous forms of participation.[98] The methods applied for such statistics and evaluations

---

97 Marek Krajewski, "Kompetencje kulturalne Polaków", in Rafał Drozdowski, Barbara Fatyga, Mirosław Filiciak, Krajewski, Tomasz Szlendak (eds.), *Praktyki kulturalne Polaków*, (Toruń: Wydawnictwo Naukowe UMK, 2014).
98 Tomasz Szlendak, "Formy aktywności kulturalnej" in Rafał Drozdowski et al., *Praktyki kulturalne Polaków*.

often failed to capture actual cultural practices, also because the respondents themselves, as a result of the domination of "high culture" discourse, were unaware that they were participating in culture. To allude to the metaphor of Molière's Monsieur Jourdain, who did not see that he was speaking in prose, the respondents completing various questionnaires often had no idea that they were engaging in cultural activities. For examples, cities such as Gdańsk, Łódź and Katowice are famous for the fantastic murals created on the elevations of ordinary housing blocks and townhouses. The residents of the cities come into contact with them every day, but participation in culture in a traditional sense would entail the need to formally cross the threshold of an institutionalised art gallery. This leads to the conviction that culture does not play a major role in daily life. Barbara Fatyga writes on the official data concerning participation in culture that: "*contact* with so-called *culture and/or art* [original emphasis]: was mentioned as one of the five most important values in life by 0.7 % of respondents, and by NOBODY in first place. People educated to degree level put this value in only 20th place, and inhabitants of the largest cities in 23rd. This means that *contact with culture and art* is no longer an element of *education*, or an element of urbanity. This result can also be regarded as a censure of cultural education programmes, as well as a contribution to the discussion on the uncertain place of culture and art in their traditional sense in the lives of contemporary Poles".[99]

The processes triggered in the course of the ECOC competition also contributed to a change in this discourse in several dimensions. Firstly, the efforts were accompanied by an intensive process of self-diagnosis and self-reflection on the state and role of urban culture, manifested among others by the popularity of research into the situation of culture in the city and the part it played. For example, in Szczecin the publication *What about Culture? Report on an Exploratory Study of the State of Culture in Szczecin*[100] concerned research commissioned by the local institution preparing the ECOC bid, the first such study in the city's history. This permitted a diagnosis of the key problems related to the operation of culture and its role in the city-building process:

> As a result of these activities, which were previously not practised, the institution had such
> a strong impact on cultural life in the city that it commissioned its own research on culture

---

99 Barbara Fatyga, "Wartości jako generatory żywej kultury", in Rafał Drozdowski et al., *Praktyki kulturalne Polaków*.

100 Magdalena Fiternicka-Gorzko, Marek Gorzko, Tomasz Czubara, *Co z tą kulturą? Raport z badania eksploracyjnego stanu kultury w Szczecinie* (Szczecin: Wydawca Szczecin 2016, 2010).

in the city. We presented that publication at a session of the city council. The research showed that the average resident of Szczecin takes part in cultural events once a year at the Sea Days festival [laughs]. (SZ03)

Studies on participation in culture are becoming an increasingly common practice for city authorities, and the ECOC competition certainly had much, although not everything, to do with this. How much is this research used for making improvements to the local cultural policies,[101] and how much is it harnessed for purely marketing objectives and to secure long-term and independent funding? Where such studies are funded by local government institutions alone, there is the danger of a clientelistic relationship, with all the consequences this entails. Both problems were addressed by most respondents, irrespective of the city, which would suggest that this is a systemic problem:

The research was supposed to be larger-scale, then it suddenly turned out there was no money. Besides which, you know, politicians aren't keen on neutral evaluation, because they never know what will come out in the end, so it's not an inordinately popular issue. In Wrocław an important step was taken. We'd previously done research not only on culture, but a social diagnosis on a large sample – 5,000 people, and from that we had interesting data on how people live and what they expect – perhaps that will be continued, but these are costly matters, and often left till the end. (WR09)

Secondly, the communitas sphere in which the teams preparing the bids operated allowed artists and cultural organisers to be attracted from spheres that had hitherto eluded the traditional classifications of "high culture". As a result, areas of art that had previously functioned outside the mainstream began to enter wider public circulation, especially the fields of design, alternative theatre and street art. What made this important was that these were the areas of art that were taking an interesting approach to processing local identities, asking questions about what the city meant and developing new urban narratives:

[The officials] were certainly more open to various initiatives. For example in my case of street art, the question of painting on walls, at the beginning it was completely blocked by the city council, but after many discussions we managed to do a lot of things. We went through this process from simple, sort of aestheticising activities, to more difficult, critical ones, where the officials weren't afraid, for example, that a mural by Łukasz Surowiec was being made, which would be very critical of the situation of the miners' strikes that were going on, and lots of initiatives like that. So definitely, the officials learned something, including the mayor, who, to put it crudely, was always perceived as a kind of village chief

---

101 A detailed analysis of urban policies in the context of the ECOC bidding process is presented in the chapter "Cities' Cultural Policies in the Light of the ECOC Bidding Process".

who knew everything best, but now had to be open to Marek Zieliński's vision, and it's great that at the time Marek was fully independent. The officials didn't interfere, because they could see that Marek and the people working with him knew better and it would be better for the application if they didn't interfere. [. . .] Design is an example of that. We have a very decent, or even more than decent Fine Arts Academy, which educates very good graphic designers and designers. It was a real explosion, there are so many people making reference to the local roots, and apart from design there's also architecture. [. . .] A book also came out, New Silesians. City. Design. Identity, *which is a PhD thesis published at the Fine Arts Academy. It's interviews with people who became active as a result of the ECOC, so it nicely shows the generational change. The identity today, certainly people identify more with Katowice than they used to. There's a growing group of responsible people who want to take responsibility for the city and don't want to leave.* (KA03)

Incidentally, artists are also often going out into the city space, mostly through murals. There's a whole route. Neglected neighbourhoods are becoming the object of interest for artists – in one of those neighbourhoods a nice mural has been painted, "Residents' Faces". (LU03)

The Nowy Theatre company put a huge amount of work into that kind of thing, for years they've been organising meetings with local artists, ordering scripts from local artists, successfully or less so, but it was unprecedented. The late [director of the theatre Zdzisław] Jaskuła was aware that the city needs cultural texts, written from the inside. Now the Powszechny Theatre are putting on the play Tango Łódź, *which personally I don't like, but it's a play about Łódź, about the workers' strikes. You can see that there's such a glut of these texts in recent years that a theatre scholar I know even complains that everything's only about Łódź and he's had enough.* (ŁÓ02)

More and more people have learned to do these city games that strengthen the reflection about the city. Recently I really like a play from the Współczesny Theatre, Singing of Toothless Seagulls, *excellent, nuances pulled out of the city's life. So that trend is here, especially as it's based not only on fictional literature, but also autobiographical, historical – there are even sections in bookshops where you can find stands just about Szczecin.* (SZ03)

The ECOC competition, largely as a result of the makeup of the teams preparing the bids, legitimised alternative cultural spheres, thereby allowing the new urban narratives created in these spheres to reach a wider circulation:

The ECOC and what happened later introduced a ferment that had an indirect effect on consumers, a large number of new consumers of culture appeared. Interesting studies came out concerning participation in culture, where the results were very interesting, it turned out that this official culture that absorbs 90 % of the budget has a small audience, that people participate in culture in various ways, in niches, that the largest potential can be found where enthusiasts have managed to create a kind of micro-community, and traditional events don't manage to do that. In Poznań it coincided with urban movements, grassroots activity of NGOs, the explosion of club life, an ideal synergy, everyone wanted to do something together, and there were people around that. (PO04)

Introducing alternative domains of art to the mainstream by no means that the traditional domains lose their power to shape local identities. The names of recognised artists, their works, art schools, important artistic institutions, and orchestras, all have an influence on the feeling of local pride:

> *There are outstanding artists who identify with Silesia: somebody was born some-where, settled somewhere. What's also important then is the identification of artistic accomplishments. Additionally, it adds value if such an eminent person is from Silesia. Then they're not assigned to a given place or city, but simply to Silesia. There are people who didn't grow up from Silesia, but those who went to university and started their career, spent their entire professional and creative lives in Katowice and very much identify with Katowice. If someone has any idea about music, history of music, events and people, they'll say that [Wojciech] Kilar and [Henryk] Górecki are from Katowice, not from Silesia. Whereas [Artur] Rojek and [Szczepan] Twardoch are from Silesia. (KA07)*
>
> *In terms of literature, quite a lot of books have come out written in Silesian, e.g. a series of crime novels about Commissioner Hanusik, there were three books, the first crime novels in Silesian. A book about Silesian cuisine came out, various Silesian dictionaries, published by Gryfnie, which promotes "godka", the Silesian dialect. That started to be present, and godka stopped being shameful to use, young people don't know it as perfectly as the older generation, but use it on the streets, they put the odd word in. I remember at the start of my studies, when someone spoke godka, it wasn't a reason to be proud, but now that's changing. (KA03)*

Creation of new urban narratives made it possible to break through the previous discourse of thinking about culture as a ceremonial, sacred thing, as the fol-lowing response illustrates:

> *The changes that are the most noticeable for residents, it was possible to bring culture into the public space, we didn't have that before, but since the time of the ECOC residents have got used to the fact that culture has become an everyday element of city life, and it's pre-sent both in the lives of residents and in the fabric of the city. I also think that the presen-tation of culture in the press has changed, if we look at the newspaper headlines, we see it there, and that didn't use to be the case, so the media importance of culture in Gdańsk has grown. (GD02)*

Culture has gained a wider, pro-social significance, which has translated into a feeling of greater responsibility among residents for their city and increased awareness of their agency:

> *The awareness of place has grown. People are thinking in broader terms now. The urban character is important, and stems from the increased awareness of place: homes, work, using what the city has to offer, shops. At one time it was the case that everybody wanted to have a flat, a job... I'm making a living, that's enough. Not much was said about how people spent their time. The situation looks different now. The other side, how to spend time, how to develop your interests, is slowly becoming an equivalent value. Public transport,*

access to schools, pre-schools, nurseries, taking advantage of cultural events. People have
bigger expectations. And rightly so. We're moving forward, and we also expect greater sat-
isfaction in the reception of culture. (KA05)
It seems that the ECOC competition started a process of residents identifying more with
their city. It was noticed that it's not just officials who are responsible for the city, but it can
also be a common good. This change in empowering residents hasn't happened everywhere,
so there's also disappointment that nothing has changed or that the change isn't obvious.
Residents don't feel invited to manage their city. Where they did feel invited, the relation-
ship between the local authority and residents was set up better, or in a more positive light,
or this made it possible to produce a phenomenon of joint responsibility for what a city is
supposed to be like and what kind of city we want to live in. (KA07)

As a result, the residents of cities increasingly felt themselves to be empowered
agents in urban processes, as well as being able to articulate their needs more
effectively:

There's an awareness that we need to fight for our common good. And that is the char-
acter of the city. There's increased openness to the residents, there are more events going
on in the city. Today there's no disputing the fact that we have the right to space, that these
initiatives are shared, that's also linked to discussions on transport. For example the ques-
tion of the fountain on Dąbrowski Square. It was put up a few years ago and is supposed to
be being removed. That project began without contact with residents, imposed from above.
Public consultations took place in August. People don't like it, don't want it, it's imprac-
tical, it's becoming a kind of exhibit, you can't do anything there. Besides which the shape
puts people off, it looks like a giant vagina. People don't like it aesthetically, but the main
objection was that it doesn't have any function in that place, it disrupts the character of
the square, as it can't be used. The authorities took the arguments on board, and now the
project's supposed to be changed. (ŁÓ08)
It doesn't just apply to Gdańsk, but to most city residents. It's manifested in a much greater
sense of agency in the city, responsibility for the city, belief that you have an influence on
the city in all the projects concerning residents – one of the results of which is the partici-
patory budget. Thinking about the aesthetics of the city, the right to use the city – that's it.
Definitely to a large extent the ECOC triggered that. (GD05)

Increased agency also means the development of a network of institutions in
local and neighbourhood communities. Although other factors certainly have an
effect on this state of affairs, in the case of Wrocław and its implementation of the
ECOC programme it was noted by respondents, especially those representing
the institutional sphere:

We're probably one of the leaders in Poland when it comes to networks of seniors' clubs,
estate clubs. It's a dense community, absorbed into the whole operation of being the ECOC,
and very nice things come out of that. I mean, the ECOC for that network – numbering
hundreds of entities in the city (around 70 seniors' clubs alone), estate clubs, and school
initiatives, outside-school ones – is a real boost. (WR10)

We're considering how to bring culture closer to our own residents... That's happening because at the moment local cultural institutions are opening that have their own task: not only to have tradition, but also to be a kind of social centre. That's taking place in the Nadodrze neighbourhood by placing NGOs there which have been given this job: do culture, but try to do it with the residents. That's taking place, and will certainly be continued. (WR09)

As a result of all these factors, culture has begun to play a city-making role, contributing to the construction of social capital and to shaping cities' identities. There has been a marked change in the previous discourse dividing urban reality into the area of high culture and that of everyday culture. These two spheres have clearly begun to merge, creating the unique blend of local urban culture.

The image of the cities

Joanna Orzechowska-Wacławska
Paweł Kubicki

Among the most important sociological theories concerning the process of identity construction is the concept of the so-called "looking-glass self", developed by Charles Horton Cooley on the basis of American social psychology. This theory posits that individuals construct their identity based on their perception of how others view them. The "other" is of fundamental importance in this conception, although it is not its actual evaluations that are important. The "other" functions as a metaphorical looking glass in which the individual looks at him or herself. The identity is thereby constructed in relation to this "other", and demands the ability to interpret its behaviours and considerable reflection.

Although, as we wrote above, the city is not an anthropomorphic entity, and is therefore not capable of reflective self-analysis, individuals/social actors function in its space, creating it. It is therefore possible to relate theories concerning construction of identity, including the concept of the looking-glass self, to research on a city's identity. The "others" in this case will be the residents of other cities, all the social actors located externally. The identity of the city analysed according to this conception will not therefore be geared towards self-diagnosis and self-reflection (as in the case of the urban narratives analysed earlier), but will refer to the *external image of the city seen through its residents' eyes.* In other words, how do the people living in the city think that it is viewed from the outside?

It is worth noting that this understanding of identity not only differs from the perspective discussed so far, which demanded that residents concentrate on themselves and produce a certain story about themselves (a narrative about the city), but is also considerably different from the conventional understanding of the image of the city. The latter refers to the assessment made by outside entities, meaning that the fundamental question is how the city is perceived by its external surroundings, i.e. by residents of other cities.

In our study, the description of a city's external image (including the description and analysis of the city brand) did not fall under our research interests. The reasons for this were the methodology we adopted and the subject matter of the project. The influence of the ECOC on changes to the external image of the city (in the eyes of others) could only be studied in relation to a city which had actually held the title of ECOC, and this would also require the project to be longer in duration. A separate issue is testing the *perception of a city's external image by its own residents*. Here, taking into account the diversity of initiatives implemented within the framework of the ECOC applications, it is certainly possible (and legitimate) to analyse residents' perception of how their city is seen from the outside.

Having adopted this perspective, we can note that in all the cities we studied, the respondents actually pointed to an improvement to the external image of their cities that had taken place in recent years. Most people thought that this was a consequence (direct or indirect) of the ECOC bidding process. The reason for this was that, as we have seen, the competition helped to "open people's eyes" to their own resources – although the scale of this varied. In Szczecin, for example, where the idea of the ECOC bid was not attached to official marketing strategies, the respondents did not associate the change in the city's image with the ECOC itself:

[Szczecin] on the outside is known as a city that's developing very energetically, and not only because there are new buildings going up, but because they're filled with ideas, people's work. I take part in meetings about the future of Berlin, where leaders in transport, culture, education and many things meet leaders in Szczecin to have a dialogue. The result of that is supposed to be better communication between cities, perhaps finally creating a new railway line, that's a process. But the fact that Berlin has begun to think seriously about Szczecin means that the city is noticeable, that it can become a partner. Previously maybe there were discussions, but not at this level, so Szczecin has changed its image, good things are being said about Szczecin externally. It used to be the case that teams from Poland didn't come here, I know, because it has contact with artists, now they come, because there's infrastructure, e.g. the philharmonic, and everyone says that Szczecin has changed a lot, that it's a different city from what they remember. In Szczecin itself we're starting to go back to the idea that in the communist era Szczecin was a window to the West, and that's a change in thinking too. (SZ07)

As for Łódź, where the ECOC bidding process has contributed to a radical change in the residents' perspective on the city, the respondents were aware that the stereotype imposed upon the city from outside remained strong:

I don't think so, because the ECOC application ended in defeat, after all [. . .]. With people from Łódź, as soon as they leave the city they immediately start being negative about it, especially when they move to Warsaw, to justify their decision. So generally bad things were said about Łódź, and the ECOC didn't change that. I have the feeling now that it's a bit better, but I wouldn't go too far. Especially people who have never been here have negative opinions, that it's like Wałbrzych [i.e. unappealing], it's depressed, the airport's empty, you can get beaten up, it's anti-Semitic. That image changes when someone arrives here and spends a bit of time here. But it wasn't the ECOC that was the reason, it was later initiatives, although they were often put into place by people associated with the ECOC. (ŁÓ04)

The majority of responses in Łódź, however, pointed to a gradual change in the city's image, although this was not necessarily directly related to the ECOC competition itself.

In my opinion, the ECOC is a closed chapter in Łódź, and now we're applying for the small EXPO 2022, and the revitalisation initiatives are a driving force. And what's happened thanks to the new investments, renovations, new investors arriving, such as OFF Piotrkowska, and creation of hipster places, promotion of a kind of slow life. . . But that's also related to the fact that there's money appearing in the city, more than the ECOC. The period that happened between the application and 2016, a lot went on. As for the image, an important moment was the "Greetings from Łódź" campaign, when Łódź was presented as a kind of slow life place, a place to have a great life, and I feel that that's actually happening and a few people from other cities have told me that it's a really great, pleasant city, but also authentic. (ŁÓ01)

Of all the cities we analysed, participation in the competition had the least impact on their image in those which were already recognised cities with a distinctive individual character. A good example here is Gdańsk.

I think that Gdańsk always had a strong brand, abroad too. Perhaps not the word Gdańsk itself, but Wałęsa, Solidarity, those were words that were very well-known. I get the impression that it's one of the four or five most recognisable Polish cities; after Krakow, Wrocław, Warsaw. But it wasn't all that much associated with culture, so that could be a change. I don't know if that's the case, though, or whether in other cities they associate it with culture these days. (GD01)

It might have helped a bit, to get something moving, but in my opinion it wasn't a key factor. At least my acquaintances from outside of Gdańsk, they identify it now just as they did before. Perhaps it had some effect on those who didn't know anything about Gdańsk before. (GD03)

More among residents than on the outside, I think. [. . .] Because of Gdańsk's image, more closely linked to the modern heritage, we didn't quite manage to change it. On the other hand – because we're doing research on Gdańsk's image – we see a change in terms of the fact that the city is perceived as one today with more to offer, stronger institutions, ground-breaking projects. (GD05)

I'm not sure whether it's my wishful thinking or whether it's really the case, but definitely Gdańsk has to an extent been restored as an unalienated city, not only as a space producing the power elites, but also as young and culturally active areas. Politics was a very large burden in Gdańsk. Politicians were absent here. This acceptance of democracy that's going on in Gdańsk is often uncanny. You almost wish the mayor would stamp his foot and give someone orders. (GD07)

The same applied to Wrocław, which already had an established external image before the competition. To a great extent, this was a consequence of the intensive marketing efforts performed on the city's behalf. Opinions are divided as to how necessary this was.

Everyone I know from outside of Wrocław stresses that Wrocław is very good in marketing terms, but the people there are a bit tired of that. Too much money goes into promotion – promotion never quite reflects reality, but the perception here is that the dissonance is too big. The people in Wrocław are often irritated by the promotion. (WR02)

According to the people responsible for creating Wrocław's image, however, such actions are still essential:

The city is becoming more and more international, people are coming to work from northern Italy and Germany. It's recognisable. The number of virtual and printed guidebooks in 2016 – there's a lot in them about Wrocław. Warsaw's the most recognisable because it's the capital. Krakow's no doubt even more recognisable, or at least as much. It's a wonderful city, plus it has everything: Wawel, the pope, Wieliczka [salt mine]. . . Krakow is recognisable on the international map. Gdańsk, because it has the Solidarity history, the sea and Westerplatte. Before our eyes, Wrocław is taking its place on the world map. It's extremely strong, it's happening really fast. The ECOC allowed us to make leap forward. (WR10)

Wrocław has gained strong external identification as a strong centre of culture, and European culture, because we're noticed in Europe too – we know that. There's an incredible amount of press materials and reports from the events that have taken place in Wrocław, in the Polish, European, and even global media. That will certainly have an impact on the city brand. We see it with the increased tourist traffic. But even with Wrocław residents, I hope so, although it's hardest to be a prophet in your own country. And there's a very intricate and vociferous debate going on in the local media, the basis of which is in my view pure politics. I'll say this: the local media do very little to make Wrocławians proud of living in the ECOC. And as a result the impression's formed that it's not the case. Studies are done which will show us, because otherwise we have to rely on our intuition. But I get the impression that many residents are proud of it. (WR09)

The influence of the ECOC bidding process on the city's image is more visible in those cities which were previously seen as peripheral and without much to offer. Lublin and Katowice are good examples:

I remember that whenever I used to meet someone from Wrocław, for example, and say I was from Lublin, he'd say, "Oh yeah, that's a town near Ryki", because he'd once been to Ryki and remembered that Lublin was nearby. Not many people knew where Lublin in. But now if you say you're from Lublin it's, "Oh cool, I'm jealous, apparently it's really great living there and such a cool city, there's so much going on". A lot has changed, and if we'd got the ECOC. . . (LU01)

When we were applying for the ECOC, the city changed its way of talking about Lublin, advertising externally, and as a result of all that Lublin certainly changed its image among people from outside of Lublin, and that's very visible. There are more tourists coming here, for example, and they leave with a high opinion, it's not just people I know talking about that, even just normal conversations you hear on the train. Recently I heard a man talking to his wife on the phone, saying it's an extraordinary city, and that he hadn't expected that. (LU02)

It was the first project in which we really made a mark. Before that Lublin was associated with the East, Poland B, sometimes with [rock band] Budka Suflera. Various studies showed that suddenly the city had been noticed. It's good what happened afterwards. There was one and a half [mayoral] terms of intensive development: the airport, highways, all the EU investments. Thanks to the ECOC, Lublin made its mark, and then everyone saw that was being confirmed somehow, that there were some more activities happening. (LU05)

[. . .] we have the sense that previously Poles didn't associate Lublin with anything. At best they associated it with Budka Suflera, or [pop group] Bajm, or the Catholic University, or trolleybuses (Gdynia and Tychy – those cities still have trolleybuses), and apart from that a black hole. We did research with the City Marketing Office, and the city began to be associated with culture. (LU07)

The participation in the ECOC changed the image of the city of Katowice, lots of good things happened, and that had nationwide and European repercussions. The Rava Blues festival received international awards. That all became stronger. Of course, it's not some incredible amount, because generally in our country it's hard to get sponsors for musical events. But here we could clearly see a positive impetus. (KA05)

The image of the city definitely changed externally and internally. A physical reflection of this is the enormous popularity of various local brands that produce that culture. For example "Gryfnia", a clothing company producing T-shirts with prints in Silesian. They run a fan page promoting Silesian culture, and they're also present at various events, and the people who come here from various cities to festivals or events buy the T-shirts, buy the clothes and it's cool. It translates into design, or clothing, and it's a positive approach. I heard recently that there are lots of local brands that sell themselves to other cities more than here, so it's a reflection of popularity. I know a lot of people from other cities who come here, because they want to go to the Silesian Museum, for example, and you can see lots of really positive reaction in their opinions. (KA07)

Social capital

Paweł Kubicki

In recent years, the concept of social capital has become extremely popular and used in various contexts. A simple consequence of the popularity of a given term is that it soon becomes ambiguous. It is therefore necessary to first clarify the meaning of "social capital". It can be understood in two ways. On the one hand, it is a tradition referring to the works of Pierre Bourdieu, which sees social capital as belonging to individuals and expressed in the network of their mutual relations, harnessed, among other purposes, for building a social and professional position and achieving one's life goals.[102] In the second case, social capital is a social good characteristic of local communities. Scholars such as James Coleman, Robert Putnam and Francis Fukuyama pointed to the nature and quality of social bonds, the capacity to work together and mutual trust. For our subsequent reflections, the second approach will be particularly important. In his groundbreaking publication (1993) *Making Democracy Work: Civic Traditions in Modern Italy*, Putnam explains this approach, proving that innovativeness and development are largely determined by the quality of local social capital, produced in a longue-durée process. In his opinion, the best-developed regions of northern Italy, as a result of the character of their trading cities, from the early Middle Ages onwards began to incorporate into exchange networks, becoming the cradle of republican and civic ideas; something which is today expressed in the innovativeness characteristic of these regions. Southern Italy, on the other hand, was dominated by feudal relationships, forming separate cultural models. The feudal ties of personal vassalage were weakened in the North, and reinforced in the South. The people in the North were citizens, while their counterparts in the South were serfs.[103] Even today, the divisions formed hundreds of years ago continue to divide Italian society, determining the nature of individual regions' identity.

The historical processes described in the previous chapter have had a decided impact on the weakness of social capital in Polish cities. This problem has been discussed by almost all scholars dealing with these issues, from the now classic work[104] that introduced the concept of the "sociological vacuum" into the lexicon

---

102 Pierre Bourdieu, *Distinction: A Social Critique of the Judgement of Taste*, trans. Richard Nice (Cambridge: MA, Harvard University Press, 1984).

103 Robert Putnam, *Making Democracy Work: Civic Traditions in Modern Italy* (Princeton: Princeton University Press, 1993).

104 Stefan Nowak's aforementioned analysis of the "sociological vacuum": Nowak, "System wartości społeczeństwa polskiego".

of sociology to more recent research. In an analysis of the Polish values system, Barbara Fatyga noted that in terms of social capital, the current situation is little different from that which Stefan Nowak described in his research in the 1970s. This points to a withdrawal from wider social orders and concentration on survival with one's closest social circles.[105]

Owing to the noble-peasant cultural model and the "sociological vacuum", Polish cities tended to be perceived as collections of private property rather than a common good where social capital could develop. The ECOC bids unleashed civic energy, thereby making a major contribution to penetrating this discourse. And yet we should remember that the scale of this mobilisation varied widely according to the city. It is particularly telling that the largest social mobilisation occurred in those cities for which the transformation period was particularly painful, and where the symptoms of the "trauma of great change" – apathy, withdrawal, mistrust etc. – were most tangible. Below we present characteristic responses from cities whose image shaped in the post-transformation discourse pointed to a crisis of identity and social apathy. The bidding process enabled these cities to discover and appreciate their own local resources.

Lublin:

*In Lublin it was one big popular movement. A ton of circles connected to culture came together. I can speak for those circles connected to culture, because I know them. But not just them, I think that many residents of Lublin who weren't previously interested in culture and didn't do anything really cared as well [. . .] People began to get organised, the SPOKO [COOL] committee formed, I don't know if it was official, but that's what happened more or less. There were meetings of various communities, collection of signatures. The city set up an online mailbox where you could leave ideas, and a lot of people sent emails. And they weren't simple wish lists, they were actually professional proposals, how much money you could do it for, what they thought. There were all kinds of things, loads of things. (LU01)
That experience shows just how involved we were. As editors for a few months we put something to do with culture on the front page every day, there was always someone saying why they thought Lublin should become the ECOC. All the media were involved in it, everyone knew about it and I doubt there are many cities where the people cared so much about the ECOC as Lublin. (LU01)
The ECOC process started off, or united, quite a few citizens' groups. Those people started to feel then that by creating something together they had more clout. Everything associated with the citizens' budget, I think it's an effect of the change that's been taking place since the moment when we started to apply for the ECOC. But it's also a case of looking at what's*

105 Fatyga, "Wartości jako generatory", 43.

happening in other cities, searching for new possibilities. You can see a desire from people to change the reality around them. I have the sense that people in Lublin feel that these social, cultural initiatives are a huge driving force, a way of changing the world around ourselves, I don't want to say it's the only effective one, but one of the more effective ones, because in Lublin we don't have any big business, and that gap is filled by culture, opening a lot of doors connected to quality of life. (LU02)

Łódź:

It turned into this Thing, a big Łódź Thing. From my perspective, Łódź was a kind of lost city, with no idea for itself, of course after the decline of industry and people losing hope. I remember the story of my parents, who were students at the polytechnic – textile manufacture, 300 people in the year, big lively city, and they were sure that it was the kind of city they could bring their children up in, yet it turned out that things turned 180 degrees. People were disoriented and despondent, they didn't know what to do, and that was a good foundation for this idea, and the idea meant that everyone believed that this was it and now things would work out, and there was a big residents' movement, especially people from the culture sector, who got things going on the PR side [. . .] It was that power of the people, residents, the belief that the people would really be involved in it, they came out of their homes, grouped together, took part in picnics, and really wanted it, wanted to be included in those initiatives. (ŁÓ01)
For me those changes are gigantic, and after the ECOC there was a 100 % increase in engagement, lots of grassroots initiatives, often pro bono. (ŁÓ05)

Katowice:

Our application, unlike the Wrocław application, wasn't written by three or four people locked in and isolated from the outside; ours was written on the streets, in cafés, with the people who helped to produce culture here, felt responsible for the application, and got more involved as a result. That was a very big group. (KA03)
And when the ECOC finale happened, there was a crowd of people on Mariacka Street, they came of their own accord. The city put up big screens and people came and waited to see who would win. In Wrocław apparently they had to round people up for that kind of event. (KA01)

In addition, in Gdańsk's case, the ECOC competition provided fertile ground for the so-called "Euro effect". In sociocultural terms, Gdańsk had been the biggest winner from being a host city for Euro 2012, the European football championships, which took place a year after the conclusion of the ECOC bidding process. Respondents noted that this had marked the beginning of intensive development of social life in cafés, restaurants etc., as residents had begun to look at their city through the eyes of others. Although major sporting events had already come in for thorough and largely warranted criticism, in Gdańsk's case, Euro 2012 arrived in a suitable context, much of which was shaped by the processes that followed the ECOC bidding. The following responses show examples of this trend:

> *I don't know how much it had to do with the ECOC, because the Euros took place here in 2012, and that was a really great time in Gdańsk, the level of identification with the city, of hospitality, we had the fortune of mostly hosting the Irish and the Spaniards, and as a result the city really came to life then.* (GD01)
>
> *Two things overlapped: on the one hand, the ECOC application, and on the other, much more important from the perspective of the region, Euro 2012, which gave the region a bigger injection of development.* (GD04)

A characteristic regularity observed in the course of the research was the fact that in cities which had come out of the transformation period relatively painlessly, and entered the ECOC competition basking in the glory of being cities of success, the bidding process did not bring such strong social mobilisation as elsewhere. A particularly striking example here is the eventual winner Wrocław. According to the respondents from this city, social engagement during the process tended to be more elite-driven than a mass-participation event.

> *The residents were not very aware of the whole process of applying for the ECOC. Although there were various forums held here, the participants were the same people, artists, people who are fixtures in this community. Rarely residents themselves.* (WR06)
>
> *The only reason I knew an application was being produced was that I was an activist in urban movements. I doubt at this stage that most citizens knew there was an application being put together. I don't remember any open calls to create the application.* (WR02)

The ECOC did not prove to be a catalyst unleashing mass social energy, as it had already been unleashed. The generational experience that had precipitated mass social mobilisation in Wrocław was the flood of 1997. Also at this time in the city, intensive processes had been launched to shape local identity, reconstruct the memory of the city and build social capital.[106] The reason why the flood became a generational experience was because it took place at a unique moment in the city's development. Wrocław had already experienced several events since 1945 that had mobilised the city's inhabitants, potentially offering good conditions

---

106 Wojciech Sitek, *Wrocławianie wobec wielkiej powodzi. Wspólnota i zagrożenie. Socjologiczny przyczynek do analizy krótkotrwałej wspólnoty* (Wrocław: Wydawnictwo Uniwersytetu Wrocławskiego, 1997); Jacek Pluta, Piotr Żuk (eds), *My wrocławianie. Społeczna przestrzeń miasta* (Wrocław: Wydawnictwo Dolnośląskie, 2006); Kubicki, "Nowi mieszczanie – nowa generacja".

for generating community social ties, such as the chickenpox epidemic of 1963 and the activity of the democratic opposition in the 1980s, which was especially strong in the city – in particular the Wrocław-based phenomenon of the Orange Alternative underground movement. Yet these events did not translate to building of strong social bonds across the whole city, and especially breaking through the trauma of the alien post-German heritage. The context in which they operated made this impossible. But the context would prove decisive in the case of the flood. Firstly, the third generation of migrants were growing up in Wrocław and treating it as their home, free of the concerns and traumas that had accompanied the first generation of settlers. Secondly, in the new market reality, the city acquired a new dynamic, entering the new millennium amid its own "golden decade" stimulated by the process of European integration.[107] It was not insignificant that at this time the city authorities, with a good command of marketing methods, were busy boosting the belief that this was a unique city with unique inhabitants. From now on, they developed intensive campaigns working on Wrocław's image, setting ambitious goals for the city. But whereas around the millennium, during the period of reconstruction of Wrocław's identity, such initiatives mobilised residents, with time they were received increasingly ambivalently. At the stage when bidding for the ECOC was beginning, Wrocłavians saw their city as one of the most European in Poland.[108] They no longer had the complexes of a peripheral, post-migration city, and were particularly interested in increasing the quality of life, developing a so-called "slow life", rather than competing for big events. The following response illustrates this well:

> *The impulse that came from urban movements, for building the city's identity through grand projects such as the World Games, the stadium, the National Forum of Music, creating big events, had come to an end. It was this idea that we'd had enough of all this ECOC and World Games. Whereas the ECOC still has positive connotations, because on the one hand it was extravagant spending, but on the other this Europeanness, the World Games is a typical example of wasting money on big events. And now there's this strong movement against such big events, focusing on quality of life, on small neighbourhood issues, little initiatives in the space of the local estate or yard.* (WR03)

Mateusz Błaszczyk makes similar observations, noting that the policy of building the brand (image) of a city by hosting major social, cultural and sporting events has been practised in Wrocław since the mid-1990s. The overture to such events was the Taizé European young adults meeting in 1989; the same event returned

---

107 Kubicki, *Wynajdywanie miejskości*, 308–336.
108 Kubicki, "Nowi mieszczanie – nowa generacja".

to Wrocław in 1995. The Eucharistic Congress took place in the city in 1997. The next mega-events were strictly commercial/consumer-based. Wrocław's authorities applied to host the World EXPO in 2010, and, when they were unsuccessful, reapplied (again without success) to host a specialised EXPO in 2012. Wrocław was successful, on the other hand, in achieving host city status for the European football championships in 2012, and this was seen as a great achievement of city policy. On the back of this success, the local authorities lodged bids to hold other major sporting events: the European University Games in 2014 (losing by one vote), and the World Games, held in the city in 2017. Wrocław also hosted matches of the men's basketball European championships in 2009 as well as the men's handball world championships in 2014. The city has also not been immune to the phenomenon of festivalisation. The official city website lists some 72 cyclical artistic festivals of varying status and types: 32 musical, 11 theatre, four film, seven literature, 13 "interdisciplinary" and five art.[109] As a result of the intensification of large-scale events and festivals, the ECOC competition was perceived as one of many events, meaning that in comparison to other cities where "nothing was happening" beforehand, the social mobilisation was relatively much smaller:

> *It was just another application by Wrocław for another major, European-scale event that was to take place in Wrocław. To be honest, these beginnings of the application for the ECOC didn't bring any particular enthusiasm, there wasn't even any shared belief that it would work, that we'd succeed; the attitude was: OK, the mayor and authorities have unfulfilled ambitions, let them try, but probably nothing will come of it. I think that was the atmosphere that accompanied it. (WR05)*

In a certain sense, it was a similar situation in Poznań, where the ECOC bidding process itself initially failed to bring any social engagement. The capital of the Wielkopolska region was one of the cities we studied which did not appoint a formal ECOC team, rather employing an external PR company. Such actions would suggest that the local authorities looked upon the process in marketing terms, and were mostly interested in building the city brand. Apart from Krakow, all Poland's largest cities entered the bidding. From the point of view of marketing brand strategies, therefore, Poznań would have lost out by remaining

---

109 Mateusz Błaszczyk, "Zanim kurtyna pójdzie w górę. Reprodukcja miejskiego spektaklu w kontekście Europejskiej Stolicy Kultury Wrocław 2016", in Mateusz Błaszczyk, Jacek Pluta (eds), *Uczestnicy. Konsumenci. Mieszkańcy. Wrocławianie i ich miasto w oglądzie socjologicznym* (Warszawa: Wydawnictwo Naukowe Scholar, 2015), 43–44.

outside the competition. Among people in the fields of culture and activism, therefore, there was scepticism regarding the city's decision to enter:

> *An external agency was hired to prepare the bid, and that was in keeping with the spirit of how the city was being run at the time. The city promotion office was working at the time like an ordinary advertising agency, and that was why they hired a firm to do it effectively, but it turned out not to be so easy.* (PO02)
>
> *The previous team and the entire city elite didn't meet in theatres, but at the football stadium in the VIP section, there were local politicians, business and the media there, and that was the message of what was important. [. . .] And then Poznań comes up with this idea [ECOC], that amused me, it was a joke. They didn't care about culture, just about prestige, money.* (PO08)

The procedural requirements of the ECOC bidding process demanded that largescale public consultations had to take place during preparation of the application. The PR agency selected to produce the bid therefore had to perform such consultations with the local community. Yet these consultations had a consequence unforeseen by the local authorities, resulting in integration of the hitherto atomised milieus functioning in the broad cultural sphere. All the respondents involved in these activities highlighted this effect:

> *A positive that came from the application was that many people and organisations met, having previously not known that each other existed, and people learnt to work together. That collaboration also went beyond social contacts. There was a kind of recognition of what was going on, people got to know each other.* (PO04)
>
> *The contractor that was managing the ECOC, a private firm that it was commissioned to, invited us to meetings, discussions, panels, kind of think-tanks, as they're known these days. And they selected a dozen or so people without any key, but various people from various fields. The most interesting thing was that before that we didn't talk to each other. [. . .] Those meetings were extremely interesting.* (PO03)

After some time, the social capital built up during the work on the application became the germ of community mobilisation with the aim of reforming Poznań's culture. This resulted in the formation of a Poznań culture crisis centre, which organised the Poznań Culture Congress – events perceived as a generational experience. Poznań's experiences in the ECOC bidding process can therefore be described as a "glorious defeat". This oxymoron has become a popular one in Poland, not only among sports commentators, but also in political discourse, and it is also useful in this context. Poznań's candidacy dropped out of the competition during the first selection stage, which was seen as a painful reverse. From the point of view of building social capital and strengthening local identity, however, it was turned into a success. An acute failure in a prestigious competition had a mobilising effect on the Poznań community, which acknowledged that it exposed the ills in the city's cultural management system and demonstrated the need for thorough reform. In this sense, the inept application became an impetus for grassroots social mobilisation. Asked about the causes of the public mobilisation after the ECOC bidding process, the respondents shared the following reflections:

The results of the first stage, I think. Then everyone knew that it wasn't good, that we were going round in circles, and now we'd received confirmation of that, quite forcefully, although I feel that both then and now Poznań is in the top league culturally, but then we were relegated to the second, or even third division. (PO01)

So when the ECOC debacle was announced, in some circles there was the idea that never mind the ECOC, since nobody was going to wave a magic wand to bring us good culture, then in Poznań style we'd start doing it ourselves. (PO02)

The failure with the applications was good in one sense, in that it mobilised the grassroots communities. There were various movements, of course there were various institutional political interests at play unfortunately, or fortunately. But what was good about that was that in this artistic-cultural community, which is small here, a need arose to change something. The application showed Poznań's blandness, the weakness of the culture it was offering, and that's the positive effect of the ECOC competition. (PO06)

This social mobilisation was possible to a great extent thanks to the previous (unintended) integration of local communities at the time of the bid consultations, as one respondent points out:

At those meetings at first we looked at each other fairly mistrustfully, but the selection of those people really hit the mark. It lasted a whole year, a lot of reports were written on the state of culture in Poznań, and also the type that wasn't being taken into account at the time, alternative culture, was noticed. At that time too a commission for civic dialogue was set up, which, you could say, was responsible for crushing the concrete. Although the ECOC application completely fell through, a lot of interesting things happened around it, especially the Congress, which drew a great deal from the work started up for the ECOC. (PO04)

Nevertheless, the groups who were invited to take part in the consultation as the bid was prepared in fact had little bearing on it, as all the respondents involved in the process emphasised:

We didn't have any influence on the application, we just received the printed materials. (PO03)

The application, which was de facto written by a PR firm, did not become an attractive narrative that could set off a process of self-reflection on local identity. It was interpreted as one of many marketing products, and not an especially successful one at that.

I remember one of the first meetings I took part in, where there was a discussion on how to build the strategy, grasp what's characteristic of Poznań. It was a strange meeting, because the agency that prepared it had some ideas and they wanted to discuss them. [. . .] I thought then that the concept of the strategy was dreamt up at a desk, and not listened to and observed in the city [. . .]. And the idea with the agency, which was a Poznań-Warsaw firm, came from someone from Warsaw,[110] who told us some rubbish, reproduced stereotypes. He had no idea what the genius loci is here, he'd come as a guest [. . .]. The application was simply badly prepared. But I don't want to seem like a critic of the agency, that's not the point. I was surprised that the authorities entrusted it to an agency, and not their own structures, or didn't call for a popular movement. (PO07)

It [the application] was so wishy-washy that there weren't any important points of reference, Poznań wasn't associated with anything, it was just this insipid city, without any focal points. Gdańsk had its shipyard, its history. Poznań had history too, of course, but that wasn't used. I'm embarrassed to admit it, but I don't remember anything from the application now. (PO06)

The mode of preparation and the content of the bid became one of the impetuses for grassroots social mobilisation:

There was a lot of grumbling and questions about the way the application was put together, that it was a bad idea, that a company did the application. And the boom that took place later, the crisis centre, was a kind of response saying that we should have written the application, not a firm. (PO05)

In Poznań's case, it was not the ECOC bidding process that was the generational event, but what came afterwards: the convocation of the culture crisis centre in the city and the Poznań Culture Congress. The respondents noted that this was one of the most important events in the city's recent history, bringing together various communities that, for various reasons, had previously been unable to integrate:

I'd say the congress was a very important experience, it brought together almost the entire Poznań community, from those who still see culture in communist terms to those for whom it's a promotional tool, to activists who prefer grassroots approaches. The subject matter of those six groups was extremely important, it boiled down to the key question of what a modern cultural institution should look like. The congress was hugely significant for those who worked on it, for their self-development and self-reflection. If we're asking how it affected cultural management directly it's hard to find, but at the level of awareness it had an enormous impact. (PO03)

---

110 As late as June 2016, a website for the Poznań ECOC 2016 bid gave a telephone number for the project manager starting with a Warsaw dialling code (22): http://www.2016poznan.pl/kontakt,41,1.html (accessed 6 June 2016).

The spontaneous and very intensive integration of the local communities that occurred after the atomisation of the transformation period meant that some respondents compared this time to the period of explosion of grassroots social capital of the period of the initial Solidarity movement:

The centre was a grassroots thing, it was set up one night at Meskalina [a café/club], there was a kind of atmosphere of a return to the '80s. (PO05)

These initiatives in Poznań were successful because of the awareness of the importance of creating procedures allowing the ideas and emotions of a grassroots social movement to be turned into concrete policy. The Poznań crisis centre was set up spontaneously, thanks to the efforts of public leaders, yet from the outset, its activities were subject to procedural rigour:

As my friend put it: I thought we'd be doing the Wielkopolska Uprising, and here we were with the November Uprising again. But at the centre were was an incredible value, especially the procedures. That's an unpopular term, but the fact that everything has to be made public, after every meeting there need to be notes, you have to invite everyone who fancies it. That was mostly down to one man, Marcin Mackiewicz, who put everything in order, who introduced corporate working methods to the procedural side, as some people accused him, but he turned out to be right. (PO03)

The grassroots social movement had a significant impact on the change to the discourse: thinking about the mutual relations between the city and culture. Yet functioning outside of the official structures meant that the potential for reform was severely limited. The response quoted below provides a model illustration of how grassroots social capital dissipates when confronted with a bureaucratic structure with no interest in reform:

And here you have the issue of the authorities' reaction: it turns out that a social organ that isn't incorporated into the local government legal structure can't function in any way if it doesn't encounter the good will of the administrators. If they want to use it, they will. And the mayor in charge of culture at the time easily played us with two methods. Firstly representativeness, although it was a hyper-representative council, he always found groups that weren't represented, and for example said: "I need to ask the photographers' association still, you're not the only ones", etc. And secondly, throwing work at us. We were working voluntarily, they threw work at us, asked us for expert reports, so we worked, e.g. they asked us how to organise a festival office like the Krakow one, so we worked, brainstorming, contacts and so on for three months, and after three months the mayor says the subject's not important any more. So all our energy goes up in smoke. (PO03)

In the long run, though, these initiatives brought significant changes for the local sociocultural, but also political sphere. The biggest success turned out to be not short-term changes concerning the city's cultural policy, but the change in

discourse and creation of new frames of reference. This gave Poznań a completely
new dynamic:

> *I think that now we have a period that's been going on for about three years, maybe two and*
> *a half. It's also connected to the shake-up on Poznań's political scene and the fact that urban*
> *movements have become stronger. The fact that people have begun to come together, discuss*
> *the city, and some of the people who initiated those discussions are currently in prominent*
> *positions in the city council, and they include the mayor and the two deputy mayors, who*
> *come from urban movements. In its fullest form, the debate has been going on for a year*
> *and a half, but of course it didn't happen overnight.* (PO01)

The unleashed social capital and change in discourse became some of the most
important factors leading to important changes, one of the example of which was
Jacek Jaśkowiak's election as mayor in 2014, declared one of the biggest surprises
in local government. Poznań, which for many years created a stereotype for itself
as a "city of closed curtains", according to some respondents is now becoming
one of Poland's most progressive cities: "Free City Poznań".

In a certain sense, it was a similar story in Łódź. Here too, defeat in the
ECOC competition was seen as a spectacular failure. Unlike in Poznań, however,
the application was written on a grassroots basis, thanks to enormous public
mobilisation:

> *The whole idea for how the ECOC was to be put together came about over countless*
> *discussions, workshops, so the application doesn't have one author, it's an application*
> *written by cultural managers, NGO people, people from cultural institutions, and those*
> *who would appear in the city's sociocultural life, I don't know if they can be called elites,*
> *probably they can, but rather a group of active citizens. So that all came about from the*
> *grassroots, that had a huge value.* (ŁÓ03)

For this reason, the city's defeat in its efforts to become European Capital of
Culture was regarded as a defeat for the whole community:

> *In that respect, the situation is different from the one that arose in Gdańsk, where there*
> *was really good team dealing with the ECOC, and on the basis of the team the city decided*
> *to build a City Culture Institute, which is putting the premises from the application into*
> *practice, and that was preserved there. Here it ended with the team responsible for the*
> *application being given the role of scapegoat; the accusation was that not everything*
> *was professional, that the dreams were overhyped, that we bit off more than we could*
> *chew.* (ŁÓ02)

Nevertheless, the social capital unleashed during the ECOC application process
proved to be a lasting resource that was not based solely on short-lived emotions:

> *After the initial crisis, just after our defeat was announced and the search for someone*
> *to blame happened, a desire for joint activities remained in people, and I think that the*

outcome of the application for the ECOC is people who want to change something. Whether those changes are good or not is another matter, and not up to me to judge. But I'm not denying that activity. (ŁÓ04)

Similarly to the situation in Poznań, the integration of communities that were allowed to see themselves as the subject of social processes thanks to the endeavours to become ECOC led to the Regional Culture Congress. One of the major experiences of this congress was the self-diagnosis of the role that culture should play in the process of forming local identity. In Łódź's case, the intensive but often chaotic attempts to search for new narratives to break through the negative stereotype of a city in crisis often resulted in imitative activities. Replacing the working-class heritage with bourgeois or creative narratives failed to produce attractive frames of reference for residents, who found it difficult to identify with such values:

That energy accumulated during ŁESK, the social capital that really was generated, something needed to be done with it, it had to be forged into something. [. . .] We were left with social capital and people with competencies, but that wasn't quite in sync, and the idea for what to do with it was the Regional Culture Congress, which gave us a certain diagnosis. For example, it turned out that Łódź didn't need culture that reproduced nineteenth-century models of bourgeois culture; they're needed and have an audience, but aren't able to be pro-development, they're unable to go further and attract a new audience. (ŁÓ06)

The polar opposite was Szczecin. This was an extreme example where the social capital that the ECOC competition had stimulated was almost entirely squandered. Of all the cities we studied, it was in Szczecin that the application process had the most grassroots, civic nature. Whereas in most cases the actual idea of entering the bidding came from the local government authorities, in Szczecin it was a local female activist who mobilised local communities, ultimately succeeding in convincing the city authorities:

In my opinion the biggest asset was the fact that it was a civic initiative. It was born in the head of one person, who infected 22 institutions with it, through these ideas, and later the decision of the City Council, the decision was made that Szczecin would be entering. (SZ03)

As a result of the grassroots nature of the whole process, the institution preparing the ECOC bid became a kind of incubator of civic activity:

The ECOC attracted various people who found out about each other. The ECOC institution gave micro-grants of several thousand zloty each, and some of them are still working together. I can't say that nothing good happened. But the energy that was awakened, OK, it fell to 10 %, but how many people got involved, that showed it could be done. The ECOC let people believe it could be done. (SZ04)

Creating a space for civic activity as well as overcoming the fatalistic discourse were extremely valuable experiences in Szczecin. Owing to the city's post-migration history, it continued to grapple with the problem of its identity and suffered from a distinct deficit in social capital. These problems appeared in almost every response:

> It's a consequence of our history that we came from various parts, and especially rural communities. It was different with Wrocław – they had professors and lecturers arriving, and no one was bothered because they all knew each other. And here there was a myth that the Eastern Borderlands came here, but that's not true, because only around 20 percent of people from the Borderlands came here, but everyone came from another region too, nobody knew each other. It wasn't whole communities coming here, but individuals, and moreover mostly the illiterate countryside. That was how it looked, more or less. No one was thinking about building – the whole time there was a fear that the Germans would arrive. Young, ambitious people came here, but with the idea of just thinking about themselves, and that lived on, it was passed on bringing children up. It's a working/money-changing city shaping the myth of a marine city, but that's a myth [. . .]. In Poland generally there's a problem with lack of trust, and that's terrible here, and the worst thing is that nobody reacts to it. (SZ02)

This was also confirmed by the research commissioned by the team preparing Szczecin's ECOC application in 2010. One of the research team's conclusions was that a negative discourse had formed in Szczecin, made up of six types of rhetoric that overlap and influence each other. These are the rhetoric of a lack of identity, the rhetoric of provinciality and abandonment, the rhetoric of a lack of a big-city character, the rhetoric of weakness and alienation of the social base, the rhetoric of the lack of direction of the urban space, and the rhetoric of organisational incapability.[111] The ECOC application offered an excellent basis for the formation of an origin myth for civic Szczecin, but ultimately this could not be created. The decisions of the local authorities taken after the defeat squandered the opportunities to exploit the social capital unleashed by the bidding process. The Szczecin 2016 institution which coordinated the work of the team preparing the ECOC application was dissolved, and there was no continuation of the process of integration and self-diagnosis of the local communities. Of many similar responses, the two presented below provide a good description of the situation in Szczecin following the city's defeat:

---

111 Fiternicka-Gorzko Magdalena Gorzko Marek Czubara Tomasz, 2010, *Co z tą kulturą?* in: *Raport z badania eksploracyjnego stanu kultury w Szczecinie*, (Szczecin: Wydawnictwo Szczecińskie), 28–34.

We were lacking a kind of shake-up, a redefinition of us. It's a pity that wasn't there, because we could have made a real change. [. . .] With our ECOC, to use marine language, there was no hitting the bottom; the ship sailed into a strait, turned on its side and rusted. It was all too tepid. When the diagnosis was made,[112] what was missing was someone pounding on the table to have a discussion over whether it was a bad diagnosis because the surveys weren't carried out properly, or whether it gave cause for thought. (SZ05)

The saddest thing was what happened afterwards. The institution cost 400,000 zloty, so not much. The institution was set up on the basis of buildings that became free that needed a proprietor, and one of them was taken over by the ECOC. And nowadays that beautiful building is going to waste, and the second, less beautiful one has been successful, because there were a lot of organisations and it was hard to throw them out, so the city set up the Culture Incubator there, and that was the idea of ECOC people, for it to be a place for various people, freelancers who can come there. The effect of the ECOC is an incubator, although not in the same form as it used to be. I remember the meeting very well – the mayor was there, several dozen organisations and a lot of unattached people came, and they came, in short, to ask the deputy mayor not to close the ECOC institution. [. . .] It was a painful issue, a kind of clipping of the wings, people stopped believing in it, it was a huge opportunity to catch the wind in the sails, there was really huge potential. (SZ04)

In most of the cities competing for the title of ECOC, the social capital created during the bidding process was preserved, in both the institutional and the non-institutional dimension. The model example was Gdańsk, where the team responsible for preparing the bid was renamed as the City Culture Institute (CCI). The respondents from Gdańsk agreed on the value of the CCI's activity, mostly geared towards strengthening local identity:

The immediate result of the application was the fact that the team responsible for it was later institutionalised, and the City Culture Institute was established. This is an institution under the auspices of the city that implements urban projects. They have several very, very interesting projects, slightly transferred from the practices observed in other cities. What that did was to shift culture in the thinking of officials, whose understanding of the importance of culture is growing and who are talking about it with increasing awareness. (GD01)

There was an acceleration, because a mechanism was set up in the form of the City Culture Institute, and not just that, because the revitalisation office was also important. But that mechanism definitely helped residents, and that was very much visible, especially in the Lower Town, where the CCI was able to provide effective assistance to a little association that managed to completely change the image of this district in the eyes of residents. More and more people are coming there to a district that was thought of as non-existent, so those initiatives can be seen there. (GD03)

Thanks to the ECOC and thanks to the CCI, most of the people who worked there have been retained; apart from the big flagship events that it's continuing, the CCI also inspires

---

112 A reference to the aforementioned study on the state of Szczecin's culture.

and co-organises many local events, such as neighbourhood walks, it promotes events on a local scale. Not much in terms of the scale of the activity, but they reach many places. I don't remember that kind of scale previously [. . .] The CCI also shows the city, pulling them out from a strictly touristic image, and I see that residents are interested in discovering the city in that way. But we're talking about a micro scale, they're not spectacular events. And that's what the ECOC left behind, because it was an important element of the application, and the CCI is applying itself to unearthing the culture and identity of the city, and it's acquiring increasing numbers of people who are interested in that. (GD04)

The institutionalisation of social capital as seen in the case of the CCI in Gdańsk was something of an exception, yet this is not to say that it was wasted. It was usually manifested in the non-institutional forms characteristic of the activities of informal social movements. The residents of cities, who began to look at their city differently as a result of the ECOC bid, also felt themselves to be agents in the processes going on there. A good example might be Katowice, where residents protested en masse against the anachronous plans for repairing one of the city's main arterial roads. A local journalist explained this as follows:

Following the ECOC experience, it ought to be clear to officials that residents don't want to have an ugly city. And the behaviour of the residents of Kościuszko Street, who threw a spanner in the works for the city. That was a PR failure for the city, but also the strength of the ECOC; we live in the city centre, so we want to have greenery, benches, pedestrian crossings, because it's our city – that was the message from residents. And in my view that's what the ECOC has done, because a few years ago, if they'd tarmacked it, nobody would've said a word; new and even – it would've been simply Silesian – is good, and if not, then that's how it needs to be. No, they won't put up with that now. I think that now people care more about how their city looks. It's a culture of, I won't say the everyday, but I think that people after the ECOC want to use the city more, go somewhere, meet up. (KA01)

The specific process of institutionalisation of social capital and of the changes in cultural policies in the various cities will be described in the following chapter.

Bożena Gierat-Bieroń, Paweł Kubicki

4. Cities' Cultural Policies in the Light of the ECOC Competition

In the European political tradition, cultural policy is the responsibility of the state or representatives of a three- or four-level local government. Its principles are determined by the constitution and the relevant parliamentary acts. A city's culture policy is part of the local governments' cultural policies, as is that of the regions (voivodeships in the Polish case). Local authorities do not operate in a vacuum, but are an expression of the institutional order and long-term processes of decentralisation of competencies and tasks. The most important law regulating cultural activity in Poland is the *Law on Organising and Conducting Cultural Activity* of 25 October 1991 with later amendments.[113] In accordance with this law, the minister acts as state patron in charge of the national cultural institutions and the national heritage. Local government institutions also provide patronage within their competences. "Territorial local authorities organise cultural activity, creating local government cultural institutions for which such activity is the fundamental statutory objective. Conducting cultural activity is a mandatory duty of territorial local government units. The entities forming cultural institutions are known as organisers".[114] City authorities therefore play a statutory role in the operation of culture in Poland, and their contribution to public revenue depends on the amount of activity allocated to them. Statistics show[115] that the contribution of urban and rural municipalities to funding of culture in Poland is high, at around 3 billion zloty, which comprises 43.30 % compared to the 80 % funding by territorial local government, i.e. half (compared to districts (*powiat*) and voivodeships. Cities with district rights spend 2 billion zloty (34.5 %), districts 124 million zloty (1.8 %), and voivodeships 1 billion (20.5 %). The Ministry of Culture and National Heritage funds culture to the tune

---

113 Law on Organising and Conducting Cultural Activity of 25 October 1991 (Dz. U. [Journal of Laws] 1991 no. 144, item 492).

114 Ryszard Borowiecki (ed.), *Perspektyw rozwoju sektora kultury w Polsce* (Kraków: Oficyna ekonomiczna, 2004), 28.

115 Data from: GUS Kultura w 2015. Culture in 2015 (Warszawa: Główny Urząd Statystyczny, 2016).

of 1.8 % of the total.[116] Generally, the duties of urban municipalities are divided into five groups: obligations to subordinate cultural institutions, obligations to the city's residents in terms of provision of cultural activities, obligations to artists, protection of national heritage (monuments), and promotion of the city and its artists, including care for the city's image and brand.

The transformation period in Poland was largely characterised by implementation of laws and a reduction, followed by an increase, in the amounts of the city budget spent on culture. Culture was first subjected to a process of depoliticisation, before being repoliticised. Attempts at reform leant towards decentralisation based on insufficient budgets, followed by a return to concentration of decisions at a lower level, leaving a limited space for the activity of non-governmental and volunteer organisations. Irrespective of the dynamic of the changes, the transformation process, according to Joanna Szulborska-Łukaszewicz, brought about a greater role of culture itself in society's economic development.[117] "There was increased emphasis on freedom of choice of cultural goods and cultural education, thereby enabling free and conscious choices in the cultural sphere".[118] We now know that local governments spend the most money on the upkeep of the institutions themselves, and since this is their statutory duty, they stick rigidly to these rules, which makes formal changes more difficult.[119] As a result of the complexities of the public sector in the Polish political system, local governments are unable to make use of various instruments for streamlining effects on art and thereby generating creative impetuses for culture. This concerns at least three instruments: the possibility of supporting private owners, assuring NGOs greater continuity in realisation of their projects, and creating an effective volunteering system. Until recently, many Polish cities had no strategic documents concerning cultural development.[120] Changes in

---

116 Proportions based on GUS (Statistics Poland) data: Ministry of Culture and National Heritage – 1.493 billion (1.8 %), local government – 6.754 billion PLN (82.4 %).

117 Joanna Szulborska-Łukaszewicz, *Polityka kulturalna w Krakowie* (Kraków: Wyd. Attyka, 2009), 47.

118 Ibid., 63.

119 Local government authorities spend the most on maintaining cultural centres and institutions (29.4 %) and libraries (19.0 %), while the Ministry of Culture and National Heritage spends the most on museums (28 %) and protection of heritage (14.4 %). Data from: GUS Kultura w 2015. Culture in 2015 (Warszawa: Główny Urząd Statystyczny, 2016).

120 Artur Celiński, co-author of the publication *Miejskie polityki kulturalne* ("City Culture Policies", ResPublica Nowa, Raport z badań, Warszawa, 2013), calculates that at the time of the research, between 2010 and 2012, on city policies in the field of culture, of

this field took place very slowly, and therefore in many urban and rural municipalities culture is an extremely neglected sector. The situation improved as a result of the end of the transformation period in Poland, the implementation of EU Structural Funds by voivodeships, the convening of the Polish Cultural Congress in 2009, the Citizens of Culture movement, and exposure of the issues in conjunction with publications on culture and economics.[121] As many researchers have shown, the cultural policy of Polish cities retained an extensive[122] and sector-based model during the transformation period. It was not subject to thorough administrative reform, a state of affairs that has often come in for criticism. With time, cities' cultural policy became resistant to change and contributed little in relations between municipal council, cultural operators and recipients, while reinforcing paternalistic-clientelistic relations. Undoubted positive aspects included increased budgets for culture, open calls for managerial positions, greater care for the state of buildings, and a relatively rational employment policy. For years, cities have been taking care of their national and international image, implementing marketing strategies, and constructing promotional brands and lines that are particularly important for tourists and investors. The regulation of the cultural sphere through fundamental laws has given it a specific position in the local government setup. Since it was additionally seen as

---

66 large and medium-size Polish cities only 12 had a separate strategy for developing culture, six of which had only started in the previous two years. The remaining cities included very general ideas for culture in their development strategies.

121 The socio-political circumstances and their influence on cultural policy in the last decade and first years of the new one were described in: *Kultura w dekadzie przemian*, eds Teresa Kostyrko and Marcin Czerwiński (Warszawa: Instytut Kultury, 1998); Dorota Ilczuk, Wojciech Misiąg, *Finansowanie i organizacja kultury w gospodarce rynkowej* (Gdańsk: Instytut Badań nad Gospodarką Rynkową, 2003); Jerzy Hausner, Anna Karwińska, Jacek Purchla, *Kultura a rozwój*; as well as the articles: Bożena Gierat-Bieroń, "Kierunki rozwoju polityki kulturalnej w Polsce po 1989 r. Koncepcje ministerialne (I)", *Zarządzanie w kulturze* no. 16 (2015), 3, 205–221; and Bożena Gierat-Bieroń, "Kierunki rozwoju polityki kulturalnej w Polsce po 1989 r. Koncepcje ministerialne (II)", *Zarządzanie w kulturze*, no. 17 (2016), 2, 91–107.

122 This concept was first coined by Jacek Purchla and Andrzej Rottermund in their joint publication "Projekt reformy ustroju publicznych instytucji kultury w Polsce", *Rocznik Międzynarodowego Centrum Kultury*" 1999, no. 8, January-December. There was a similar theme (może lepiej problem considered in: in Dorota Ilczuk, Wojciech Misiag, *Finansowanie i organizacja kultury* and Katarzyna Plebańczyk, "Prawne aspekty działalności kulturalnej w latach 90. – projekty reform ustrojowych", *Zarządzanie w kulturze* (2002), vol. 3.

an autotelic field, the area of the collective-national idea, it was not regarded as being entitled to pragmatic actions such as evaluation of the effectiveness of tasks and objectives, public opinion research, or even provision of specific statistical data. When the city council is nothing more than a perfect guardian of the public budget without any development plans (not to speak of a city strategy in the field of culture), monitoring systems, or methods for measuring cultural success or failure, the cultural sphere cannot attain the anticipated dynamic. The ECOC competition in Poland made local government authorities aware of a fundamental question – that culture in large urban areas should be considered from the point of view of development,[123] and that it is necessary to be able to programme development. The competition therefore helped to shine a light on an entirely new perspective according to which culture must respond to modern-day challenges, and can and should become the catalyst of broader changes in reference to various spheres of urban reality, as well as a building block of the new local government order.

One of the main issues that emerged from the research on the effect of the ECOC in the context of urban cultural policies was the question of the impact of the application process on the administration system used by the local authorities as well as institutional changes in the various cities. Above all, as Wojciech Kłosowski notes, "[. . .] the beginning of serious reflection on the role of culture as a development factor in metropolises can probably be linked to the moment when Polish cities started to apply for the title of European Capital of Culture 2016. [. . .] The bidding period in all these cities was a time of intensive debate among circles associated with culture, the authorities, residents, the media and scientific communities, resulting in a radical intensification of perception of the role of culture. In the applications of the various cities, culture was treated as a tool for comprehensive social change".[124] The ECOC competition posed the question of how a city attains success and what use it makes of this success, as well as eliciting a discussion about the indicators of success. As a result, the Polish local government elites quickly, but often also uncritically, assimilated ideas

---

123 The concept of culture as a pro-development element had long been a favourite subject of Jerzy Hausner, who presented his forthright position on the matter at a meeting of the Polish Cultural Congress in 2009 (Warsaw), and subsequently in numerous academic publications.

124 Wojciech Kłosowski, "Kultura jako czynnik rozwoju społecznego a polityki kulturalne polskich metropolii", in: Stanisław Szultka, Piotr Zbieranek (eds), *Kultura – polityka – rozwój. O kulturze jako „dźwigni" rozwoju społecznego polskich metropolii i regionów* (Gdańsk: Instytut Badań nad Gospodarką Rynkowa, 2012), 70.

about the creative class (Richard Florida)[125] as well as Charles Landry's creative city.[126] However, the superficial conclusions drawn from such publications led to a wave of criticism of municipal governments, which for years had perpetuated the model of their role as accountants of culture, thereby hindering genuine creativity and innovativeness. It is therefore hardly surprising that the responses in the study on the ECOC 2016 competition are critical when it comes to cities' culture policies, as it turned out that the respondents' activism on behalf of the city soon achieved much more interesting solutions for the city and its residents than many years of work by local officials. What was particularly interesting in this context was the question of whether there had been qualitative changes and if culture had begun to be prioritised by local authorities. Was culture now important for local government officials who had taken the step of allowing activists to participate in administration of the city and begun to notice the actions of the third sector and/or integrated the various initiatives? In most cases, no long-term change had been experienced. What seemed to happen, of course in certain respects, was a carnival phenomenon, in which for a brief, ceremonial period, relations in the sphere of government had changed, followed by a return to the old, established state of affairs. The initiatives undertaken during the ECOC bidding process were often given special priority, and respondents frequently stressed that during the competition a distinct qualitative change in administrative workings had been apparent:

> And many of the people who were working on the ECOC at the time noticed a major difference between how things had been previously and how they were at the ECOC, and noticed that the administration can work faster and better, that you don't have to wait months for every response, but you can get it by email the next day, and that was a kind of culture shock for us. But after losing the title, everything went back to the old procedures; when the pressure fizzled out everything went back to the way it was before [...]. It was completely wasted. Unfortunately it happened in the usual way; at first we go in all guns blazing, then later there's nothing left and I have the feeling that we're left with a big void, just the memory of how great we were and what a good application we had, because we did. (KA02)

The mechanisms of institutional change initiated during the ECOC bidding process began to falter after it came to an end, as they turned out often to be task-based rather than systemic. Such views were raised especially in the cities

---

125 Florida, *The Rise of the Creative Class*; Florida, *Cities and the Creative Class* (New York–London: Routledge, 2005).
126 Landry, *The Creative City*; Landry, *The Art of City-Making* (London: Sterling VA, 2006).

holding the highest hopes for profound, long-term change of local cultural policies. Responses from Katowice and Łódź are good examples:

> But in my opinion it's still the old policy that triumphed, the desire to spend lots of money
> doing spectacular things. You can criticise it or not, but the city abandoned culture a little
> and went for business tourism. When there's something going on in the city, usually there's
> a city grant behind it, buying big events. It's an effective policy, because seats are filled, but
> it annoys me, because the city's funding a fashion show. (KA01)
> I have the feeling that we can hardly talk about lasting effects. It was a nice piece of work,
> a job well done, but it was mostly then shelved. If it has any effect, it's just the fact that
> the people who wrote the application are now active, and are higher up than they used
> to be, so that had more of an impact on the people involved in it. But as for the applica-
> tion as a document, nobody cites it, it's not a reference point, no one uses it as a policy
> document. (ŁÓ03)

The ECOC competition stimulated the hopes and aspirations of many local
communities which, for various reasons, have not been entirely fulfilled. This is
the reason for the dissatisfaction expressed by many respondents regarding city
officials, or civil servants more generally, for their inability to harness the energy
and creativity of the people working on the ECOC teams to exact lasting changes
to the system. They often responded in similar terms when asked to evaluate the
systemic changes the bidding process had brought about:

> As for the administrative sphere, the change was momentary, and later everything was
> business as usual. (KA01)

In this case, though, the problem is with the system, and we should not link it solely
to the ECOC competition. To simplify somewhat, we can identify three systemic
causes that limited the scope of the institutional changes in the bidding process.
First, the lack of long-term institutional thinking. In the modern era when public
institutions were developing, the Polish state did not exist at all following the
partitions that divided the country, and later no sovereignty. As a result, Polish
society either lacked such institutions or perceived them as foreign, and thus was
profoundly distrustful towards them. As a result, it was unable to make use of
grassroots social capital in an institutional fashion. The short lived moments of
social mobilisation usually bore the hallmarks of carnival, the best example of
which is the term "carnival of Solidarity" that functions in the official discourse
to describe the largest social movement in Poland's history, from the early 1980s.
Secondly, this problem was conditioned by the contradictions inherent in the
ECOC competition procedures. Rational, bureaucratised structures are not conducive to innovation and creativity. In a classic work analysing the antinomies of
modernity, Shmuel Eisenstadt points to the inconsistency between the creative

dimension intrinsic in visions leading to the crystallisation of modernity (pro-moted by the Renaissance, Enlightenment and revolution) and the fact of their fading, *disenchantment* of the world, resulting inexorably from the advancing routinisation of these visions, and especially from the bureaucratisation of the modern state.[127] If the structures of the European Union have changed anything in this context, it has only been by consolidating routinisation and bureaucracy. In the EU discourse, such ideas as creativity and innovation function more as "keywords", metaphorical objects for opening the treasure chest of funds. After a grant is awarded, however, innovative, creative and prosocial activities are replaced by a bureaucratised and routinised accounting procedure. These antin-omies were also revealed by our study. For example, one of the requirements of the ECOC competition is social participation and reinforcement of local social capital. This assumes inclusion in the application process of the highest-possible number of local communities. On the other hand, however, the com-petition logic requires that the application forms be written according to the rules of the grant, governed by specific rules of bureaucracy, and wide-ranging participation is at odds with such demands. Two extreme examples illustrate this antinomy: Wrocław and Łódź.

The strength of the Łódź candidacy was tremendous social mobilisation and participatory procedures adopted for the writing of the applications. And yet this also turned out to be a serious shortcoming. By emphasising participation, Łódź's application had 80 authors but no editor, and this was one of the main reasons why the city, treated as something of a "dark horse", was eliminated in the first stage:

> Like any document resulting from teamwork, it has various inconsistencies, it's hard to put everything together, and the time spent on writing that kind of application is also longer. I remember how the people were working then, the last days before submission of the appli-cation were non-stop work with no sleep, and despite corrections and our efforts, the little faults like typos occurred, and some journalists cited them later when it turned out we hadn't advanced to the next stage. (ŁÓ03)

A few months after Łódź's defeat in the first stage of the bidding process,[128] the local supplement to the *Gazeta Wyborcza* newspaper printed a critical article by

---

127 Shmuel Eisenstadt, *Utopia i nowoczesność. Porównawcza analiza cywilizacji* (Warszawa, Oficyna Naukowa, 2009), 379.

128 Designation of the European Capital of Culture 2016 Selection Panel Report on Pre-selection Warsaw, 12–13 October 2010, Ministry of Culture and National Heritage, http://www.mkidn.gov.pl/media/docs/esk2016/101115_Polska_raport_preselekcja_EN.pdf (accessed 1 August 2019). See also: Selection of the European Capital of Culture

Jędrzej Słodowski summing up the city's ECOC application with the striking title "The ŁESK 2016 application: chaos, sloppiness and waffle".[129] This article and other similar ones provided the impetus for an appraisal of Łódź's bid that resulted in a significant reduction in the social energy that the application process had unleashed:

> Unfortunately, what we called the areas of intervention were later squandered owing to the psychological aspect and the losing mentality: searching for culprits and all the negative repercussions, the negative witch-hunt, we hadn't got it so we wouldn't do it any more. The investment in people, knowledge, awareness – that survived. The people pulled themselves together after the "defeat". (ŁÓ07)

In Wrocław, the application-writing process took place in reverse. The head of the team was selected on the basis of his experience and proficiency in writing such documents. After brief consultations required by the procedures, a small, well-oiled team set about professional work:

> Prof. Chmielewski's team was set up then, and it was an administrative decision when it became clear that Poland was going to have the ECOC, and the calendar showed that it needed working on, and then I think Mayor Dutkiewicz made an administrative appointment, in the sense that there weren't any consultations – at the time there weren't such standards as consultations. (WR02).

Wrocław laid the emphasis on efficiency, and this was instrumental in its success. But this was also one of the factors that had an impact on the relatively weaker social mobilisation of residents described above. The professional preparation of the application failed to excite public emotions. The opposite was true in Łódź, where an excessively participatory application captured the public imagination.

The third and final factor was the lack of coherent urban policies on a national scale.[130] After Poland's accession to the EU, its cities were saturated with capital, and the lack of such policies often resulted in numerous dysfunctions, causing such problems as uncontrolled suburbanisation, so-called urban sprawl, privatisation of public spaces, and depopulation of city centres. For obvious reasons, this state of affairs was not conducive to development of the cultural sphere, which does not function in isolation, but is closely associated with the urban

---

for 2016 in Poland. Selection Panel. Final Selection report. Warsaw, 20–21 June 2011, https://ec.europa.eu/programmes/creative-europe/sites/creative-europe/files/files/ecoc-2016-panel-poland_en.pdf (accessed 2 August 2019).

129 http://lodz.wyborcza.pl/lodz/1,35136,8597871,Aplikacja_LESK_2016__chaos__niechlujnosc_i_wodolejstwo.html (accessed 31 July 2019).

130 Jacek Gądecki, Paweł Kubicki, "Polityki miejskie", in: Politeja (2014), no. 1, p. 135–156.

system. In addition, the very organisational logic of the ECOC competition did not provide the systemic foundations for lasting institutional changes. The organisation of the teams preparing the bids was crucial here. As described above, the characteristics of the communitas sphere in which these teams were located meant that they made a significant contribution to dynamising the ECOC effect. The problem was, however, that in the case of lasting institutional reforms this proved to be a shortcoming, for two main reasons.

Firstly, lasting institutional change depended on a combination of chance events, especially regarding the individual predispositions of leaders propelling the ECOC effect, and not systemic initiatives. In certain respects, the social mobilisation triggered by the ECOC competition resembled the mobilisation of social movements, where the key role is played by charismatic individuals and emotions. In this case, the dominant role of individuals was displayed in two dimensions. On the one hand, it entailed the engagement and/or charisma of social leaders that lent dynamism to the ECOC applications. On the other, it resulted from the very strong position held by the mayor of the city in the local government power structure. The involvement of the authority of the mayor, or lack thereof, played a decisive role in the ECOC effect, as illustrated by the below responses:

> *The mayor saw benefits for himself and his public administration in the ECOC, and therefore made a point of supporting and budgeting for that work. Because it soon turned out that the quality was very high, the administration weren't interfering, and there was a big media effect.* (KA02)
> *I suspect that the officials didn't want the ECOC, for two reasons. Firstly, it's good as it is, and everyone's comfortable with the situation. Secondly, it means extra funds, extra working hours, extra checks in Brussels, from the ministry etc., so I don't think that the people working in the public administration in Wrocław had that will. But on the other hand, there was the prominent voice of Mayor Dutkiewicz, who simply really wanted it. So I think it happened as a result of the authority of the president, and not because thinking had changed in official, administrative circles.* (WR04)

Furthermore, when the extraordinary situation caused by the ECOC competition came to an end, priorities also tended to change, and according to some respondents the city's cultural policy returned to its position from beforehand. As we shall see in the next section, in certain cities there was a noticeable qualitative change. However, excessive emotions and aspirations, if they are not institutionally harnessed, often lead to a number of dysfunctions, and not to the institutionalisation of social capital. A particularly characteristic phenomenon was that the emotions and hopes that were aroused were sorely tested in the post-competition reality, providing fertile ground for the development of a culture of mistrust – the antithesis of social capital. The responses from Szczecin and Łódź cited below provide an adequate illustration of this situation:

> But when the institutions were scrapped, everyone threw up their hands and went their own way, there was no glue. There was a lot of disappointment, because a lot had been promised, that we'd be able to implement our ideas even if we lost – the people felt cheated because they'd sold their ideas. (SZ03)
>
> When we organised the Regional Cultural Congress in 2011 and tried to make contacts with the people who'd worked on that application, they were clearly traumatised. They had problems later too, I don't know if they were formal, but concerning funding – people were also criticised for putting big money into an application which was ultimately useless. Socially, it was a big disappointment after the defeat, and a lot of time was needed before we started doing other things. (ŁÓ02)

Secondly, the position of the teams preparing the ECOC bids meant that local government administration and institutions were less likely to become so-called "learning institutions" in which reflectiveness – observing one's own thinking – plays a key role.[131] The reason for this was that in certain respects, the operation of many local authority cultural institutions can be compared to autopoeitic systems, which are not interested in communication with their surroundings, but close themselves off, legitimising the existing status quo. The processes triggered by the ECOC competition inevitably demanded reflectiveness and openness to the outside world. From this point of view, it was perceived as violation of the status quo. In certain cases, the teams preparing the ECOC application were treated as competition, rather than as a partner stimulating new tasks. This problem is illustrated by the below responses:

> What surprised me most was the fact that institutions began to be afraid of this project, for a simple reason. Some institutions could be persuaded, but others were opposed, because they were scared that we'd take their money away and enter their space. (SZ04)
>
> Very soon it turned out that those left behind were cultural institutions; it turned out that they didn't see what could be done within that kind of project, they were probably the most anachronistic element of the network. The directors of those institutions are struggling to preserve their status quo and prestige. The directors saw their institutions as something separate, and not nodes in a network, they didn't know what they could offer or what they could get by being open to a proposal from outside. It's not surprising that the main driving force of ŁESK was people from the creative industries, cultural educators, rather than people from professional cultural institutions. (ŁÓ06)

---

131 Peter M. Senge, *The Fifth Discipline. The Art and Practice of the Learning Organization* (London: Century, 1990).

In analysing the process of institutional change, we can refer to the term "hacking the system". This expression is often used by urban movements to describe the process of systemic change through collaboration with local government administration offices and institutions. By bringing their own knowledge and experience to local authority institutions, urban activists change the system from within, opening it to more participatory procedures. The ECOC competition was highly significant in this case. As we have seen, the bid teams occupied a special place in the structure – between the formal offices and institutions that are subject to their own bureaucratic logic and the spontaneous, amorphous social movements that were undergoing dynamic growth at the time in Polish cities. This position resulted in the creation of a genuinely creative space where new ideas and urban narratives could be forged. But also, and particularly importantly, it allowed them to be implemented in the formal structures of offices and institutions. This circulation of ideas was possible because the people with experience accumulated while working on the ECOC applications began to enter the local government structures. The scale of this phenomenon varied, from Lublin and Gdańsk, where one could practically refer to a generational change[132] in local authority culture management, to Szczecin, where the local government structures were exceptionally resistant to appealing to the people involved in the ECOC and benefiting from their knowledge and experience. This process took place on various tracks and not everywhere, and it was not always possible to "hack the system".

In Szczecin, the City Council was almost completely closed to the ideas and social energy that the ECOC team had engendered, as practically every respondent highlighted:

The fact that it was a grassroots initiative ultimately had a consequence. Maybe it wasn't an unwanted initiative, but a kind of abandoned child of the City Council. The mayor couldn't oppose the European Capital of Culture, but I don't suppose it was easy for him. Our city authorities didn't have much idea what to do with it and it floundered. (SZ05)

At the other end of the scale were Lublin and Gdańsk, where the ECOC bidding process resulted in the aforementioned generational change in the institutions responsible for cultural policy. This was largely due to the fact that the people engaged in the competition, as well as those recruited from the activist community in its widest sense, over time often became full-time employees of these structures, which enabled them to put the energy and creativity unleashed during

---

132 If the ECOC competition can be treated as a generational event, then Lublin is the best example, and it is in this sense that we use the term.

the bidding process to good use. The following statements from respondents from Lublin and Gdańsk offer an appropriate illustration of this process:

Then things opened up, we're going forward, we're looking for legal and financial instruments to allow us to proceed. There were an awful lot of problems with public tenders, for example. That meant that we needed to employ new people in the Culture Department and acquire new competencies. That department transformed completely, because it had to adapt to the new realities. A completely new organisational structure was needed. When it started, there were nine people here, and now there are 25. People had to adapt a bit. They had to learn a few things in this way or that. The officials were always all right, so it was a question of changing the means of management and setting new objectives. It turned out that many people suddenly unleashed their potential, the conditions changed and people began to operate differently. (LU05)

Culture, the reliable worker it is, did its job, and we have what we have. When I look at how the culture department works in this city, and the roads and bridges department, I'd swap the workers so that those from roads and bridges would go to the culture department, because at least they'd learn something and not break anything. (LU06)

At a certain point, it was a team of around a hundred people directly involved in the actual writing of the application, creating it in various areas. As time has told, today a lot of those people hold important positions in the administration and cultural institutions. I became the director of the Culture Department, and I started out as one of the people in the ECOC office in Lublin together with Mayor Wysocki, then I was section manager, then deputy director of the Culture Department, and finally director. Piotr Choroś is now head of the public participation section at the Mayor's Office. At the time he was a member of the Homo Faber Association. Rafał Koziński, who was then an ordinary staff member at the Culture Centre, is now responsible for the whole Coalition of Cities in Wrocław. I could name many such people. The process that appeared in 2007 in Lublin resulted in these people meeting, integrating, preparing the application, and later, even though the title went to Wrocław, they mostly remained in those areas or found other areas of activity, such as Piotr Celiński - today a professor at the university. Those people really were well chosen and the most active. (LU07)

In my opinion, the ECOC efforts attracted people to Gdańsk - that was the case with our ECOC office too. Diverse groups were working in accordance with the key determined by the European Commission. Gdańsk took the original decision to announce a contest for the post of project leader. The contest was decided and the project was run by the two who came out on top - they later selected people... Roman Pokojski and Ola Szymańska. That was very interesting, because Robert's from Toruń, and Ola's from Warsaw, from very different fields. That worked magnificently, and attracted many diverse people. (GD06)

These examples from Szczecin, Lublin and Gdańsk mark the extremes of the scale. In reality, the institutionalisation of social capital largely depended on a combination of factors characteristic of a given city. A certain pattern could be observed, however. During the bidding period, it was mostly the people in the ECOC teams who were learning and building individual social capital. The knowledge, competencies, experience and contacts these people obtained while working on the ECOC are now generally being put to use outside of local government structures. The responses listed below were characteristic of the majority of the cities we studied:

> It's interesting to see what all those people are doing. Practically all of them have settled down in an interesting cultural institution or are doing something interesting of their own, or are working with an NGO, because of the group that was working at the time there's hardly anyone left in the current office. (KA03)
> The institutions that prepared the applications in other cities were turned into other institutions. In Łódź it was a project started up by an NGO and implemented – on the basis of a tender – but still by an NGO. Unfortunately, in my opinion it wasn't a conscious transition – from the moment of writing the application to an institution that could later implement certain projects. (ŁÓ08)

The opinions of respondents in other cities, in which changes did take place, can be divided into several types of answer: a) the administration offices changed their style of work, making minor internal administrative reforms in the cultural sector, which is satisfactory; b) the offices made minimal changes to their administration methods, in particular introducing cultural issues (taken largely from the ECOC application forms) to the city development strategies; c) the changes were significant in the ECOC process, but are now no longer satisfactory. We treated the statements of the respondents from Wrocław to an extent separately, since during the research this city held the ECOC title, and therefore de facto was in an intensive process of change. On the one hand, Wrocław's ECOC victory is an undoubted success, but on the other, as a result of this achievement, the city is subject to particularly careful and often critical public appraisal. The respondents were interested in the impact holding the title had on the place of culture in city policies today, and how the prognosis for the future looked. The various positions are presented at length below:

a) In this case, alongside the examples from Lublin and Gdańsk outlined above,[133] significant changes in the operation of local government administration and institutions were also observed in Łódź:

> The approach to cultural institutions changed. They were institutions that were managed in a very authoritarian way, without evaluation. They were big museums in which the

---

133 During the research, the subject of positive changes in the operation of council offices and local government institutions was often highlighted in Poznań. In this case, however, the ECOC bidding process was only of indirect significance, superseded by the decisive, relatively recent change in the city authorities, including the mayor.

directors were selected without an application process and they were directors until they retired. Now there are application processes – of course there are a few exceptions that the media have seized upon. A positive example – when a theatre had no application process, the media and residents immediately latched onto it. The standard is that applications are invited and new cultural managers appear, a fresh team. At a certain point it turned out that the majority of managers were from outside of Łódź. People appeared who showed with their CV, achievements, experience, that you can win a contest without any local context. Previously it was just people from Łódź with some close connections with the city authorities and cronyism in the world of culture, and that's gone now. (ŁÓ07)

b) The city changed its administration style slightly, in particular introducing cultural issues (largely taken from the ECOC application forms) to the city development strategies. The respondents operating directly in the cultural sphere note a significant change corresponding to the needs of residents and people of culture, as illustrated by the statements cited below:

When I look at various Polish cities, the strategy that came about during the application for the ECOC later becomes the one in place for years. We wrote an application in which we set the bar very high, which it was possible to jump over only by obtaining major additional funds. As a result, even the thinking of those who decide on the shape of the budget is changing. They recognise the great importance of what the ECOC brings with it. In my opinion we hit upon a very interesting time. Only then did it begin to be recognised in Poland that culture wasn't a square peg in a round hole, but a value in itself. Perhaps culture could drag the economy with it. Secondly, that in fact to a great extent culture could be a Polish speciality, that we had something to show, and finally that culture is an instrument, but not only that. (GD06)
There was supposed to be a turn towards culture, with culture as one of Gdańsk's priorities. An additional strengthening of culture took place. That's also manifested in an increase in the budget. If we compared Gdańsk from six years ago to Gdańsk today, it's certainly reflected in the budget designated for culture. Greater empowerment of artists. (GD06)

Respondents also noticed that the city's cultural policy had become a subject of public debates and an important aspect of the urban reality. Several example quotations show the scale of this phenomenon:

It was a complete turning point, because previously concepts like the city's cultural policy weren't even being used. It was activity sponsored by chance, festivals in which the best-known names were the ones shouted about the loudest... There wasn't any multidimensional, strategic thinking, about the entire city policy. It was thinking about a single event, festival, concert..., no one arranged those blocks into any strategic action. (ŁÓ07)
We wanted to put all the experiences recorded in the applications, especially the first one, into one document. That strategy allowed us to put a lot of things in order in terms of the decision-making level – we're not surprised by various types of decisions. We prepared a map of the city, added all the cultural institutions to it and considered where there were institutions missing. That kind of document also makes it easier to apply for various

European funds – it's always possible to point to a strategy and show that it's considered and coherent with the overall city strategy. (LU07)
As for participation in the ECOC, it strengthened and gave some order to thinking about culture in Katowice. Every contest is governed by its own rules, it has procedures, formalities, so in fact it's necessary to produce a coherent project for the needs of the ECOC that takes all aspects into account. The social aspect and public engagement was important in this project. We made use of that too. For us it was an instrument for implementing the city's cultural policy. (KA05)
There were changes in cultural policy, in the way of thinking about culture as a part of the city's broad strategy. In a sense you can see a departure from a sectoral understanding of culture, based strongly on supporting institutions. Certain studies and diagnoses that we carried out during the application were used. There might still be a lot of "buts" regarding how it's being put in place. But I think that if we take the document about the strategy of the city of Gdańsk today, the role of culture in the city's strategy has definitely increased, and stopped being just a segment. (GD05)

Nowadays, the cultural strategies that cities possess or are working on are undoubtedly designated by the directions of development. As we saw earlier, this phenomenon is relatively new and raw. Yet designing and planning of cultural policies in Polish cities is progressive in nature. The way in which strategies are amended and modified is the source of doubts mostly from the institutions that are overlooked in the strategies or people who have no influence on their content:

The thing with culture management is that for years – in keeping with what we say at ideological level – we've been trying to make sure that the various cultural institutions are free. We expect some shared responsibility from them, and that usually works, but not always. And there's still lots to do here. There's no democratic form or referendum here. . . You have to try to do everything to keep up with others in culture. Often that means rows, and they can be destructive to all sides. (WR09)
Certainly culture is one of the key areas, domains in Gdańsk. There was a chance for it to be the first domain. . . When you decide to enter that kind of competition, inevitably you take responsibility for the fact that you have to put a stress on culture now. In a way that puts pressure on officials and councillors. You have to put money behind that. (GD07)
Łódź's cultural policy. . . A document was produced – rather turbulent consultations were carried out on it. It's kind of halfway between what's supposed to be institutional in culture and what's being implemented. You can't be good at everything. Flagship institutions were chosen that weren't quite chosen to show what's important from the point of view of a historical policy or one being created. What should be in the cultural policy is what sets Łódź apart. We have the avant-garde, post-industrial heritage, elements of a material, but also spiritual history, and we have film. There's the question of whether film, the studios, will ever regain the renown they had in the '70s. I'm sceptical. Warsaw and Wrocław probably took films away from us a long time ago. (ŁÓ10)
The application for the ECOC and now the application for EXPO 2022. There's a continuation here. I can say many common aspects that were in our application and now they're in

> *the EXPO project. It focuses on rebuilding and reinventing the city, but also – and this was important in the application for me – that it's not focusing on the event itself. It's supposed to be an idea for the city. (ŁÓ08)*

A change in the way city councils operate is visible, although not in the sense of a revolution in administrative structures, but rather openness to the needs of people working in the cultural sector or needs of non-governmental organisations and their important functions for the development of civil society. The respondents frequently highlighted this state of affairs:

> *The cultural policy of the city of Łódź has become more open. The city administration has become very open. There were lots of people involved, then they got jobs in cultural institutions. Every city had some kind of cultural policy. What changed was that people really started to discuss something, it started to be publicised. Now there are different budgets, a different way of working with NGOs. There are meetings where NGOs are invited, there are contests consulted with NGOs, the civic budget. Sometimes it's hard to say how much that was solely an effect of the ECOC bidding process. It was a series of events going on at the same time. But the increased budgets, more independent institutions. . . that was in our applications. The council realised that this was what was needed. (ŁÓ08)*

An important change within municipal administrations was the aforementioned recognition of independent research concerning the operation of the cultural sphere, which provided concrete data pointing the way for further steps, directions, trends and needs. It is not a common phenomenon in Poland for local authorities to fund studies on the cultural sphere. The example from Szczecin described above was an exception. In Wrocław, however, in particular in the context of implementation of the ECOC programme, research on culture has been and continues to be carried out.

> *In Wrocław an important step was taken. We previously did research not only on culture, but a kind of public diagnosis on a large sample – 5000 people – and from that we had interesting data on how people live and what they expect. It might be continued, but these are costly things, often left till the end. It's not always possible to get the numbers. There's a problem in museums – some have high attendance, others low, and they need to work out why that's the case. It's similar in galleries – great, interesting art, and no people. (WR09)*

c) The changes were considerable in conjunction with the ECOC process, but are now unsatisfactory. Such opinions were expressed by respondents from various cities and diverse circles:

> *Going back a few years, Gdańsk didn't have a Culture Department, just a Sport Department, functioning for a few months, which equated cultural policy with promotion of both sport and culture. Cultural policy was equated with maintaining a few museums, a few cultural institutions and ones which are identified with Gdańsk's cultural heritage. The Culture Department now constantly has insufficient mechanisms for supporting the creativity and*

activity of the non-governmental sector. The department didn't emphasise initiatives asso-
ciated with the various forms of culture. Gdańsk didn't recognise and still doesn't see the
potential that lies in the possibility of promoting the city through culture, which is impor-
tant for the overall city policy, focusing on various areas. (GD06)

In a sense we also have the ECOC to thank for the fact that we have a plenipotentiary for
non-governmental organisations, the city is more open to working with NGOs, and they
have greater influence on what's going on. So we have a genuine influence from the third
sector. (KA07)

What worries me today about culture in Łódź? That it's used instrumentally for promo-
tional and entertainment activities, culture's confused with entertainment, lots of money is
spent on entertainment, and less on cultural, social and educational activities. It's kind of
keyword thinking. Łódź – city of four cultures – and we do a festival, we have institutions
that take care of the traditions – especially the Jewish ones – so a Dialogue Centre. At the
same time we get into things that shouldn't be taken into account at all, like these super
picnics etc. I understand the need for entertainment, but that's not it. Not all initiatives go
together, there should be some selection, you need to be able to rank it. It's a difficult process,
because the City Hall is a participant and the creator of various cliques and procedures,
and you need to be able to link certain things together. The most important thing in this
cultural Łódź is the avant-garde, the industrial character and the films. Who will make
the choice? What's the flagship institution? Of course I could do that arbitrarily, but imme-
diately there's a conflict between the various groups. Although we work together, everyone
looks after themselves a bit. (ŁÓ10)

A negative consequence of the changes caused by the ECOC competition was the
monopolisation of activities by one institution. According to the respondents,
such approaches fail because they do not change the overall cultural landscape,
as well as leading to antagonisms between artistic communities.

I'm against a situation whereby there's one leading institution that has a gigantic budget
and various other institutions, and that one makes the decisions on distributing funds. It's a
policy error. That institution has become an instrument of the city's cultural policy. (KA07)

A further important factor was that the people involved in the ECOC often
spontaneously took the initiative. Seeing that the good practices they had started
would probably not be implemented by the public authorities, they attempted
to make use of them themselves, which helped with cooperation. The following
quotation provides an apt illustration of this mechanism:

Most importantly, experts appeared from outside and started talking about the city's cul-
tural policy, thematic working groups appeared. Unfortunately, what we called the areas of
intervention were later wasted as a result of the psychological aspect and the losing men-
tality: looking for a someone to blame, and all the negative repercussions, a negative ap-
proach saying that we didn't get it, so we wouldn't do it any more. The investment in people,
in knowledge, in awareness – that survived. The people pulled themselves together after the
"defeat". Two years later various movements sprang up around the theatre, film community

etc. The result of that was that people began talking to each other. Before that it was a kind of fragmented community, so the communities integrated with each other... (ŁÓ07)

The difficulties referred to in this statement regarding the changing cultural policy in Łódź also resulted from the independence of the institution preparing the application form, since it was not later incorporated into the city structures or transformed into a city institution, as was the case in places including Gdańsk and Katowice:

> *The institutions that put the applications together in other cities were converted into different institutions. In Łódź it was a project initiated by an NGO and implemented – on the basis of the competition – but still by an NGO. Unfortunately, in my opinion that wasn't a conscious transition – from the moment of writing the application to an institution that could later put certain projects into practice.* (ŁÓ08)

A further factor that it is important to address in this context is the question of metropolitan cooperation in the regions. The two cities that declared an interest in metropolitan issues, Gdańsk and Katowice, continue to raise the subject today, albeit to varying degrees. Katowice defined collaboration within the framework of the Metropolitan Association of Upper Silesia, an agglomeration of 14 towns and cities with a total population of around 2 million. A resolution was passed on this issue, the association was registered in 2007, and work was commenced in conjunction with the voivodeship. Horizontal directions of collaboration were designated, including cultural issues. One objective was to build a metropolitan consciousness based on the tradition of the region. However, respondents noted that the project was "frozen" as a result of excessive discrepancies regarding the leading role of Katowice in the Upper Silesia conurbation. The Gdańsk application form referred to "Gdańsk and Metropolis 2016", even envisaging a joint candidacy for the ECOC title between the city and the remaining parts of the Tri-City conurbation (especially Gdynia and Sopot). The ECOC was meant to be an instrument for integrating the region and creating a metropolis. The metropolitan area numbers approximately 1 million residents, a combination of regional and national interests.[134] Ultimately, however, little was done in this respect, as a result of the rivalry between the three main cities in the agglomeration, differences in budgetary spending, certain events and personal animosities.

> *Gdańsk's main slogan was "Gdańsk and Metropolis", which of course raised doubts, but previous experiences showed that one can engage the region. That resulted in the Culture Commission being set up as part of the Metropolitan Association. The feeling of the largest city in the region that it owed something to its partners, smaller towns, is very powerful.*

---

134 More on this in the Appendix.

Next year another Metropolitan Culture Forum will take place – that shows a certain type of agitation. You need to remember that the largest financial outlays on these things come from Gdańsk. It's not easy, because the local government law clearly regulates the way money can be spent. (GD06)

The cities signed up, but the whole time we were struggling, trying to sort our relationship out, because the main subject of contention was what the name of the project was and how much it would involve events from the other cities. It was a procedural problem that it was one city applying, and not the region. We asked a few times whether it could be done differently, and received an absolutely clear answer. The conflict became evident. I still believe that the Tri-City's cultural potential is huge as soon as you think of it as a joint venture. Unfortunately, the ECOC didn't manage to construct that. (GD06)

It was at a diagnostic level. To be a city of culture or not to be? Why suddenly a city of culture and not ecology, or for example a city that will be a kind of centre. Because the level of services, of commerce here could become something for the whole agglomeration to trade on, or for example a services centre for the whole agglomeration, because there are the best doctors, dentists etc. The thing is that when the decision was made that Katowice would also be going for the "beauty contest" for the title of European City of Culture..., at least something at the level of diagnosis should be treated seriously. (KA06)

Our study showed that the work on cultural policy taking place at present in the majority of the cities we examined results from specific ideas contained in the application form. A response from Katowice, for example:

On 15 December last year [2015] Katowice became the first city in Poland, and I think the first in Central Europe, to join the network of UNESCO active and creative cities in the field of music. That's a continuation of what came before inasmuch as the final verdict on the bid stated that Katowice is definitely the capital of music. Everything we defined in the application in terms of a platform and musical space, from very many smaller projects, via large ones concerning spectacular festival ventures, to educational initiatives and workshops, will be implemented in the framework of the creative city. (KA06)

It was a similar story in Gdańsk, where the question of opening the city towards "water" was one of the application's strategic tasks. However, respondents noted that the discussion on this subject is not yet complete:

Gdańsk's turn "towards the water" is an ongoing process. The city policy is changing here. Gdańsk is trying to make use of its water. The city is thinking of starting up water routes... What can be rescued and have its importance restored is being done. Is it effective? That's debatable. (GD05)

The respondents also highlighted the need to diversify the system of funding culture. This was frequently perceived as an immediate result of the ECOC. Many of the people working in the broad cultural sphere and NGO sector and collaborating with the City Council on the ECOC acquired knowledge on city budgets, outlay on culture, and the impact of public consultations on division of funds, and recognised the importance of transparency of finances in this regard. This had a certain impact on the empowerment of dialogue partners, but also raised doubts as to how long such a situation could last.

> *Usually there's official culture and civic culture, and they often don't overlap. Although we have a single budget, it's passed on to the institutions, and the directors make decisions individually. On the other hand, we have a system for NGOs, and here it's not the council that decides on the subsidies, but a group of people – a grants committee. A great deal of decentralisation. On top of that there are funds from the Ministry of Culture, which awards grants. Plus there are sponsorship funds. That was the kind of culture we were aiming for – well funded. (LU07)*
>
> *If the leaders of the city are consciously emphasising development, they need to understand that it requires a culture, investment, repair infrastructure. But it also means working with the community, discussing finances, openness to collaboration, negotiations. The income to the budget is regularly increasing. When we were embarking on the project, we adopted a resolution about its funding – because that was a formal requirement. When we didn't get the title, those conditions changed. But the increase for culture, for initiatives, so for these soft projects, was retained. (KA05)*
>
> *A social dialogue box was set up in the structure of the City Council for the ECOC – it was a kind of new tool: a resident could write something and put it in the box. It's another matter that the whole system wasn't able to just transform as if touched by a magic wand under the influence of culture. In the application there are plans that we'll change the whole system for managing culture and the city, that culture will become an impetus for improving institutions, democratising them, listening to needs – that was the kind of thing we wrote in the application. The Culture of Space Council was set up too, which was people who started to get involved in designing the city, urban planning – that's still functioning now. Then there was the Culture Council, mainly with representatives of the world of culture and non-governmental organisations. NGOs made a lot out of it. But the question is whether it was just then (because the budgets increased), or whether they're still using it, and whether young organisations are able to do so too. It's a question of whether the ECOC was geared towards the specific beneficiaries that we know and that we nurtured ourselves, or whether there was a self-acting mechanism. I don't know if we can answer that. I can have a crack, because I have arguments for both sides. (LU06)*

The appearance, or promise, of extra money for culture for 2016 raised artists' hopes of a better situation in cities' artistic and cultural lives. Culture, it seemed, could be important after all, and artists could be appreciated. Poland had for many years nurtured the belief in the "messianistic" ethos of the Polish poet, taken directly from Romantic literature and enjoying great popularity in the communist era. In the first years of the political and social transformation, artists and writers lost out in terms of finance and prestige, as artistic studios were abolished, the activity of artistic unions was questioned, the wait continued for a new law on cinematography, low wages were prevalent, there was no social security for creative professions,[135] and copyright laws dated back 40 years. For a long time, Polish local authorities failed to grasp that a city's capital was also built from its artistic capital, for which it is essential to develop the appropriate infrastructure and institutional sphere. The situation changed markedly only when Poland began to absorb Structural Funds (from 2004 onwards), i.e. de facto only in recent years. The respondents' statements show that, although support for artists was the last link in changes to cultural policies, to a certain extent it now exists. The ECOC competition certainly transformed the awareness of local governments in this area too. The responses listed below show exactly how it did this. The ECOC was favourable to artists, but mostly those who already had their own established brand and a solid professional position:

> *I have a case of artists who, organising in various types of associations, aren't particularly happy about the support, because they have a different status. Some more recognised artists – I'm particularly thinking of painters – get good prices for example for renting a studio. (WR08)*

Artists benefit from the fact that cities are becoming major centres of artistic life, equipped with modern artistic institutions, with prospects of employment, and consequently of creative development:

> *The city leaders know that the cultural, investment and repair infrastructure is important, but also collaboration with the community, discussions on finances, openness to cooperation. That comes with negotiation. Collaboration with the Music Academy and Fine Arts Academy: we supported the Fine Arts Academy's investment initiatives and building of the Music Academy's Concert Hall. Certain academic projects are supported financially by the city. The university rectors are very positive. They say good things in their forums. We really want the city to be a supporting partner, including with logistical support. But very often that entails financial support. (KA05)*

In certain cities, the cooperation situation has improved on the artist–cultural institutions axis:

> *It's always a difficult subject, because every city has to choose. Just as a coach selects a team – some play, others don't. And when we were putting the ECOC project together, we couldn't invite everyone to work with us. There are always some negative voices, the*

---

135 Good descriptions of the situation of Polish culture in the first decade of transformation are provided by: Marian Golka, *Transformacja systemowa a kultura w Polsce* (Warszawa: Instytut Kultury, 1989); Jerzy Damrosz, *Kultura polska w nowej sytuacji historycznej* (Warszawa: Instytut Kultury, 1998); and Teresa Kostyrko, Marcin Czerwiński (eds), *Kultura polska w dekadzie przemian* (Warszawa: IK, 1999).

proverbial sticky situation. In Gdańsk it wasn't very sticky – especially after they lost. The artists began working a little closer to cultural institutions and participating in cultural life, going outside of their area. It's a bit hard for me to talk about that now. I like the fact that the City Culture Institute has a cultural observatory – research evaluating and forecasting – that's going very well for them. The city really needs that. Observing from the outside – definitely the situation hasn't worsened. (GD08)

Artists' experiences from the ECOC competition gave them the opportunity for greater support from public funds:

As for hard factors, the grant policy in the city changed, grant contests emerged, festivals that paved their own way in behind-the-scenes discussions had specific funding. After the ECOC there were three contests: for big events – over 50,000 PLN, small events – less than 50,000 PLN, and contests for artists' grants – so-called small grants. Proper instruments appeared, the mayor's grant. (ŁÓ07)

There were no programmes supporting mobility. A programme concerning artistic studios emerged. . . There were instruments for supporting creativity, which Gdańsk hadn't had previously. In that sense it's seen as a certain change. The institutional landscape changed a lot, artistic venues are more open to initiatives that have a direct impact on artistic activity. More important than the amount is the change in thinking about the role of institutions, how this institutional potential can serve individuals. New spaces also appeared in residential programmes. Contrary to appearances, a lot changed in Gdańsk's cultural policy. I have the sense that a conscious cultural policy has just begun. The situation still needs action and changes. (GD05)

Analysis of this study showed that, as activities in cities became generally more dynamic as a result of the bidding process and frequent visits from Polish and international experts and artists, sharing good practices in matters including space, rental and other issues regarding investment in artists, practices of artists being provided with rooms, studios and exhibition spaces became more common:

Two major infrastructure instruments have also emerged. The first is spaces for creative people along Piotrkowska Street, and the second is the Księży Młyn artistic district, which also came about as an idea in our application. We wanted there to be artists' studios in that historical district – several dozen studios have opened there over the last four years. There's also EC1 – the biggest flagship cultural institution, which is continually developing. Yesterday it won a National Geographic *prize for the biggest miracle in Poland in 2016.*[136] (ŁÓ07)

---

136 *National Geographic Traveller Poland* "7 Miracles of Poland" prize.

The respondents also noted that during the application process, which were focused on discovering a city's own resources, increased importance of local artists could be noticed:

> *That changed too, although sometimes it took a long time. This year people are only just becoming aware that it's worth backing Polish artists. It's not just about inviting artists from other cities, but maybe it's also worth constructing a policy to allow Łódź's artists to develop. (ŁÓ08)*

From the point of view of issues connected to cultural policy, above all we have the ECOC competition in Poland to thank for generating a new language of discussion on the role of the city in the contemporary world and the role of a city's cultural policy. It is evident today that the current debates are not dominated by the previous burning questions of maintenance of cultural institutions, leaking roofs, actors' wages or the problem of emigration of opera soloists. A multifaceted discourse began on the creativity of individuals and of the city and its residents, including artists. In this context we can again cite the theoretical concepts of Pierre Bourdieu, who wrote that "creativity is fundamentally about generating new ideas and new forms, and much of this is dependent on new labor pools who bring forth fresh ways of interpreting the world".[137] With this in mind, it seems that the ECOC bidding process created favourable conditions for building trust on the local government–artists axis. For many years, this relationship was dominated by a historically grounded syndrome of mutual distrust: the authorities towards artists and vice versa.[138] In order for new relations and procedures to emerge, the city must be open to pragmatic visionaries – decision makers but also artists, activists and consumers of art. This horizontal placement of the active entities operating in a city paves the way for development of practices of a partnership-based and participatory mechanism of joint responsibility for the city understood as a common good. And even if art as such is not necessarily subject to the laws of democracy (this much has been clear since antiquity), its creators can join the pro-democratic process of its dissemination and usage, launching a constructive dialogue with other entities creating culture. In the globalising world, everybody is dependent on each other like communicating

---

137 Elizabeth Currid, *The Warhol Economy. How Fashion, Art, and Music Drive New York City* (Princeton–Oxford: Princeton University Press, 2007), 13.

138 In terms of the artists, this was justified by many years of restriction of their creative freedom by censorship, while for the authorities, it was based on a perception of artists as irresponsible aesthetes.

vessels – without art there is no culture, and without culture there is no art. And it comes full circle.

Andreas Billert wrote that we are functioning today in a strange tension "[...] between discovery and a return to the 'inherited city' and 'shooting' new impulses of the global economy into its structures".[139] Billert is correct in this view, illustrating the entire process through which the ECOC competition allowed cities to discover their own resources. As we described in the chapter concerning the identity of the city, the bidding process triggered self-reflection and self-diagnosis in the cities. A further factor in the processes of "discovering" the place's urban character and "opening one's eyes to the city" was the inclusion of specific cities in the European debate on the role of European Capitals of Culture in the development of European societies and the creativity of Europeans. This is significant because of the synergy that exists between the operation of the EU's cultural policy and its other policies, meaning that the ECOC has a certain relationship with the cohesion policy and programmes supporting creative industries. The respondents were very much mindful of European trends in thinking about culture in their cities. Even if they did not put a direct name to these phenomena, they had assimilated concepts of integrated planning and strengthened territorial cohesion, i.e. the fundamental premises of the EU's cohesion policy. As we know, European cities are the main engine of economic growth. In order to help them to function more smoothly, the Union provides ready-y-made proposals and recommendations. One of these was the document *Cities of Tomorrow – Challenges, Visions, Ways Forward*[140] from 2010, which noted, for example, the need to implement management solutions "based on people, and not on places",[141] or to "combine the formal structures of administration with flexible, informal structures of management corresponding to the scale of occurrence of a given challenge",[142] as well as to "create systems of management making it possible to build joint visions combining competing objectives and opposing models of development".[143]

---

139 Andreas Billert, "Kultura i rozwój społeczny i przestrzenny miasta. Doświadczenia niemieckie", in Stanisław Szultka, Piotr Zbieranek, *Kultura – Polityka – Rozwój*, 22.

140 European Union, Regional Policy, *Cities of Tomorrow – Challenges, Visions, Ways Forward* (2011), https://ec.europa.eu/regional_policy/en/information/publications/reports/2011/cities-of-tomorrow-challenges-visions-ways-forward   (accessed 27 June 2019).

141 Anna Augustyn, "Polityka miejska w Polsce w świetle polityki spójności UE na lata 2014–2020", in *Problemy Rozwoju Miast* (2012), 9/2, 2012, 7–15.

142 Ibid., 10.

143 Ibid.

According to the respondents, however, the various innovative methods of implementing cultural policy in cities had not received an immediate response from Polish local government officials, and in some cases there had been no response at all. The strength of being accustomed to working methods in use for years took precedence over the possibility of adjusting them. The creation of urban spaces as areas of artistic activities was often met with some resistance, albeit perhaps somewhat less as a result of the general increased acceptance of new art forms, as described in the previous chapters. In certain cases, grassroots creativity in parallel with institutional initiatives is welcomed in Polish cities, while in others it is intentionally ignored. One might assume that the ECOC process led local governments to be open to a change in culture, but they do not fully recognise its function for the future. Furthermore, in many cities there is a lingering belief among officials that the municipal council is an emanation of the urban community. According to many of our respondents, however, it remains an institution with a tendency to be closed to the reality of the city. The participatory approach to cultural initiatives as an expression of egalitarian responsibility of people for a community is something new in Polish cultural policy, and continues to be more a proposal than an everyday standard.

There is no doubt that local authorities' investment policy resulting from the implementation of Structural Funds changed the possibilities in the cultural sphere. Many modern facilities, museums and concert halls were built, some of them becoming a permanent fixture in the landscape of Polish cities and important elements of their structure. The cultural aspirations stimulated by the ECOC competition only heightened the impact of such institutions. Nevertheless, the utilisation of these sites remains an important question, along with clarifying their role in the strategies and plans for sustainable development of cities in the future. This problem will be discussed in detail in the chapter "Infrastructure: New Cultural Institutions".

Bożena Gierat-Bieroń, Paweł Kubicki

5. Urban Networks. Coalitions of Cities

Among the most important characteristics of the Western city is reflectiveness, which stimulates thinking, creating favourable conditions for the development of innovation.[144] Reflectiveness is formed in part thanks to networking, which stimulates the movement of people and ideas. For a resident of a city incorporated into an exchange network, the experience of "otherness" is an everyday occurrence that gives food for thought and stimulates reflection on oneself and one's group, thereby supporting the formation of a local identity. The networking that is so characteristic of modern times has a long tradition in Europe. One of the specific characteristics of European urban civilisation was the creation of city networks. Europe as a sociocultural space emerged and was able to integrate largely as a result of cities incorporated in networks of mutual relations. Town rights and everything related to them spread in the framework of European city networks. They were codified in the so-called *mother town*, and disseminated into *daughter towns*.[145] It was thanks to exchange and cooperation that Poland at the dawn of its statehood was able to participate in Europe's most important political, economic and sociocultural processes. The country's gradual exclusion from this network, resulted in its subsidence to ever more distant peripheries. Being outside of exchange networks is tantamount to stagnation and marginalisation.

These relationships in contemporary European integration make networking extremely important. The integration process stimulates cooperation at many levels and in a wide sense, the most concrete expression of which is the establishment of foundations and associations of an international or transnational nature. To an extent, Europe's cultural networking was connected to the lack of a formal cultural policy in the European Community (until the Maastricht Treaty), and the consequent weakness of the cultural sector regarding the public policies included and developed in the unification process. The formation of sectoral groups, consortia, elite clubs, organisations, federations, various leagues or forums was, and still is, supposed to provide the opportunity for exchange of ideas, thoughts, knowledge and experience within sectors and across borders.

---

144 For more on this subject see Kubicki, *Wynajdywanie miejskości*, 30–40.
145 Robert Bartlett, *The Making of Europe: Conquest, Colonization and Cultural Change* (Princeton: Princeton University Press, 1994), 173–175.

In a sense, this is an extension of the international or intergovernmental cooperation to which culture was subjected, which also creates an entirely innovative way for institutions and people to communicate with one another.[146] The notion of a "good practice" is one of the EU's oldest indicators produced to define common searches going on within the processes of integration. Practitioners were meant to exchange practices, since even within one field (e.g. medicine), practices had various accomplishments depending on the level of a country's development as well as the degree of professionalisation of research and scientific discoveries. In fact since the early 1980s, Western Europe has been covered by a network of cultural associations and organisations,[147] which have gradually transformed into a platform of exchange of knowledge and experience. Over time, professional sector consortia have begun to develop, becoming flexible cosmopolitan organisations implementing the working methods in place at the time and responding to the challenges of the era of new economics and creative industries.

The Resolution of the Council and the Ministers of Culture Meeting within the Council of 14 November 1991[148] was the first document to call for development of this type of non-governmental activity in the cultural realm, as well as for its support by the European Commission as proof of the growing awareness of the European dimension of culture, increasing integration processes and the creation of new forms of collaboration at supranational level.[149] Article 167 of Title XIII of the Treaty on European Union from Maastricht expressed full support for the idea of networked culture, stating that: "Action by the Union shall be aimed at encouraging cooperation between Member States and, if necessary, supporting and supplementing their action in the following areas: improvement of the knowledge and dissemination of the culture and history of the European peoples; conservation and safeguarding of cultural heritage of European

---

146　J. Mark Schuster describes the process astutely in the book *Informacja w polityce kulturalnej. Infrastruktura informacyjna i badawcza* (Kraków: Jagiellonian University Press, 2007), 19.

147　Council of Europe, *Forum of European Networks of Cultural Centres* (Strasbourg, 1988).

148　Resolution of the Council and the Ministers of Culture Meeting within the Council of 14 November 1991 on European cultural networks (91/C 314/01).

149　Kazimierz Waluch, author of the book *Sieci współpracy kulturalnej w Europie* ("Cultural Cooperation Networks in Europe" (Warszawa: Difin, 2012)), traces the history of cooperation networks to former times, at least the eighteenth century, and focuses particularly on the work of the International Museum Office (IMO), founded in 1926, and the International of Library Associations and Institutions (IFLA), established in Scotland in 1927.

significance; non-commercial cultural exchanges; artistic and literary creation, including in the audiovisual sector".[150] Cultural networks were included in
"non-commercial exchange", since the crux of their activity was confrontation of
views, problems, information, knowledge, and experiences, as well as promoting
joint forms of activity. Networks are characterised by independence and the
profound personal engagement of members. Gudrun Pehn (1999)[151] lists four
main characteristics of network organisations: 1) strong interpersonal relations
that go beyond purely competence-based issues, 2) lack of hierarchy, 3) openness to development and change, 4) innovativeness of structures and actions.
Rod Fisher[152] attributes the increased popularity of networks to the fact that
they permitted flexible communication, which translated into solving specific
problems in the field of culture at low cost and in a horizontal manner. What
was new was their non-institutional character and independence. Among the
typical features of the activity of a network, the Coalition of Cities which we
will describe below was characterised by advocacy, since, as Małgorzata Sternal
writes (2012), such organisations are "an important voice of the community in
the forum of European institutions, advocating for the introduction of legal
and financial solutions favourable for the cultural sector in Europe".[153] In the
Coalition of Cities, this "advocacy" would also take place in the national forum –
calling for specific solutions in cities' cultural policies. Over time, the specific
Polish proposals in this regard could be transferred to the European and international forum. Research shows that European cultural networks followed a path
from a visionary decade, via a pragmatic decade to a decade of new regulations,
becoming increasingly large and more effective, but also increasingly subject to
the political lobby. Researchers underline the benefits[154] that European cultural

150 Treaty on European Union, Official Journal C 326, 26/10/2012 P. 0001 – 0390 https://
eur-lex.europa.eu/legal-content/EN/TXT/HTML/?uri=CELEX:12012E/TXT.
151 Gudrun Pehn, *Networking Culture. The Role of European Cultural Networks*
(Strasbourg: Council of Europe Publishing, 1999), 29.
152 Rod Fisher (ed.), *Arts Networking in Europe* (London: The Arts Council of
England, 1997).
153 Małgorzata Sternal, "Sieci współpracy kulturalnej – czym są, jak powstają i jak działają?",
in: *Pod lupą: Europejskie sieci współpracy kulturalnej w praktyce* (Warszawa: Cultural
Contact Point, Adam Mickiewicz Institute, 2012), 10.
154 Among others: Silvia Bagdadli, "Museums and Theatre Networks in Italy: Determinants
and Typology", *International Journal of Arts Management*, Vol. 6, no. 1 (Fall, 2003),
19–29; Tanja A. Börzel "Networks in EU Multi-Level Governance: Concepts and
Contributions", *Journal of Public Policy* (2009), no. 2, pp. 135–151.

networks draw from this cooperation. These include mutual and common promotion of organisations, creativity resulting from the informal structures of NGOs or the energy of the activists that form them, gaining the competencies needed to move freely in the international community (including EU regulations), ability to find partners, joint acquisition of grants and administration of international projects. At the same time, they emphasise a certain thanklessness of working in networks resulting from the difficulty in funding them, working at the grassroots, or gaining the trust of public institutions. According to Jean-Pierre Deru,[155] the director of one of the first such organisations in Europe (the Marcel Hicter Association), a major obstacle in the development of European cultural networks is the current hierarchisation resulting from the rules of competition. Over many years of formation of networks, some of them carved out a stable brand for themselves which allowed them to make extensive use of European funds. They have high recognition in the market, and are therefore dominant in the apparently democratically formed NGO community. Deru proposes a model of how networks are formed and then develop. Let us take a closer look at this in order to provide a context for the Coalition of Cities in its own process of formation. Deru mentions five stages: "Forming: start, network's beginnings; Storming: initial chaos, ideas result in the first phase of activity; Norming: network begins to appear and stabilize; Performing: network knows where it is, how it should perform, and who are its members; Adjourning: the most difficult and delicate stage – network must become aware that its life has come to an end and either the work should be started anew or it is time to do something new".[156] Indisputably, cultural networks are regarded[157] as an innovative phenomenon in cultural management in Europe, not least because they promote self-organisation and modern management of "small costs", demonstrating the high self-awareness of the organisations associated with them. Furthermore, they contribute to the creation of lasting supranational connections; they lobby, strengthening international bodies in the collective protection of the interests of culture and cultural operators; and in a certain sense they are an ally to the EU in generating original, non-state organisational solutions and building a civil

---

155 Jean-Pierre Deru, *Powtórka z kultury; Sieci współpracy kulturalnej w Europie*, http://wiadomosci.ngo.pl/wiadomosc/672703.html (accessed 3 January 2017).

156 In making this distinction, Deru was inspired by the works of the American economist Neil Wallace. Jean-Pierre Deru, *Development of Cultural Networks in Europe: Challenges and Trends*, http://www.culturecongress.eu/en/ngo/ngo_bestpractice_deru (accessed 27 June 2019).

157 Waluch, *Sieci współpracy kulturalnej.*

society. For many years, they were a symbol of a post-political model of collaboration. This model was based on an innovative method of joint administration of many equal entities stemming from various national and political realities and creating new structures breaking the state monopoly on cooperation in Europe. According to Kazimierz Waluch,[158] networks now seek to play more of an important role in the mainstream of EU cultural policy and national policies. They want to offer a different type of collaboration to the Union, which shows an inclination towards institutions with a suitably stabilised political position. This should be built not on statism and bureaucracy, but on interactive work for joint enterprises and exchange of knowledge.

From tournament of cities to coalition of cities

The decisions made by the various cities to enter the bidding to become Poland's representative as European Capital of Culture were taken in context. Simplifying somewhat, we can venture the assertion that a ranking discourse was dominant. This was a time when both the media and local government authorities placed considerable emphasis on various ranking lists, using them to measure the level of cities' development. Such lists of course have their uses, especially as gauges of the evaluation and reflectivisation of local urban policies. In the first years after Poland's accession to the EU, however, it became very clear that certain actions of local governments were influenced more by a desire to improve short-term ranking indicators than to develop long-term policies providing foundations for lasting development of cities. In this context, the ECOC competition, entered by all Poland's major cities with the exception of Krakow, initially triggered a spirit of competition, as the words of one respondent demonstrate:

> There was kind of rivalry mechanism set off, like when there was once a "Tournament of Cities". Unfortunately, thinking about culture in the heads of the decision makers is often thinking about rivalry. The decision was made to enter the competition because everyone else was entering it. (PO03)

In practice, the process of applying for the ECOC had the opposite effect. Rather than ambitious rivalry geared towards improving short-term ranking indicators, it turned out to be a networking mechanism. It allowed the various cities to work together, stimulating the diffusion of ideas and good practices, and made a major contribution to a change in thinking about the role of culture in the city-making

---

158 Ibid., 40.

process, and especially its role in the formation of local identities. The networking cooperation that developed over time in the shape of the Coalition of Cities proved to be one of the more important long-term effects of the ECOC bidding process.

The character of the communitas sphere outlined in previous chapters also contributed to greater reflectiveness, and this in turn permitted the creation of a networking forum for exchange of good practices in the cultural sphere. This reflectivisation is illustrated by many similar responses:

> In the course of ŁESK, the process of examining each other was very important. I remember well discussions about what Katowice or Lublin were doing. Those were good experiences. In addition you're left with contacts, we learned various things, exchanged specialists. Those experiences show that that kind of coalition makes sense. Plus, in my opinion no Polish city has the resources just to do things on its own. (ŁÓ02)

The result of this thinking was the Coalition of Cities, the framework of which emerged during the bidding process. The Coalition of Cities is an unprecedented initiative in the history of the European Capital of Culture programme. It emerged from a desire for authentic collaboration among the cities applying for the title of ECOC 2016, and particularly thanks to the strong ties formed between the teams responsible for putting the applications together. From the outset, the participants in the initiative were both representatives of the local authorities and people from the ECOC offices, i.e. the authors working on the application forms or the co-authors of the main artistic and cultural concepts. There was an emphasis from the beginning on open collaboration and exchange of ideas and aesthetic concepts, which are an overriding value compared to the temptations of intercity rivalry and competition. The initiators met on several occasions (at conferences in Lublin and Wrocław, a workshop in Gdańsk and the Congress in Łódź) before the programme for presentation of the cities at Wrocław 2016 was determined – an artistic platform of the Coalition of Cities for the ECOC Wrocław 2016. A joint document was published, *Coalition of Cities. Collaboration Project as part of the European Capital of Culture 2016 Wrocław*, outlining the conditions of the collective initiative and operationalising the cooperation. Prior to the final adjudication of the competition, in October 2010, the candidate cities signed a declaration in Szczecin entitled *Civic Partnership for Culture 2016*,[159] denoting collective cooperation with the winning city, whichever it might be:

---

159 For more on this subject see *Koalicja Miast. Projekt współpracy w ramach program Europejskiej Stolicy Kultury 2016 Wrocław*, n.d. (brochure).

The first initiative for the teams to meet and shake hands came from Szczecin, and the first meeting took place in Szczecin, where representatives of the cities applying for the ECOC signed a letter of intention saying that they'd observe and support each other and exchange experiences, but also that, after the selection of the city that would hold the title, they'd support that city and help to produce its programme where possible [...]. After the first meeting in Szczecin, we met in Łódź, then in Lublin, then in Wrocław, and the Coalition of Cities project refers to that idea, as it's based on lively contacts between still active people working in various cities. (SZ08)

The aspect of collaboration between the cities was one of the most frequently mentioned topics, especially in the statements of those respondents who were directly involved in the work of the competition teams and saw for themselves the added value that cooperation and exchange of experiences could bring. This cooperation developed at various levels, applying to both the institutionalised sphere and direct contacts and relations between the people involved in the work of the ECOC bid teams. The following responses illustrate this:

It came from the sense that it was worth swapping experiences of the changes that were taking place. At some point it's worth building programmes concerning city strategies. There are certain mechanisms that can be used, it's worth looking critically at your own cultural policies, looking at what works and what doesn't. At first when we met, it was with the idealistic idea that we believed it should be not just a presentation of the city, but also show the potential of the whole country. We all knew that one city would win. (GD05)

I remember my own first reaction when I saw Łódź's core points. I read [...] that they had Captain Culture to promote Łódź, that Miss Poland would be there too, and Captain Culture in a yellow cape would be giving stickers out in the city. I sat down and wrote an email to Cendrowicz. I wrote that it was absolutely stupid, because Captain Culture was a formula from American culture. It had nothing to do with European culture, and it wasn't about promoting culture per se, but doing something really new and innovative, and showing off to Europe that we had a different Łódź, design, photography... etc. But I didn't send the email...! I got hold of Cendrowicz at some congress, pulled him over to the table and asked why they were doing it like that. [...] And I told him that for us it was about a change in culture. I just cared about Polish film or design and creative industries – if Łódź won – for it to go, spill over Poland, but also to teach something to Europe. And then I thought it made more sense to work together than to argue. And it's good that I didn't send the email, because we might not be talking today. (LU08)

In the course of our research, the idea of the Coalition of Ideas was generally accepted. In fact, none of the respondents doubted the value of developing a network of cooperation. Where doubts did arise, however, was regarding the question of the Coalition's future. The two most important issues that arose in the respondents' statements concerned independence and representativeness. It was possible to formally establish the coalition as a result of the institutional support of local authorities, yet its dynamic stemmed above all from the social capital released during the ECOC bidding process. On the one hand, therefore, the respondents pointed to questions of funding and organisation. For example, the following quotation came in response to the question of whether the interviewee thought that the Coalition of Cities should continue to operate after the conclusion of Wrocław's tenure as ECOC:

> *Yes, that would be good, but it would have to depend on the authorities, and everything comes down to funding. As long as that kind of entities are financed solely from public funds distributed by the local authorities, they won't be able to free themselves. You can fight and talk about ideals, but when you take public money, in my opinion it's not quite possible. It becomes possible if you at least diversify the funding sources and have city, state funding perhaps using social economy mechanisms, and EU funds, for example. If you have that kind of funding, you can think about independence.* (WR04)

The strength of the social capital fuelling collaboration within the Coalition of Cities is highlighted by a number of similar responses:

> *Throughout the whole ECOC process a lot of fantastic friendships were formed, positive relationships between people. That's hugely significant at the level of officials and employees as well as that of residents.* (LU07)
> *Apart from the fact that a desire for joint projects arose, human friendship came about too.* (ŁÓ07)
> *The feeling that the cooperation and relations that came about make sense lasted. In very many cities the people who coordinated the initiatives changed, although there's a core – the few people who became kind of liaisons and built the Coalition.* (GD05)
> *It's important when building a coalition to build trust. We build trust among people who don't know each other, among communities, not only artistic, but also managerial. Suddenly we need to create something together in a group that don't have each other within reach. We speak different languages because we have completely different cities and needs. And that's the challenge.* (WR07)

This social capital is undoubtedly a very precious resource. Without it, the Coalition would not have been formed, and even if a similar project had been established, it is likely that it would have collapsed soon after the verdict of the jury announcing the winner of the ECOC 2016 competition. This was shown clearly by the first meeting after the end of the bidding process, which took place in February 2012 in Lublin. Despite the emotions associated with the final result, the decision was taken to carry on working together – cooperation which continues to this day.[160]

---

160 For more on this subject see Paweł Kubicki, "Efekt ESK", in *Kultura Enter. Miesięcznik wymiany idei* 2012, no. 43.

During our study, the respondents who did not take part in the work of the bidding teams pointed out that the effectiveness of the Coalition ought to be founded on bridging social capital. In other words, in order for the Coalition to play a significant role in the sphere of urban cultural policy, it must be perceived as an institution open to various communities. The problem of representativeness – not only of the Coalition, incidentally – was a topic that was often raised in the course of the research. The comments of one respondent quoted below are an example of this:

> For me, the biggest problem in all these grassroots initiatives that try to organise themselves is the mechanism of representativeness [. . .]. And it's the same with the Coalition. It's great that cities are trying to talk to each other, but who's representing them? And it's always the case that some people start to decide, so others feel discarded. So it's important to make it as open as possible to new communities, or is the Coalition supposed to be collaboration between local authorities, or between cultural operators, or theoreticians? I'm really missing a level to clarify that. Although what's going on, I think it's interesting. (PO03)

The problem of the Coalition's representativeness was particularly emphasised by respondents from urban movements, who were critical of local authorities' so-called "sham activities". The idea of twin cities came to represent something of a symbol of such initiatives.

> It's like the institutions of twin cities, whose only function in my opinion is to put up a sign at the entrance to a city with the names of twin cities. That's all I can see in the fact that the twin city of Katowice is Cologne, for example – all in all a very nice city with which a lot of things could be done. (KA02)

The Coalition's effectiveness, and particularly legitimacy, will depend on whether it is open to wider circles representing various spheres of city activity, which could be a guarantee that it will not share the fate of the idea of twin cities:

> When we were organising the First and Second Congress of Urban Movements, we stressed the need to end the rhetoric of competition between cities. So the idea of building the Coalition of Cities is of course very nice. Except that [. . .] if it's going to be a kind of programme exchange, that's great, because a lot of people can't afford to go to another city for a show or concert, but there's also the danger that it'll be another scheme where we exchange good practices, so we talk ad nauseam and nothing comes of it. The answer to the question depends on what it's supposed to be based on, which institutions will be taking part, if it's going to be based on the councils, it'll be a similar story to twin cities. (ŁÓ02)

Nevertheless, it was the same respondents, originating in urban movements, who also pointed to the major potential opportunities that the Coalition could have in the sphere of city policies. One of the factors upon which the formation of the Congress of Urban Movements in 2011 was based was the belief that only the power of lobbying of an integrated community could become an effective tool in the pursuit of an effective urban policy. Despite its declared decentralisation and increased power to local authorities, Poland de facto remains a strongly centralised country. When confronted with centralised ministerial machinery, individual local authorities tend to be in a losing position. The experience of activity in networked urban movements has therefore resulted in a realisation of the role that the Coalition of Cities can or should play:

> *I think it would be great if it was a kind of pressure group that would push through things that are important at culture at central level. Or a group that could produce joint documents modelled on the urban culture strategy, where some initiatives could be prototyped too. (KA03)*
> *I think that it doesn't just make sense, it's essential. For instance from my experience in urban movements, their greatest strength is in collaboration, in the fact that we're learning methods of action, we know how to react, we have mutual support. So cultural operators who are in a very similar situation have achieved a lot as a result. But I don't really see that activity. (WR01)*

The responses to the questions regarding the sense and nature of the Coalition's work in the future can be distilled to one main theme, which can be described using the idea of the think-tank, i.e. an institution that collects and develops good practices concerning public policies, produces expert reports and takes part in the public debate on the culture of cities. For a number of reasons, in Poland there are no think-tanks oriented towards urban policies in the broadest sense. According to the respondents, this gap – of course only in part – could be filled by the Coalition of Cities:

> *It ought to be a platform of exchange of good practices, sharing good solutions, showing what the paths to deal with something are. Sometimes it seems that something can't be done, but then we look at other cities and see that it can. And that's a very good argument for officials, just like the CSK [Centre for the Meeting of Cultures] will now be fighting to put beehives on a roof, and for a couple of years there have been City Council resolutions prohibiting beekeeping in the city centre. So what arguments to use, you could say that bees don't bite, but the main argument will be that you can in Krakow, you can in Wrocław, and in New York there are millions of those bees. If it was a platform of exchange of experiences, that'd be cool. (LU01)*
> *The most interesting thing for me is watching each other, what our organisation looks like, what paths have already been covered in other cities, what we can take from others and what we can infect others with. (LU02)*
> *Every good, well-networked cooperation makes sense. You can make use of so-called good practices, and you don't have to find everything out yourself. Secondly, you can form interesting cooperation based on exchange, so who does what in fact. Participation in networked projects really helps us. We have recipients throughout Poland and internationally. (KA05)*

The field of exchange of experiences and networking in the field of culture itself, that worked great – the Coalition of Cities and the instruments behind it brought us closer together. We met up, all the cities that went out in Wrocław and we were invited to work together. There was no rivalry, no bitterness. (ŁÓ07)

Some of the respondents pointed to specific ideas of how such institutional cooperation should develop:

The Coalition – like any – is a good idea. In Liverpool there were always coalitions in various fields and at various levels, and that worked fantastically, except that things function at a different level there. I don't know how it'll work in Poland. In culture, a coalition makes sense to create a framework of cultural strategy, to develop models and good practices. Everything's based on the quality of the work that's done and the people who are involved. I'd expect that with a coalition the good practices would stay, some formal or informal body would be established to work for cultural development, collaboration, and not rivalry. Rivalry is our eternal ailment. The general idea of the ECOC was for the candidate cities to work together and talk to each other. I'd expect every city to have a designated person with some level of decision-making competence, and for those people to form a coalition at the start, and later for it to broaden. It would be good if the cities could be closer together in future. There's strength in their diversity (the cities have various histories, budgets etc.), and they can create many fantastic things together. Just a simple thing like spending EU funds, of which there'll be less and less. Poland has a very low index of spending of funds. There was also the proposal for further collaboration based on the specific goal that will be the 700th birthday of the city of Lublin in 2017. The coalition partners therefore made plans for cooperation. This kind of targeted and short-distance work of the coalition seems to make sense as it marks the short-term perspective of joint enterprises, and in the meantime allows us to make proposals concerning further activity. (LU07)

Respondents also noted that the institutionalisation of the Coalition will make it necessary to identify a strong leader to coordinate its activities and designate its objectives:

It depends on a strong leader of the project (as practice has shown). In Wrocław, in conjunction with Impart and the main organisation working on the ECOC, when there's the will to continue the project and some leader appears, I think that we can carry on meeting, because genuine cooperation has emerged and in these few years we've really grown to like each other as cities. It was a community of problems, in every city we had that context and similar problems dealing with the city authorities. We supported each other and exchanged experiences, and that worked. I think that at human level that will remain, but when there's a strong project leader that will also remain at the level of continuation of the project. (ŁÓ07)

The presentations of the festival year 2016, comprising series of exhibitions of a given city in Wrocław's urban space (streets, trams) or untypical institutions (at the City Arsenal, in a town house or at the foot of a hill) demonstrated collaboration within the Coalition of Cities in exemplary fashion. The Coalition of Cities presentations, which took place from May to September 2016, totalled seven exhibitions with very diverse names: "Lublin: City of Inspirations", "Szczecin: Space of Joint Dialogue", "Katowice: City of Music", "Poznań: Next Stop", "Gdańsk: Friends from by the Sea", and "Łódź: Woven Renewal". A separate project consisted of presentations of Wrocław in all the coalition cities, with the slogan "Wrocław for Culture". Although this aspect was not covered in our research (as it concerned the festival year 2016), it often cropped up in respondents' statements, especially those from Wrocław, who had the opportunity to see the culture on offer in the cities making up the Coalition of Cities. It was evaluated positively, as the following response reveals:

> From Wrocław's point of view, it's working really delightfully. It's a question to the Ministry of Culture to see what the Poland-wide value is. It's clear that culture arises in dialogue, in joint exchange of ideas. I don't think that cultural operators and artists are that keen to exchange, work together, have a dialogue. Sometimes people are open, but generally on their own patch. If that turned into some kind of network of exchange, so that we could watch each other, that would be something. I am proud that we initiated it, but the thinking that not some fairs, but proper art and investment in culture build the position and brand of a city, that started from the competition. It happened on a wider scale. The effect is wonderful, because it'll stay in thinking and in materials. (WR09)

The Coalition of Cities, functioning as a think-tank stimulating cooperation networks, could potentially become a more invigorating impetus for the operation of the cultural sphere in cities. It is rather obvious that networking stimulates social and cultural diffusion, as well as contributing to changes in relations in the governmental sphere, which is significant in the case of cultural policies in cities. Culture is a sphere that demands particular reflectiveness, as otherwise, it can evolve in the direction of autopoeitic systems – closed to external contacts and the outside world. This limits possibilities of development, innovativeness and creativity. Intensive, mutual relations within a network of cities also contribute to strengthening of local identities. The process of forming identities always requires relations with partners. In order to discover oneself and appreciate one's own resources, it is essential to have – as we saw earlier – a metaphorical "other" through whose eyes one can examine oneself. This is the role of networks, within which cities "examine each other". The Coalition also has the chance to become an organisation supporting cities in constructing local cultural policies and implementing innovative development practices.

Our study showed that the Coalition of Cities, to refer to the classification cited by Deru, is in the "Storming" phase, i.e. that of brainstorming and initial chaos. None of its members is quite sure whether the project will have a continuation and whether it will ultimately attain its objectives. Over time, according to the dynamic of development of European networks, they either become a significant and common voice of the community, or, as a result of financial instability (the most frequent reason for abandoning further work), they are dissolved. The Coalition of Cities bears all the hallmarks of an organisation with an invigorating character, which, owing to its independence and transregional, and in future potentially trans-border structure, has the chance to become a free network promoting modern European cities, in which the role of culture is to participate in the formation of local policies. As we have seen, networks can be urban, regional, or national, and either thematic or sector-based associations. Irrespective of the profile and public mission, their greatest merit is incorporation in the process of building civil society, and as a result of their democratic structure, learning democracy on a daily basis.

Joanna Orzechowska-Wacławska

6. Infrastructure. New Cultural Institutions

Between Bilbao and Valencia

Bilbao and Valencia have become contrasting symbols in contemporary Europe of cities illustrating how investments in culture can stimulate development. In order to further analyse the role of culture and cultural infrastructure in the process of urban regeneration, it is necessary to first provide a basic outline of these two Spanish cities. In both Bilbao and Valencia, an ostensibly similar strategy was adopted – the development of the city was to be stimulated by investments in cultural institutions. In fact, though, the implementation of the strategy, the selection of specific solutions, and the combination of this strategy (or the lack thereof) with the wider development plan and local context, all differed markedly. As a result, the consequences of the policies also contrasted. Bilbao, in which the chosen strategy contributed to the successful repositioning of the city in the international arena, is held up even today as a model for other post-industrial centres to follow. Valencia, on the other hand, became a symbol of an incompetent and badly implemented urban strategy characterised by overinvestment in large-scale buildings of cultural institutions.

It is important to remember that when Polish cities, at the peak of post-accession optimism, were entering the ECOC competition, their Spanish counterparts were starting to experience the painful effects of the financial crisis, largely brought about by the burst of the speculative bubble on the real estate market. It was at this time that Valencia, investing in spectacular but very expensive buildings, was proclaimed the land of white elephants. Bilbao, though characterised by no less spectacular investments, was not unduly affected by the crisis, and managed to retain its development impetus. The key question is therefore not *whether* to build spectacular investments in culture, but *how* to weave them into the urban fabric to allow them to become the driving force of development.

Even in the late 1980s, **Bilbao** was still a dilapidated post-industrial city whose glory days seemed far behind it. The city had experienced a boom in the late nineteenth and early twentieth centuries, when it went from being a port and trading town into a buzzing industrial and financial centre, the capital of the flourishing so-called Bilbao metropolitan area (*área metropolitana de Bilbao*, BOM), as well as one of the most important post-industrial port cities not only on the Iberian Peninsula, but in the whole of Western Europe. The reason for the economic transformation of Bilbao's profile was the remarkably intensive process of industrialisation, ushered in by legal and systemic reforms from the mid-nineteenth century.[161] The city in fact retained its industrial profile until the 1970s, and during the dictatorship of General Franco was a major centre of Spanish heavy industry. In the international arena, however, its economic significance was minimal, largely as a result of Spain's economic policy at the time and the country's distinct economic marginalisation. The situation was further worsened by the oil crisis of the 1970s, which had a major impact on Spain as a whole, and in particular on its most industrialised regions, especially the Basque Country. It is important to note that for Spain the consequences of this crisis coincided with profound transformations of the political system and the process of democratisation following Franco's death. The far-reaching changes throughout the country's political and economic system from 1975 onwards were not accompanied by a suitably circumspect (restrictive) economic policy, which the economic situation of the time called for, and this had catastrophic effects for regions dependent on industry including the Bilbao region. The process of deindustrialisation of the late 1970s and early 1980s was extremely tough. It is estimated that in the first decade of reforms, i.e. between 1975 and 1985, employment in Basque industry fell by 24 %, corresponding to approximately 94,700 job losses.[162] Many factories in the iron and steel production sector as well as in the shipbuilding industry were closed down. In 1986, unemployment in the region reached a level of 21 %.[163] Bilbao in the 1980s became not only a city struggling with structural problems, but also simply an ugly city – the activity of the port gradually shifted in the direction of the river mouth, leaving many abandoned, devastated and neglected post-shipyard areas in the centre. The city's political significance was also reduced, with the smaller city of Vitoria-Gasteiz in the province of Álava being chosen over Bilbao as the capital of the Basque Autonomous Community. The image of the decaying post-industrial city that Bilbao was associated with in the 1980s was supplemented by a certain infamy in

---

161 For more on the process of industrialisation in the Basque Country, see Joanna Orzechowska-Wacławska, *Baskowie. Powstawanie współczesnego narodu* (Kraków: Jagiellonian University Press, 2014).

162 Gerardo del Cerro Santamaría, *Bilbao. Basque Pathways to Globalization* (Amsterdam: Emerald Group Publishing, 2007), 63.

163 Data based on: Eustat (Banco de Datos. Poblacion en relacion con la actividad (PRA)).

the international arena: as Iñaki Zabaleta's research shows,[164] its main connotation was with the activity of the Basque terrorist group ETA. The need for change in economic and social terms, but also regarding the image of the city (and de facto also that of the entire region) became apparent in the late 1980s, and revitalisation initiatives have been put into place consistently since the 1990s. The strategy adopted in the city was based upon four main foundations: long-term, strategic planning, engagement of public-private institutions as key agents, expansion of the city infrastructure, and implementation of large-scale projects.[165] The flagship of the project was the Guggenheim Museum. The decision to build this iconic structure was taken in 1991, with Abandoibarra chosen as its location – a seafront, centrally located part of the city and previously the site of industrial and port activity. From the outset, the investment attracted significant media interest, and following its opening in 1997, the museum became a magnet attracting throngs of Spanish and international tourists.

There are two main reasons why the Guggenheim Museum in Bilbao caused such a buzz and captured public attention. The first was the history behind the investment, which can be described in short as something of a "misalliance" in the world of art: a very prestigious American cultural institution hit by financial difficulties decided to open a European branch of its museum in a prosperous region of Europe, yet one that was seen as dangerous and was essentially very little known. The history in itself had great potential to ignite media interest and stimulate the public imagination. The second reason was Frank Gehry's remarkable design, which stirred attention among architects from around the world. The Guggenheim Museum became the subject of the major titles of the international press, which acclaimed it as one of the most important buildings of the twentieth century.[166]

The museum was an immediate success in terms of visitor numbers. In its first three months, almost 260,000 people passed through its doors, and 1.5 million visited by the end of 1998. On average, around a million people attend the

---

164 See Iñaki Zabaleta, "The Basques in the International Press: Coverage by the New York Times (1950–1996)", in: *Basque Politics and Nationalism on the Eve of the Millennium*, ed. W. A. Douglass (et al.) (Reno: University de Nevada Press, 1999).

165 More on this subject can be found in Joanna Orzechowska-Wacławska, "Baskijskie polityki miejskie: konstruowanie nowej symboliki i nowego oblicza Bilbao", *Politeja* 2014, no. 27.

166 See Joanna Orzechowska-Wacławska, "Rewitalizacja po baskijsku. Kulturowy kod 'efektu Guggenheima'", *Folia Sociologica. Acta Universitatis Lodziensis* 2015, no. 54.

museum every year.[167] A measurable effect of this success has been the increased tourist traffic in the region, recorded from the beginning of the museum's operation. In its first year, the number of foreign visitors using hotel services in Bilbao doubled (from 61,173 in 1997 to 126,953 in 1998). In 2013 there were almost five times as many foreigners in the city as there were in 1997 (296,853).[168] A consequence of the influx of tourists is a growth in income in the region recorded year on year. It is estimated that during the first thirteen years of its operation (until December 2010) the indirect and direct income resulting from the museum increased the Basque Country's GDP by more than 2 billion euro (roughly 180 million euro annually), meaning a yearly addition to the Basque budget in the region of 25–30 million euro.[169]

The second visible consequence of the building of the museum, alongside the economic revival mentioned above, is a remarkable change in the city's image. The museum became a widely discussed revelation in the world of architecture, a genuine "must-see", and as a result Bilbao was something of an overnight success, arriving on the map of top cultural tourism destinations. Some 8500 press articles were written about the museum in the first two years of its existence.[170] With this proliferation of texts and reports about the museum came a change in the narrative of the city, as Bilbao began to be described in the same terms as its most famous attraction, as modern (!) and innovative.

This incredible metamorphosis of the city, which went from being a post-industrial town in decline to a recognised global city in under a decade, meant that Bilbao was proclaimed a success of revitalisation policy. Since the project's showcase and the new symbol of the city was the Guggenheim Museum, the "Guggenheim effect" (or sometimes more broadly: "Bilbao effect" became a popular concept. This was the idea that a spectacular large-scale investment in a cultural site making use of an innovative architectural design could, as Bilbao did, stimulate interest, attract tourists, rejuvenate the economy and bring the city into the centre of networks, assuring it global recognition. Such thinking often led to the conviction that Bilbao's success could be repeated merely by constructing a museum, philharmonic hall or opera, as long as the building housing the institution was sufficiently innovative, breaking with the standards of contemporary

---

167 Guggenheim Museum, Bilbao, *Notas de prensa*, 2000–2014.
168 Orzechowska-Wacławska, *Rewitalizacja po baskijsku*, 112.
169 Orzechowska-Wacławska, *Baskijskie polityki miejskie*, 223.
170 Cerro Santamaría, *Bilbao. Basque Pathways*, 102–103.

architecture; in short, as long as it was a stunning design that captured people's imagination.

Many cities around the world have attempted to follow in Bilbao's footsteps, investing in spectacular buildings for cultural institutions. Poland is no exception. As we shall see in later chapters, the desire to repeat the "Bilbao effect" with new cultural institutions has for years been making a mark on the thinking of local political decision makers. A frequent problem, however, tends to be the superficial approach, whereby the solutions put into place in Bilbao are treated as a "ready-made product" that can be imported. This results from a failure to understand the nature of the Bilbao transformations, with the flagship initiative of the Bilbao revitalisation (the Guggenheim Museum) being regarded as its core. And yet the "Guggenheim effect" (or better "Bilbao effect") would not have taken place if it had not been for an array of other, less media-friendly and more prosaic and systemic activities. As we have seen, the essence of Bilbao's revitalisation was founding the project on a comprehensive and long-term revitalisation strategy for the entire city (not just one district!), undertaking to create many large-scale investments, both in cultural sites and in public spaces and transport infrastructure, where an active role was played by public-private partnership, and alluding to and stemming from the cultural context.

An inestimable factor when analysing the "Guggenheim effect" in Bilbao is the aforementioned unique cultural aspect of the enterprise. It is important to remember that Bilbao is one of the main centres of the Basque Country, an area inhabited by a population with a very strong national identification. Apart from many other issues, the very choice of the Guggenheim Museum as an idea for changing the image of the city and region also had a socio-political dimension – it can be interpreted as something of a declaration of independence of Basque cultural policy from Spanish cultural policies. Furthermore, one should bear it in mind that the Basques have an extremely strong tradition of communitarianism and respect for community values and joint ownership. Initiatives expected to benefit the community – such as projects for revitalisation of urban areas – are therefore in the interest of many entities involved in the process.[171]

It is also important to remember that, although the museum was the first spectacular large-scale investment in Bilbao, it was followed by others, including the Deusto University Library designed by Rafael Moneo, the auditorium of the University of the Basque Country designed by Álvaro Siza, César Pelli's Iberdrola

---

171 For more on the cultural dimension of the "Guggenheim effect", see Orzechowska-Wacławska, *Rewitalizacja po baskijsku*.

Tower, the Palacio Euskalduna Conference Centre and Concert Hall designed by Federica Soriano and Dolores Palacios, and the Zubiarte Shopping Centre, the work of Robert Stern. The redevelopment of the transport architecture was emphasised, including building of a metro network – which, incidentally, in 1998 was the recipient of the Brunel Railway Architecture Award, the most prestigious prize in transport architecture. Finally, the revitalisation process encompassed not only Abandoibarra, but other areas of the city too (including Casco Viejo, Bilbao la Vieja and Ensache). If we take a close look at Bilbao and what actually happened (and is still happening) in the city, therefore, the Guggenheim Museum was part of a larger revitalisation strategy – *one* of the elements, but not *the only* one.

The fact that a large-scale investment in even the most spectacular cultural site is not sufficient to generate measurable economic developments and effective positioning of the city has been a painful lesson to **Valencia**. As a result of over-investment in striking cultural buildings, the city has become a symbol of the follies of white elephants – spectacular architecture that turns out to be impractical, with maintenance costs exceeding the possibilities of the institutions that administer them. The best illustration of this is the City of Arts and Sciences (*Ciudad de las Artes y las Ciencias*), designed by Santiago Calatrave in conjunction with Felix Candela. The City of Arts and Sciences is a complex of buildings intended for culture and entertainment purposes. It is located at the end of the former Turia riverbed, which was diverted after a flood in 1957, with its previous course turned into a park. In a total area of 350,000m², seven buildings were erected: 1) *L'Hemisfèric* (completed in 1998), an eye-like building containing an IMAX cinema, planetarium and laser show venue, 2) *El Museu de les Ciències Príncipe Felipe* (2000), an interactive science museum housed in a building resembling the skeleton of a whale, 3) *L'Umbracle* (2001), an open architectural structure surrounding a walkway where one can find plant species typical of the Valencia landscape, 4) *L'Oceanogràfic* (2003), an oceanarium built in the shape of a water lily, 5) *El Palau de les Arts Reina Sofía* (2005), i.e. the Queen Sofia Palace of the Arts, an opera house, 6) a bridge, *El Pont de l'Assut de l'Or* (2008), and 7) *L'Àgora* (2009), a multifunctional covered space used for holding concerts, exhibitions, congresses, and sporting events.

The idea of creating modern emblematic buildings of cultural institutions first arose in Valencia in the late 1980s. In 1989, the province's regional government proposed building a "City of the Sciences", to encompass three buildings: a telecommunications tower (later abandoned), a planetarium and a science museum. The total cost was to be 150 million euro. A change in the local authorities and the city's policy led to modifications in the project, expanded to include cultural and entertainment buildings (the word "arts" was also added to the name of the proposed zone), meaning a significant increase to the budget and, as it turned out, placing the city in serious debt.

The City of Arts and Sciences, known as "the district of the future", was meant to embody the ultramodern side of Valencia. It was intended as a space for organising major events, a contemporary showcase and calling card for the city, and, of course, a magnet attracting tourists. In 2007 the complex was named one of Spain's 12 treasures (*12 Tesoros de España*), alongside the Mosque–Cathedral (Mezquita) of Córdoba, the Alhambra in Granada, the Sagrada Familia in Barcelona, La Concha beach in San Sebastián and the Guggenheim Museum in Bilbao.

In the initial phase, Valencia's policy, focusing on major investments and major events, embodied by the City of Arts and Sciences seemed to deliver entirely measurable results (in comparison with other regions): tourist traffic in the region increased, and the economy was boosted. It is estimated that in the period between 1999 and 2007, the number of tourists visiting Valencia increased by more than 1.5 times (from 740,995 in 1999 to 1,921,197 in 2007).[172] Employment in knowledge-intensive activities in Valencia rose in this period by 27.5 % (the equivalent figure in Bilbao was 9.9 %), and employment in the sector of culture, recreation and sport increased by more than 58 % (compared to almost 32 % in Bilbao).[173]

Starting in 2008, when the Spanish economy was hit by recession, Valencia began to feel the effects of the financial and economic crisis ever more keenly. The model of city development based on a kind of "bubble" of major events and spectacular investments began to fall apart. Fewer tourists came to Valencia in 2008 than in the previous year (1,821,695 versus 1,921,197 in 2007). And this drop continued in the next few years, reaching the lowest level in 2010 (1,598,030). In 2015 (1,867,677) Valencia was visited by nearly 3 % fewer tourists than in 2007. In this period (2007–2015), employment in knowledge-intensive sectors in the city decreased by 18.8 % (compared to just 7 % in the same period in Bilbao).[174]

---

172 Data based on VLC Valencia "Estadísticas de turismo'09" and "Estadísticas de turismo 2015", http://www.visitvalencia.com/es/Datos/IdiomaNeutral/PDF/estadisticas09.pdf and http://www.visitvalencia.com/es/estadisticas-turismo-valencia/#p=1 (accessed 31 January 2017).

173 Rafael Boix, Pau Rausell, Raúl Abeledo, "The Calatrava Model: Reflections on Resilience and Urban Plasticity", *European Planning Studies 2017*, 25:1, 40.

174 Ibid., 40.

In an atmosphere of growing economic difficulties, corruption scandals and frauds associated with the investments in the city began to come to light. The majority of the politicians responsible for administration of the city and organisation of major events were suspected of corruption.[175] There was growing talk in public about the lack of financial stability of the city's investments. Santiago Calatrava became at least a controversial figure in Valencia. There were press reports of his astronomical pay (in excess of 94 million euro) as well as the enormous costs of the investment: rather than the projected 300 million euro, the City of Arts and Sciences ended up costing well over a billion euro.[176] Public dissatisfaction was huge, especially as the Valencia autonomous community – with a debt exceeding 20 billion euro and a local public finances deficit to GDP ratio of 4.5 % – was the first region in Spain to request aid from a special fund set up by the central government to help affected regions to refinance their debt.[177] Amid fierce criticism, a website was set up by a local politician entitled *calatravatelaclava*, which can be loosely translated as "Calatrava will suck you dry", in which the author listed the costs of Calatrava's City.[178] Following a court injunction, the name of the site was changed to *calatravanonoscalla* ("Calatrava will not silence us").

From being an attractive modern showcase, in the course of just a few years the City of Arts and Sciences turned into a typical white elephant – an investment that was as costly as it was spectacular, which not only did not create public value, but sucked resources out of the local system of culture.[179] Instead of being a symbol of progress and success, Valencia came to be widely seen as an embodiment of financial profligacy, an example of overinvestment in large-scale buildings of cultural institutions, and above all, a symbol of badly implemented

---

175 Ibid., 39.
176 Adolf Beltran, "Calatrava ha cobrado más de 94 millones por la Ciudad de las Artes y las Ciencias", *El País*, 4 May 2012, http://ccaa.elpais.com/ccaa/2012/05/03/valencia/1336074084_564574.html (accessed 31 January 2017).
177 Fiona Govan, "Valencia: the ghost city that's become a symbol of Spain's spending woes", *The Telegraph*, 29 September 2012, http://www.telegraph.co.uk/finance/financialcrisis/9573568/Valencia-the-ghost-city-thats-become-a-symbol-of-Spains-spending-woes.html (accessed 31 January 2017).
178 Giles Tremlett, "Architect Santiago Calatrava accused of 'bleeding Valencia dry'", *The Guardian*, 8 May 2012, https://www.theguardian.com/world/2012/may/08/architect-santiago-calatrava-valencia (accessed 31 January 2017).
179 See Joaquin Rius-Ulldemolins, Gil-Manuel Hernàndez i Martí, Francisco Torres, "Urban Development and Cultural Policy 'White Elephants': Barcelona and Valencia", *European Planning Studies* 2016, 24:1, 61–75.

city policy. Leaving aside technical issues (falling segments of the mosaic from the opera house roof, for which Valencia took Calatrava to court), the main problems of the investment were: firstly, overestimated investment costs and a simultaneous lack of awareness of economic realities – maintaining the adopted model would require a continuation of trends both in the global economy (a generally good economic situation without major fluctuations) and in fashion (major events and large modern buildings as magnets attracting tourists); secondly, a superficial and very instrumental treatment of culture.

In their analysis of the directions of Valencia's cultural policy, Rafael Boix, Pau Rausell and Raúl Abeledo show that the City of Arts and Sciences represented a departure from what they call a policy of "a leap to modernity and high culture" and a shift in the direction of "sparkling culture" (1991–2003) and a strategy of "big events" (2003–2008). According to the authors, the proposals in the field of culture and arts framed in the city project were "relatively artificial and showed structural weaknesses in terms of discursive sustainability, because they were projected and designed without taking into account the possible contributions to the city's productive system (new areas of activity) and the knowledge system (i.e. the local universities, firms, and research centres)".[180] This new leadership-based strategy, the authors continue, was complex and scarcely believable.

The shallow and instrumental treatment of culture in urban development projects derives from fascination with the idea of the "creative city", whereby the authorities responsible for implementing city policy concentrate more on constructing a brand and external promotion than on supporting the cultural activity of the local population. For Joaquim Rius-Ulldemolins, Gil-Manuel Hernàndez i Martí and Francisco Torres, this is the reason for Valencia's problems. The City of Arts and Sciences and investments in the port were the essence of the development model adopted in Valencia, and the focus of the marketing strategy and cultural policy. The authors argue that these two investments along with the major events held there "consumed Valencia's energy" and used up public funds, and the fall of the city's policy "caused the disappearance of almost all of its cultural and sports projects and the degradation of global Valencia's marketing [. . .]. When the Valencian cosmopolitan bubble burst, it became clear that the 'white elephant' was too large".[181]

---

180 Boix, Rausell, Abeledo, *The Calatrava Model*, 38.
181 Rius-Ulldemolins, Hernàndez, Torres, "Urban Development and Cultural Policy", 71.

New cultural institutions in Poland in the light of the ECOC 2016 applications

Bilbao and Valencia represent two (extreme) reference points that are examples of effective (Bilbao) and ineffective (Valencia) practices in which cultural sites have been used for development and promotion of the city. It makes sense to refer to them in the context of initiatives implemented in Poland, since in recent years Polish cities too have seen a number of spectacular cultural building developments. This is the result firstly of a certain trend reinforced by the example of Bilbao, which has spread throughout Europe. Secondly, it stems from opportunities: Poland's membership of the European Union and access to EU funds have created a real chance for funding of such ventures. A third reason is the previous infrastructural backwardness of Polish cities, which for a long time suffered from a shortage of modern cultural institutions.

The period when Polish cities began to invest major, mostly EU, funds in the development of infrastructure for cultural institutions coincided with the competition for the ECOC 2016 title. As a result, the various cities' bids devoted a great deal of attention to infrastructure. This is not to say that the construction of cultural institutions was dependent on the competition. Many such projects were already underway, with the decision to implement them taken before the beginning of the ECOC procedure, and the main reasons for this was the huge deficit of such institutions and the need to create suitable sites and conditions for the pursuit of artistic activity. Furthermore – and this shines through clearly in the Polish cities' applications – it was about using this fact to show the scale of involvement of the local authorities in the city's development and to demonstrate that culture was valued and regarded as one of the driving forces of this development. In a sense, a much more important question, in which the connection between new cultural institutions and the ECOC bidding process is visible, is the issue of the reception of these investments in society. The large-scale public mobilisation resulting from the ECOC applications that we described above stimulated interest in culture, meaning that newly built institutions often attracted new audiences.

The social resonance of new cultural institutions, incidentally, is one of the more interesting and more important themes to emerge from our research. We were interested not only in the extent to which a new cultural institution de facto contributed (or otherwise) to changing perceptions of the city, whether its existence and activity translated into development of tourism in the region, or revived the city and led to increased interest in culture – it is much too early to evaluate the economic and social consequences of building and launching these institutions, especially as many of them were opened only recently. We were more interested in how these institutions are *perceived* by social actors, especially those who create new urban narratives. In our study, new cultural institutions were analysed above all from the perspective of these social actors. These institutions were both evaluated from the point of view of the ECOC applications and also (as a result of the time when the fieldwork was conducted) discussed from the perspective of the year 2016. This is significant firstly because it influenced the way in which the concept "new cultural institution" was conceptualised, and secondly as it explained why we were only interested in the institutions that were referred to in the ECOC 2016 bids.

In a certain sense, the definition of a **"new cultural institution"** was elaborated in the course of the study. Our interlocutors themselves almost instinctively referred in interviews to those institutions to which they attributed the characteristic of "newness". Bearing in mind the whole array of cases which were mentioned and discussed, we can identify certain common points of such entities. In particular, these were always **(usually formalised) organisations employing staff, with their own base and implementing activities in the field of culture aimed at a large audience.** These encompassed philharmonic halls, opera houses, and theatres, but also museums, because a contemporary museum is no longer geared solely towards assembling collections and making them available to visitors, but also often "opens to the city", permitting active participation in culture, and frequently, as a result of its building (see the Guggenheim Museum) itself becomes an object of art. We excluded congress/exhibition centres, since their activity is not necessarily strictly cultural, although this was not always possible. For example, our respondents in Katowice often referred to the International Congress Centre, as a result of it being an intrinsic part of the city's Culture Zone, and moreover being housed in an extremely interesting architectural building which can itself be interpreted in terms of art. The question of **architecture**, incidentally, was one of the two main indicators of the "newness" of these institutions. The second was the **time of their establishment** – we only took into account those institutions that were created after Poland's accession to the European Union. As a result, in the further analyses we considered both the institutions that had in fact existed for a long time, but recently gained new homes (e.g. the National Polish Radio Symphony Orchestra and the Szczecin Philharmonic), and those that were newly founded (e.g. the National Forum of Music in Wrocław).[182]

---

182 A very interesting analysis of new cultural institutions in Poland is currently being

In almost all the cities we studied, there had in fact been a new cultural institution opened in recent years. The exception was Poznań, in which no such institution had been established,[183] which the respondents usually put down to the fact that the people who had run the capital of Wielkopolska for the previous decade or more had been more interested in the sphere of sport and recreation than in culture. Therefore, if one is to look for the "flagship" monuments of the previous authorities' government that became "flagships" of Poznań's city policies,[184] these tend to be sporting and recreational sites.

In this chapter, we shall focus on describing the institutions established in four cities – Katowice, Gdańsk, Szczecin and Wrocław – thereby omitting Lublin and Łódź. The reason for this is that it was not possible to evaluate public opinion in these two cities. In Lublin, the Centre for the Meeting of Cultures was opened during our fieldwork. In Łódź, meanwhile, EC1, an institution that was for some time in a rebuilding process, opened its planetarium, one of its flagship investments, only in 2016. Furthermore, this institution is incorporated in a broader project for revival of the city, and its potential success also depends on other institutions.

The Katowice Culture Zone. Creativity in a modernist form

The most clear-cut example of transformations of impoverished areas through cultural institutions today is the Culture Zone in Katowice. Located on the site of the former Katowice mine, the zone comprises three new cultural and entertainment buildings: the International Congress Centre (Pol. Międzynarodowe Centrum Kongresowe – MCK), the (new) base of the National Polish Radio Symphony Orchestra (Pol. Narodowa Orkiestra Symfoniczna Polskiego Radia – NOSPR), and the (new) Silesian Museum (Pol. Muzeum Śląskie). These new developments are complemented by the Spodek arena, built in the 1960s. Work on the zone began in 2006, and was completed in 2015 when the Silesian Museum was opened (June 2015). The main idea of the project was to create a completely

---

carried out within the research project: *Efekt Bilbao czy kult Cargo? Nowe instytucje kultury jako aktywatory życia społecznego, kulturalnego oraz gospodarczego* ("Bilbao Effect or Cargo Cult? New Cultural Institutions as Activators of Social, Cultural and Economic Life"; see http://bilbao.bibel.pl/).

183 Something of an exception to this is Porta Posnania, a centre of interpretation of heritage opened in 2014. This institution's unique character (it is not a museum) prevents it from fitting into the definition of a "new cultural institution" accepted here, and it is therefore not analysed in this chapter.

184 Kavaratzis, Ashworth, "Hijacking Culture", 160.

new cultural space to comprise the physical emanation of the official slogan promoting the city's transformation: "Katowice for a change". The total value of the new investments in the Culture Zone, including the costs of rebuilding the road infrastructure, is estimated to be in excess of a billion zloty.

Each of the zone's buildings is architecturally unique. Next to the Spodek, which even today is regarded as one of the most iconic buildings in Polish architecture and an unquestioned symbol of Katowice, the International Congress Centre (MCK) was erected – a building in the shape of a black cuboid crossed by a green slit designed by JEMS Architects. Work on the building was completed in March 2015. Its most characteristic feature is a roof resembling a valley, surrounded by a system of banks and natural irregularities. The ground-level strip of land running along the bottom and cutting through the edifice reconstructs the course of the historical route to the district of Bogucice. The care for the identity of the place is highly valued by the residents of Katowice, as shown by the words of one respondent, a local newspaper journalist:

> *The MCK is a phenomenal architectural project, you can walk across the building, there are green roofs. And when I write about the building, I'm always sure to note that it's a reconstruction of an old road – across the roofs – an old, medieval road that passed from the village of Bogucice to Kuźnica Bogucka, a kind of pseudo-foundry. And the architects recreated the road and Katowice's residents know about that. Besides which, there's a phenomenal view of Katowice from there, lots of young people come there on dates in the evenings. Every American town has its hill where people come on dates to look down on the town, and it's more or less the same there. (KA01)*

In terms of functions, the MCK is a public utility building, intended mainly for holding conferences, congresses, exhibitions and fairs. Thanks to its unique construction, with the "green valley" space open to the public, it also has the chance to play a social and city-making role.

In the vicinity of the MCK lies the new building of the National Polish Radio Symphony Orchestra (NOSPR), designed by Tomasz Konior's studio and completed in 2014. The NOSPR's architecture alludes to Silesian constructions: it is a brick monolith, intersected by numerous glazed sections. This building also emphasises the character and identity of the place. The crimson-coloured sidewalls of the niches invoke traditional Silesian *familoks* – workers' housing blocks built in the late nineteenth and early twentieth century, with window frames painted red. The concert hall, the most important part of the NOSPR, is a kind of "building within a building", with the black block of the hall located inside brick packaging to resemble a lump of coal. And yet it is not aesthetics, but acoustics that are the most important feature of the hall, and Kozłowski Acoustic Studio collaborated with specialists from Nagata Acoustics in Japan to ensure the highest standard. The result is remarkable – the NOSPR concert hall is regarded as one of the best in the world in terms of acoustics.

The third new building in the zone is the Silesian Museum, designed by the Austrian studio Riegler Riewe Architekten. It comprises a complex of blocks with a restrained and very elegant form. The museum's main section, its exhibition space, is underground. Yet the exhibition can be viewed by daylight thanks to opaque glass cuboids rising to the surface. The form of the minimalist blocks of the museum is not intrusive, as they fit into the post-industrial landscape. They also provide an interesting background for the historic buildings, including the tower of the Warszawa mineshaft, which soars above the building, a relic of the coal mine that used to operate on the site.

The remarkable architecture and media buzz that accompanied the development of the Culture Zone meant that the cultural institutions located there captured the public imagination almost immediately. Whereas in 2013, the NOSPR's last year in its old building, its concerts attracted 21,400 spectators (to 33 events), in 2015, the first year spent entirely in the new concert hall, the total audience was 195,000 (266 musical events were held). The Silesian Museum boasted even more impressive numbers. In the course of a year and a half (from its opening until the end of 2015), the new museum building had 175,000 visitors, compared to just 10,500 people attending the museum's old base on Korfantego Avenue in 2015.[185] This demonstrates the exceptionally important role of a site's architecture in igniting the interest of consumers of culture.

Almost all our Katowice respondents mentioned the fact that the cultural institutions of the city's Culture Zone attract a large – and often completely new – audience. Without any doubt, this can mainly be attributed to curiosity about the place itself and a certain novelty effect.

> *There's been a change in terms of culture. Projects are consistently being implemented, especially investment, because that's easier. So the MCK was built, the Spodek was renovated, the NOSPR was built for 300 million. And now there's a concert, and there are 1800 seats, you can't get a ticket. It's amazing, and the tickets cost as little as 10 zloty. Everything's sold, in an apparently industrial city. No doubt it's the power of novelty, but that works well too.* (KA01)

Also significant is the increased interest in culture, largely stimulated by the ECOC applications. A report published by GUS (Statistics Poland) in 2016 shows

---

185 Data based on: http://katowice.wyborcza.pl/katowice/1,35063,19773082,katowice-niespotykana-dotad-frekwencja-w-muzeum-slaskim-i-nospr.html and http://www.e-teatr.pl/pl/artykuly/219338,druk.html (accessed 31 January 2017).

that over five years (2009–2014) there was a discernible increase in interest in culture among Poles, including participation in institutional culture (going to theatres, operas, operettas, philharmonic halls and museums).[186]

Urban transport, access to schools, pre-schools, nurseries, making use of culture. People have bigger demands. And rightly so. We're moving forward, and we also expect greater satisfaction in consumption of culture. We expect an appropriate level of response to our needs. People who didn't use to go to the Philharmonic or the NOSPR enjoy going now. (KA05)

Although from an architectural point of view, the Silesian Museum was the phenomenon of the Culture Zone (recipient of numerous awards including the AIT-Award "Best in Interior and Architecture" 2016, the Grand Prix in the "Best Public Space of the Silesian Voivodeship" 2015, one of three Polish candidates for the European Union Prize for Contemporary Architecture – Mies van der Rohe Award 2015), in terms of cultural and social resonance the NOSPR plays a fundamental role.

The NOSPR itself is an absolute event, as we didn't get such crowds coming to the old building. Certainly they're curious about the place. Of course it's not a Bilbao effect, but we definitely have an NOSPR effect here, as people come because they're curious about the building. Musical education here is pathetic, so they're not coming to listen to music, appreciate the acoustics and appreciate the musicians, but to see the building, or to be able to say "I went there, I went to the NOSPR". (KA04)

The importance of the new NOSPR building can be considered on at least a few levels. In artistic terms, the institution's building is often praised above all for the professionalism of its execution and the excellent acoustic merits of the concert hall.

We have one of the best concert halls in the world. One of the best three in Europe. [. . .] Regardless of individual tastes, it's been very positively received. Acoustically it's magnificent – preparatory work, then implementation, a very carefully prepared design. Then amendments to the sound engineering. The hall is fantastic. Maintenance, emphasis and capable presentation of those elements that connect with the phenomenon of the place. The trade media and consumers of culture. They want to come here because they feel that they're coming to European-level events. The outstanding infrastructure does a lot, because after all we have guests who come [specially] for NOSPR concerts. [. . .] This is the European standard. (KA05)

---

186 See http://www.nck.pl/media/attachments/317440/Uczestnictwo%20ludno%C5 %9Bci%20w%20kulturze%20 w%202014 %20r..pdf (accessed 31 January 2017).

In terms of the cultural dimension, at the forefront is the NOSPR's obvious allusion (the new building's architecture as well as the institution as such) to the region's rich musical traditions:

> *I think that the residents of Katowice are very much aware of this shape of history, difficult but beautiful. [. . .] The groups of singers who had a major influence on integration [. . .] workers' communities. Musical traditions. The Silesian composers' school. [. . .] That has enormous value.* (KA05)

The music in question here should be treated not only in terms of history (music as an important element of folk culture, to which the NOSPR alludes), but also in reference to the present and the past: music is a unique form of cultural resource that can play an important role in creating the new face of the city. The new NOSPR building therefore has the potential to become emblematic for the entire transformation of Katowice and a new symbol of the city.

From the point of view of its social importance, the NOSPR building (like the Culture Zone as a whole and its other elements) should be analysed in terms of its incorporation into the fabric of the city. The key question here is whether, and to what extent, the NOSPR (but also the Silesian Museum) helps to create the urban character of the city – is it space-integrating residents, a meeting place? The answer is not obvious. On the one hand, the Culture Zone gives the impression of being an incomplete project, as the new buildings are lacking a background of other "ordinary" architecture: homes, shops, service points – in short everything that constitutes the everyday life of a city.[187] One of our respondents' most common criticisms of the project concerned the zone's monofunctionality, its dehumanisation, and a kind of isolation from the rest of the city (the very word "zone" expresses this separateness).

> *I was very critical of this investment. We nominated it for the "Concrete Block" award. We don't think it's all that bad, but we wanted to start a discussion. It's a monofunctional space, completely separated from the city, geared towards car traffic. We listed its shortcomings, but we also wanted to think about how to use it since it's there already, how to incorporate it into the city. That kind of talking about culture as a separate, elite sphere with no impact on anything apart from itself doesn't appeal to me. I also often stress that it would be much better for the city if the buildings were scattered around the city, then perhaps they'd become elements supporting revitalisation of those areas, which wasn't considered at all.* (KA03)

The majority of respondents pointed to the fact that the location of Katowice's Culture Zone had entailed typical errors of the modernism period: the aforementioned zoning (monofunctional districts), but also – as the following quotations

---

187 See http://www.szneider.eu/katowice-2015/ (accessed 31 January 2017).

show – the primacy of the car and development of multi-lane transport arteries cutting through the urban fabric.

> *Go out with a watch in your hand, as I once did, and try to reach the NOSPR ticket window. It'll take you a quarter of an hour – in a straight line it's 300 metres. This Culture Zone is completely cut off from the city, and to walk there you need to go to a lot of bother, go through the tunnel, walk up and down the steps. You'll cross an empty square where nothing's happening. If you go the other way, it'll be even worse, because you'll spend five minutes at each set of lights, even though there are only four lanes. We wrote about that a lot of times and said that it's terribly cut off from the city because it's hard to get there. It's best by car, as there's a big car park for 100 vehicles. And that's the problem. It's a kind of island. And I'm happy that the NOSPR as an architectural site didn't win any important trade award. The MCK got prizes and is great, in my opinion too. The city itself calls the district the Culture Zone, so something separate. They should have considered whether all the buildings needed to be in this place, for example whether the NOSPR couldn't have been in Załęże or Szopienice, in those post-industrial districts. That might have been a good place for it, or in Nikiszowiec. (KA01)*
> *I don't hold the cultural axis in all that high esteem. I think it's bad thinking about a city, with the huge car park, for me it's like a bigger M1 [shopping mall] in the suburbs. I'm not a critic, I think since they've built it then OK, let it be there, but I'm certainly not going to praise it. The buildings don't play as a city. They generate traffic on occasion and don't influence their surroundings, or if they do it's because there's a big event and there are no parking spaces, so all the lawns and pavements in the area are driven over, and that's the only interaction with the surroundings that takes place. But there's certainly no influence on the surrounding estates. The space is very dehumanised. (KA02)*

On the other hand, however, and surprisingly given the above remarks, the respondents report that the Culture Zone is a place to which people come, a living place:

> *It's cut off from the city, but if you go there, paradoxically it turns out that the stuff works. There's a phenomenal green space there, kids love it and often go there. There are nice benches, people come with blankets. People go there to spend their free time. The Silesian Museum also has wonderful grounds around it. When people get married, they go there to take photos, it's a pretty place. Although it's separated from the city, people go for walks there. It's a place where you can go simply to be in the place. It's not like the Main Market Square in Krakow, but it's become a nice place. It would be a lie to claim that it's an empty space and nothing happens there apart from artistic events. People go along and spend time there. (KA01)*

The reason for the Culture Zone's popularity among Katowice's residents might be the shortage of attractive public spaces in the city, but it is also a consequence of the right selection of institutions and high quality of implementation of designs:

But the zone is there, there's no hiding it, sometimes it's lively, especially the park behind the NOSPR. I live nearby and I see that people go there when the weather's nice. But it's more about the hunger for good public spaces in the city, and when that kind of space appears then people naturally appear there too. But looking more broadly at the effect the space has on the city, especially in the context of car traffic, which is increasing a great deal in the city centre, it means that people get used to going there by car even from nearby. I'm not happy about that. (KA03)

There is no escaping the impression that, from a city-making point of view, the Katowice Culture Zone is something of a paradox. On the one hand, it is a space with large potential to become an image of Katowice's cultural transformations, offering an interesting illustration of the direction in which the city is changing. On the other hand, it prevents the cultural buildings situated there from becoming "hotbeds" of city life. To a great extent, this is the result of thinking in terms of modernism: zoning and making the car the main means of transport. Consequently, the zone is a place which one has to make a point of visiting – there is no possibility of it being a space that is naturally incorporated into everyday city life – a space that one can stumble upon and stroll around.[188] Its biggest problem is the question of communications and dependence on the car, although notably, this is not an issue confined to Katowice. In reality, it is something of a leitmotif that recurs in the context of cultural institutions in other cities too. To a great extent, therefore, it should be viewed as a problem of a systemic nature – the outcome of a completely different way of thinking about urban planning and city transport links from that seen in many Western European cities.

This problem is particularly visible if we compare the Culture Zone in Katowice and Abandoibarra in Bilbao. The main points distinguishing the two zones (apart from their location: unlike the Culture Zone, Abandoibarra is a riverside area) are the aforementioned issues of functions (multifunctional Abandoibarra and the monofunctional Culture Zone) and pedestrian infrastructure: Abandoibarra is incorporated into the city by becoming a natural space for walks (it is easiest to reach by foot, tram or metro), whereas the Culture Zone as a space is cut off from the city by highways and equipped with large car parks.

This reference to the Bilbao model results from a number of similarities between it and Katowice. This concerns both their character as important urban centres of mining regions, which on account of their natural resources played a

---

188 See "Przestrzeń pogodoodporna" – a discussion with Marcin Kwietowicz, Grzegorz Piątek and Jarosław Trybuś published on *dwutygodnik.com strona kultury*, November 2015. http://www.dwutygodnik.com/artykul/6235-przestrzen-pogodoodporna.html (accessed 31 January 2017).

major role in the past, and their specific role in the region. Katowice is the central industrial hub of Silesia – a unique region politically torn between Poland, the Czech Republic and Germany, which managed to mould its own historical personality over the centuries. Bilbao, on the other hand, is one of three main cities in the Basque Country, and historically the region's most important city, the cradle of Basque nationalism. Just as Katowice is inevitably associated with Silesian culture, Bilbao is fundamentally a centre of Basqueness, inhabited by a population with their own unique cultural and linguistic identity.

Both Katowice and Bilbao were previously key administrative-industrial centres in important mining areas (coal mining in the former case and iron in the latter case). The steel industry played an important role in both cities. The decline of heavy industry led each to experience structural problems, and consequently both underwent a difficult period of socio-economic transformation. Searching for their place and struggling against the stigma that burdened them meant that they were forced into change by creating new reference points allowing them to transform into competent post-industrial centres. In Bilbao, the recipe to deal with the previous marginalisation and stigmatisation was investment in cultural institutions. The large-scale revitalisation process carried out throughout the city, with Abandoibarra – and the Guggenheim Museum on its territory – as the showcase, allowed the city to be repositioned effectively. In the space of a decade, Bilbao became an important design centre and reference point for planning revitalisation processes in former post-industrial centres. It is therefore not surprising that Katowice, with its many shared characteristics with Bilbao, began to plunder a well-tested model. Only time will tell how effective the actions taken in Katowice will prove to be, but three main issues are worth consideration. First, the essence of the "Bilbao effect" was by no means the construction of spectacular large-scale buildings, but a long-term and comprehensive strategy based on public-private partnership envisaging the creation of new cultural institutions. In other words, in order to repeat the "Bilbao effect" it is not enough just to build new cultural institutions; it is also essential to base the entire project of transformation of the city's image on a universal and systemic strategy and long-term planning. The fundamental question is therefore what other (further and wider) investments and initiatives are (and will be) foreseen in Katowice, and how they will be implemented. Secondly, of key importance in Bilbao was the development of transport infrastructure, on the one hand making efficient communications possible in the city, and on the other allowing many areas to be restored to residents via the development of pedestrian and cycle routes. From the point of view of the Culture Zone in Katowice, this aspect remains the biggest problem of the revitalisation initiatives conducted in the city. Third and finally, it is worth remembering that the investments carried out in Bilbao were very controversial from the outset. The construction of the Guggenheim Museum alone was opposed by many communities, including Basque artists. Financial issues were a particular concern – the building of the museum was extremely expensive, costing more than 130 million dollars, to which the costs of its upkeep must be added. Guarantees were made that the lion's share of the budget on Basque culture would go towards the launch of the museum. This fact is worth considering in the light of the frequent remarks about the sense of the costs involved in the development of the Culture Zone.

> *It's also an astronomically expensive investment – the whole thing cost over a billion – and the question is whether we as a city can afford such an investment and whether it's needed, and will ever pay back. I have my doubts. Buildings such as the NOSPR or the Silesian Museum are needed in the sense that those institutions needed new homes, but the question is whether they had to be quite so expensive and huge, as well as whether the congress centre was also such a needed building, or might have been combined with the NOSPR hall as a multifunctional facility.* (KA03)

Gdańsk institutions: politics and culture

An area that undoubtedly shares many characteristics with Abandoibarra in Bilbao is Gdańsk's Young City (Młode Miasto). Whereas in the case of Katowice's Culture Zone references to Bilbao resulted from the particular similarities between the two cities (the industrial past, Katowice and Bilbao's centrality as the main conurbations in mining regions, the stigma of industrial cities, a strong regional/national identity), the comparison in Gdańsk's case concerns the similarities of the *potential* of the revitalisation areas themselves. The word "potential" is intentionally emphasised here because if we compare the *possibilities of implementation* of revitalisation initiatives (and thus the question of practice), the Young City and Abandoibarra turn out not to be so similar at all.

In terms of potential, in both cases we are dealing with extremely promising areas providing significant opportunities. They are both post-port spaces located in the city centre. The central location and proximity of a river constitute a very attractive combination, as waterfront districts have long been considered excellent areas to become flagship projects in revitalisation processes. This is in fact the extent of the main similarities. What differentiates them most and has a fundamental impact on the revitalisation processes is the ownership structure in place. One of the characteristics of Abandoibarra was the fact that as much as 95 % was in the hands of public entities. The opposite is true in the Young City: the vast majority of the land belongs to private investors. This is of substantial importance because the question of ownership plays a decisive role

concerning what will be built, when, and how. The reason is obvious: the objectives of the socio-economic activity of private and public entities are completely
different. In the case of public authorities, a significant concern in decisions on
use of land owned by the city is the broad question of residents' quality of life,
which demands (at least theoretically) consideration of the social expectations
concerning the use to which the land is put as well as its cultural and historic
significance. The logic of the activity of a private business (a developer, in the
case of building investments) is based on different concerns entirely – above
all, they are interested in satisfying (their own) financial needs. Developers in
Polish cities are well known as perhaps the best exemplification of the capitalist
idea of profit maximisation. For many years now, chaotic construction paying
little heed to local traditions and peculiarities, along with at best indifference
to environmental issues (building in wind corridors, reducing air flow in cities
and increasing the problem of smog), has been a major problem contributing
to deteriorating quality of life in cities. A second, and in a sense related issue is
the completely different approach to the question of the public good. In the very
egalitarian Basque society, "common" means "belonging to everyone", and thus
what needs to be cared for. In Poland, a remnant from the previous system is the
belief that "common" means "no one's", although we might note a certain cultural
change in the approach to concepts of common goods in recent times – well-kept
urban recreation spaces and playgrounds are an example of this trend.

Our respondents often highlighted the question of land ownership in the
Young City and the problems it causes for creation of socially friendly spaces in
the city. This was also significant because one of Gdańsk's most important new
cultural institutions, the European Solidarity Centre (Pol. Europejskie Centrum
Solidarności – ECS), was located at the edge of the Young City.

> The ECS is there in an empty space that is not organised, because in practice it's private
> property on which the developer can do what they like, because the local plan allows them
> to. Anything can be there, of whatever shape or size. And no urban fabric has been estab-
> lished there. And it's standing there somewhere in the outskirts, but that's the problem of
> the whole Young City. (GD03)
> The ECS is supposed to be a kind of nucleus. The whole Young City is supposed to be devel-
> oped around it, new infrastructural solutions have appeared, a new street. But you can see
> that certain premises are no longer realistic. The idea was to turn that whole post-shipyard
> area into a kind of cultural centre, but that certainly won't work now. It'll be possible to
> develop a residential district maybe within 10–15 years. But the idea was also to build a
> modern opera house, as the current one is located miles away from the centre, in a building
> that used to be a riding hall before the First World War, and doesn't satisfy the contempo-
> rary standards for classical music, and especially opera. (GD04)

The European Solidarity Centre was established in 2007 with the mission of promoting the legacy of the Solidarity movement. Initially it was active in a temporary base in the former management building of the Gdańsk Shipyard, before, in 2014, moving to its new purpose-built home at Plac Solidarności 1. The new ECS building is a monumental rust-coloured edifice designed by the Gdańsk-based architectural studio Fort. It is supposed to conjure associations with a ship's hull, an obvious allusion to the city's history and shipbuilding tradition. The ECS has been controversial from the outset. Firstly, some critics see the building itself and its rust-coloured covering as resembling an old wreck. Secondly, the profile of the institution's activity, which has a distinctly political dimension, has been contentious. In nurturing the traditions and memory of Solidarity, the ECS refers to quite recent events, thus stirring acute emotions. These histories are interpreted in various ways, and interwoven in diverse, often contradictory narratives of contemporary politics. Our respondents spoke about these initial doubts regarding the ECS:

> When the ECS was being set up, it was the investment that was attacked most by residents. [Mayor Paweł] Adamowicz was lambasted for wasting public money, saying you can't do that, etc. (GD06)
>
> I have the feeling that the ECS is developing very nicely and proving its usefulness. At first people were very sceptical, particularly regarding the big block, which was really controversial. But that was overcome with the sheer number of different exhibitions that take place there; it's an open institution, you can go there and see it. It's one of few such institutions that earned a name for themselves. (GD01)

It is important to add that the ECS is not the only cultural institution in Gdańsk to be so heavily mired in the political context. The same is true of the Museum of the Second World War (Pol. Muzeum II Wojny Światowej). Although our respondents had little to say about this institution (since it was not yet open when our study was carried out), the references they did make almost always emphasised its political overtones. This tendency is clear in the following quotations:

> The monument of those initiatives is the ECS, which expresses the city's ambitions and activity. The Museum of the Second World War is supposed to be a symbol too. Gdańsk alludes to the tradition of Solidarity and the trauma of the Second World War, which began here. And this museum is meant to be devoted to an objective history of the Second World War. Of course, we don't know what the museum will end up looking like, which form it will present those histories in. (GD04)
>
> The Museum of the Second World War – a very mysterious building. . . we'll be adjusting it. . . . Otherwise a very important and necessary museum because of the subject it will present. (GD08)

In spite of the initial controversies, on the whole the European Solidarity Centre as an institution has been very well received. Our interviewees emphasised the number of initiatives undertaken at the ECS and its open character.

The ECS is a very good institution with a big challenge. They [. . .] see themselves as a cultural institution in a broad sense. They have an impressive permanent exhibition, but apart from that they also implement a lot of projects. When Gdańsk was applying for the ECOC, the ECS team was an extension of the ECOC team. After that the new building opened, and all the infrastructure – they have excellent facilities. (GD08)

The ECS programme and its shape didn't become a museum project – as might have been thought at the beginning – it became a living institution. The main initiatives are set up for now, constant work linked to the Eastern partnership, for example, a kind of cultural diplomacy. A very clear message that maybe at the moment, in a difficult situation, is verbalised ever so strongly – we're open and we're here for everyone. (GD06)

Yet the institution's openness and active involvement in community life does not translate into the city-making sphere. According to our respondents, the ECS, like the Gdańsk Shakespeare Theatre (Pol. Gdański Teatr Szekspirowski) – another important cultural institution established in recent years in the city, does not form part of the urban fabric. The theatre, designed by Renato Rizzi and opened in September 2014, is a modern building that alludes to the architectural conceptions of seventeenth-century English theatre: the brick building contains Elizabethan wooden interiors, and the retractable roof allows plays to be performed in the open air.

From an artistic point of view, there's a lot going on there, plus what the ESC was set up for, so various anniversaries and freedom-related events take place. The only major, mass event that the ECS organises is All About Freedom, which takes place in the ECS building. But the ECS isn't an initiator, it didn't create a new quality. The Gdańsk Shakespeare Theatre is another example. Institutions that function very well in their own right, but haven't become new kinds of centres that somehow stimulate the space around them, they're more like islands. (GD04)

I don't know if the ECS creates an urban fabric, because it doesn't have a context there, the shipyard was torn down around it, the ECS covers shipyards. The ECS certainly doesn't have a city-making action, it might have a cultural one, people like to meet there. (GD02)

Our study showed that the social and city-making effects of the theatre are smaller than those of the ECS. Our respondents appreciated the theatre's importance for increasing the range of artistic opportunities offered in the city, while also noting that it was distant from the urban reality:

They also don't need to shape the urban reality, but rather to shape a theatre world, kind of separated from reality. (GD01)

As for the Shakespeare Theatre, as a citizen I don't feel invited to join in. But the European Solidarity Centre is an institution that works very nicely, and I feel invited to the events that take place there – and it's not just me, my children and my parents feel good there too. [. . .] I hope that the Shakespeare Theatre will develop. . . (GD02)

The emphasis on the ECS as, in a certain sense, Gdańsk's "leading" cultural institution might also result from the specific context of the research – more than any other cultural institution, the European Solidarity Centre linked very coherently to the main idea of the city's candidacy for the title of ECOC 2016. In a sense, the ECS comprised the institutional emanation of Gdańsk's slogan "Freedom of Culture, Culture of Freedom".

Szczecin and the "best buildings" in Europe and the world

An excellent example illustrating the way in which cultural institutions become new symbols of cities is the Mieczysław Karłowicz Philharmonic in Szczecin (Pol. Szczecińska Filharmonia im. Mieczysława Karłowicza). The building, designed by the Spanish-Italian architectural duo Fabrizio Barozzi and Alberto Veiga, soon gained international renown. The philharmonic was opened in September 2014, but prior to this, at the design stage and when work began on the building, it was proclaimed a new icon of the city – although as with any spectacular construction, there was also no shortage of critics. Within two years, the new building was showered with a series of contemporary architecture award, including Europe's most important prize, the Mies van der Rohe Award, in 2015.

The Philharmonic is situated at the confluence of Małopolska and Matejki streets, on the site where Szczecin's concert hall (*Konzerthaus*) stood before the war. It constitutes a natural allusion to the city's musical history. There are more such references to Szczecin and its peculiarities in the Philharmonic, incidentally, although at first glance they are not obvious. The building stands out dramatically from its surroundings. It is a luminous white edifice made of opaque glass with almost no windows and without a traditional division into floors. Its shape resembles the tip of an iceberg, ostensibly not fitting the nearby buildings in either colour or form. Surprisingly, however, the white block of the philharmonic fits into its surroundings in a remarkable way – its profile alludes to the neo-Gothic buildings in the vicinity, with the towers of churches and multi-hipped roofs, and its proportions corresponds to the neighbouring constructions.

The edifice of the Szczecin Philharmonic is a very characteristic building anticipated from the outset to become a new icon of the city, a new showcase that would not only be inexorably associated with Szczecin, but would also put the city on the map of important destinations of cultural tourism.

The fact that the philharmonic was to play an important role in promoting the city's image was obvious from day one. As early as the design competition stage, the justification for the jury's decision concerned its exceptional city-making potential. "This is a philharmonic. This is art. The dynamic of the light and shadow symbolise development. The building says that it is a temple of music that will become an icon of the city and give strength to new architecture in Szczecin".[189] The investment was presented in a similar tone in the ECOC 2016 application, which suggested that it would "be a spectacular architectural composition, [. . .] which has the chance to become an architectural icon of Szczecin".[190]

The philharmonic was expected not only to enrich the architectural cityscape and add to its cultural offerings, but also – owing to the exceptionally bold building design – to meet the need for a new symbolism for the city that did not necessarily invoke the way in which Szczecin had previously been thought and spoken about.

There's this history here: the mast [one of the city's symbols] had been dismantled, and it's interesting, Katowice deliberately reinterpreted its symbolism, and here they're disavowing the mast, because it was some kind of safety concern. And now no one has the money to renovate it. The mast is the property of a museum, the land belongs to the city. And companies got in touch and said: we'll renovate it, but the mast needs to go back to where it was, because it's one of the symbols of Szczecin's maritime nature, but the city weren't that bothered about the mast. And the mast, like the remains of the shipbuilding, industrial city, is resting somewhere. The central reservation where it stood is blocked. Now the philharmonic's supposed to be a symbol, they needed something concrete, because they're concrete guys who need promotional success. They've invested a lot in the philharmonic, and I absolutely agree, fantastic design. And well, there's a chance for change. The square is illuminated. When the police saw that, they illuminated their building too. The philharmonic's lit up, and nowhere in Szczecin is so nicely illuminated. (SZ05)

This symbolic role of the philharmonic can be understood in two ways. On the one hand, the Szczecin Philharmonic was supposed to influence the city's external image. The intention was for this representative building of Szczecin to summon unambiguously positive associations with the city from the perspective of the observer. On the other hand, at least to the same extent, the philharmonic was to command an important internal function, as one of the (tangible) elements of the construction of a (new) urban narrative. Of course, to a certain degree, all cultural institutions become part of the process of creating and reconstructing a city's identity, but in the case of the Szczecin Philharmonic this

---

189 Piotr Fiuk, "Filharmonia w Szczecinie", *Przestrzeń i Forma* 2008, no. 10, 331.
190 *Szczecin 2016. Europejska Stolica Kultury. Kandydat* (Szczecin, 2010), 166.

role was fundamental since, as our respondents noted, the city's identity remains a problem. The subject of Szczecin's difficult and still unresolved history and the motif of the search for its identity cropped up on numerous occasions in our interviews.

> *Recent discussions that have taken place on the subject of identity... [a discussion] that took place at the Breakthroughs Museum, which I observed via the intranet, the best summary was that Szczecin has its identity, Szczecin's identity is based on the permanent discussion and asking questions about Szczecin's identity [laughs], our identity is about the search for identity – a kind of meta-identity.* (SZ08)

This search also concerns symbols:

> *That identity is still being searched for, be it moving closer to the sea, or using the Odra River. And the whole time we're straddling, it's not as if the city has nothing to be proud of, but it's all so superficial. [. . .] We don't have the same symbols as Wrocław with its dwarfs or Krakow with the hejnał [hourly trumpet call], you don't associate Szczecin with anything, it's a difficult city.* (SZ06)

By filling this symbolic space, therefore, the philharmonic was to become a new, attractive reference point. How much it fulfils this function is something that will become clear in the future (the new building was only opened in 2014). Yet there is no doubt that it is already a site that evokes emotions among residents and generates a great deal of interest.

> *The philharmonic had the same effect as the Tall Ships races, just at a different level, building a kind of local patriotism, pride, it really blew up. It's an institution that people of various ages and various interests have started to go to. The people who've started going to the philharmonic are those who never went to the old philharmonic, the building inspired them so much that they decided to try it out and see what was going on.* (SZ07)
>
> *It's really great fortune that the philharmonic ended up in Szczecin, because it won all the awards and it's been shown in Poland and Europe. That made it trendy. Almost every day there's some event there, almost every day a full house, it's a phenomenon – who knows how long it'll last. Also a controversial form with various reactions, the experts positive, at least officially, and various opinions from residents, some calling it a tin hut, etc.* (SZ03)

A tangible effect of this success is the audience numbers at the philharmonic: in its first two months in the new building it was visited by as many people as had come to its old home on Armii Krajowej Square in the entire previous season.[191] In 2015 more than 160,000 people attended concerts, exhibition openings, film showings, public dress rehearsals and other events held at the philharmonic. An

---

191 See   http://radioszczecin.pl/4,117886,nowa-filharmonia-bije-rekordy   (accessed 31 January 2017).

important part of the audience is made up of young visitors – more than 20,000 children, parents and teachers took part in the #EduFilharmonia series.[192] This kind of activity addressing audiences directly and engaging various groups was highlighted by our respondents:

> There are quite a few free concerts, they take care of the audience, they have a very good team managing it. They also bring kids in from the area, from outside of Szczecin. I don't think the city deals with that at all. (SZ03)

An entirely separate question is how much the philharmonic is part of the city fabric. According to some respondents, the main problem is its surroundings.

> There's a problem there because you come out of the philharmonic onto a car park. [. . .] But there's really a lot going on there, they allow events to take place in the lobby, and lots of young people come, the whole space is full. But what? They leave and disperse and there's nothing there. And in Europe when you come out of the theatre or the philharmonic there'll be a nice square, you can chat. [. . .] Does it have any references in the city? I haven't encountered any. The philharmonic doesn't go beyond its walls [. . .] And the philharmonic was situated there, and as a building it doesn't change the traffic much. Kaskada, the shopping mall that was rebuilt, changed a lot in terms of the organisation of traffic, but the philharmonic not much. On an "urban-animational" scale, to coin a term, nothing's changed. (SZ03)

The same applies, incidentally, not only to the philharmonic, but also to the nearby Breakthroughs Dialogue Centre (Pol. Centrum Dialogu Przełomy).

> At first there was loads of hate about this ventilator [a disdainful nickname for the philhar-monic building] put here. And next to it there's the Breakthroughs Museum, which is also very controversial, and not just because of the architectural form, but some people think that it evokes fears [. . .] That museum was supposed to be a breakthrough, and I don't know if it quite fulfils those criteria. The square too, previously it was a pleasant green, now there's a tonne of concrete poured down there and people don't accept that. It was a place where older poor people could sit with their friends for free, and now it's been filled with concrete. And lots of other places have been filled with concrete here too. (SZ06)

When assessing the social significance of the two buildings and the role they play in the city, it is important to make allowances for the temporal context of the research described here. Although the National Museum – Breakthroughs Centre for Dialogue was included in Szczecin's ECOC 2016 bid as one of the key new cultural institutions, work on it was concluded much later than antic-ipated (the date of completion given in the application was June 2012), and it was ultimately opened in January 2016. In the period in which we conducted

---

192 See http://filharmonia.szczecin.pl/aktualnosci/202-Rekordowy_rok_Filharmonii (accessed 31 January 2017).

the study, the philharmonic had been open for less than two years, while the museum was just opening. As a result, the material collected in the research does not reveal the city-making nature or otherwise of these buildings. Too little time has passed, and the phenomena in question are dynamic in nature. However, the interviews do highlight the controversies over the investments that arose in the initial period. These concerned both the transformations to the physical aspect of the square where the museum was built – previously a wooded green popular among residents, and now a concrete-tiled plaza – and the first problems and controversies that ensued after its opening.

> As for the surface at the Breakthroughs Museum, I don't know how much it's a true story, or if it's exaggerated, but people were roller skating there and there was some ban intro-duced, and word went round that you couldn't skate there, or be in the space, but I don't think it's formally prohibited. And that's a problem, because the space came into being and got residents active, but through some administrative and media confusion people left the area, and that's sad. (SZ07)
> The Breakthroughs Museum causes controversy with its architecture, the fact that they banned roller skaters, the fact that veterans are up in arms because the undulation of the area means the army can't hold a guard of honour because they can't stand straight. They put up a statue of an angel made by Mr Dźwigaj, which the Szczecinians jokingly refer to as "the waiter", and it's a compromise, because it clashes with the building's modern architecture. (SZ08)

Particularly interesting from the point of view of stimulating city life was the prohibition on skateboarders, rollerskaters and cyclists using the space of the square (this ban was ultimately lifted in mid-2016). Although the direct (offi-cial) reason for its issue was safe usage of the public space (the main explana-tion for the introduction of regulations for using the square, including the ban, was the safety of pedestrians and the building, as well as insurance concerns), the prohibition led to a debate on the socially acceptable forms of using a space with a specific social significance. At its heart was the question of whether such recreational activity is possible (or appropriate) in a place of remembrance. The Breakthroughs Dialogue Centre was, after all, located on Solidarity Square, a place with a unique history which in recent decades, following the events of December 1970, had become a symbol of resistance to the communist regime. The discussion regarding use of the ground-level part of the museum – the roof, at the level of the plaza – also had a broader aspect, as it was part of the debate on the ways in which the urban space should be used and who had the right to do so. To whom, in other words, does the city belong?[193] This can be seen

---

193 See http://www.archsarp.pl/6545/muzeum-i-plac-centrum-dialogu-przelomy-w-szczecinie (accessed 31 January 2017).

as a tangible emanation of the narrative of martyrdom that characterises Polish national tradition, in which there is a tendency (and preference) to commemorate tragic events (the outbreak of war, uprisings, and other national tragedies – such as the Smolensk disaster in more recent times), and places of remembrance are surrounded by an aura of sorrow, solemnity and sombreness. The debate on how the square should be used showed that there were many different views on the subject, and that cracks had appeared in the hitherto dominant tendency in Poland to treat difficult spaces evoking tragic events with gravity and ceremony. This was also the intention of the architect, Robert Konieczny, who, when designing the museum, highlighted the need to give the square to residents, inviting them to make use of the space for everyday meetings. The plaza was supposed to be a place uniting generations and various social groups.[194] This open and integrating aspect of the site was recognised in 2016, as the square was the joint winner of the European Prize for Urban Public Space. The jury justified its decision by commending the specific nature of the building, which allows residents to learn about the city's difficult history while also being a place for their everyday activity.[195]

The main idea of the museum was to showcase the key moments shaping Szczecin's post-war history. The exhibition space is located underground, meaning not only that the whole square – the museum roof – is a space open to residents, but also that the building does not obscure the adjacent philharmonic, almost melting into the background. As a result of the innovative design and the exceptional way in which it slots into the history of the city, in 2016 it received the World Building of the Year award in the Culture category at the World Architecture Festival in Berlin. According to the jury, the centre "enriches the city and the life of the city. It addresses a site with three histories, pre-World War II, wartime destruction, and post-war development, which left a significant gap in the middle of the city. This is a piece of topography as well as a museum. To go underground is to explore the memory and archaeology of the city, while above ground the public face of the building, including its undulating roof, [can] be interpreted and used in a variety of ways. This is a design which addresses the

---

194 See "Na uroczystość włożyłem rolki" – an interview with Robert Konieczny conducted by Monika Stelmach published on the culture website *dwutygodnik.com*, December 2016, http://www.dwutygodnik.com/artykul/6916-na-uroczystosc-wlozylem-rolki. html (accessed 31 January 2017).

195 Ibid.

past in an optimistic, poetic and imaginative way".[196] Solidarity Square in Szczecin thereby became Poland's most award-winning site in architectural terms, and the city became a unique place housing two cultural institution buildings boasting awards from major architectural competitions.

In terms of shaping the city space, the philharmonic and the Breakthroughs Dialogue Centre link make an interesting addition to the existing architecture, helping to create a kind of "creative quarter" in Szczecin.

> We have a place, it's a kind of crossing of the Philharmonic, the Castle, the Arts Academy, there's a space there, there's the Breakthroughs Museum too, the Traditional Museum, the KANA Theatre nearby. It's a space that generates thinking about the city in more cultural terms. And the Cathedral's in that square too, because it also creates culture, in the summer it creates the huge St Jacob's Fair, as today stalls alone are not enough, there are stages etc. (SZ04)
>
> No one used to go to Eagle Square, where the Academy of Arts is, but now there are reasons to go there. [...] But that whole Castle – Arts Academy – Philharmonic – Breakthroughs Museum section has turned into a very artistic quarter which wasn't there before. (SZ07)
>
> In the old system there was a kind of triangle there: the Press Corporation, the Militia and Secret Police, and the Pomeranian Ducal Castle as a kind of symbol of the return of the Piast lands, and there was also [the cultural centre] 13 Muses. The Breakthroughs Museum and the Philharmonic were added to that space, so it's not a new centre, it had new narratives added to it. (SZ08)

It is important to add here that the mere existence of attractive cultural institutions does not necessarily translate into active participation of residents in the (cultural) space of the city and development of what is known as urban culture. Szczecin is perhaps the most emphatic example of this fact. On the one hand, as we noted above, the city possesses remarkable buildings enjoying inter-national renown, yet on the other, as all our respondents stressed, its problem continues to be a lack of numbers visiting them.

> A city is not a dead product. The infrastructure is important and that's happening, but also significant is the human factor, and that's worse, there's a lack of audiences and flows between these institutions. [...] Most of the staff of the Academy of Arts don't live in Szczecin, but commute here, the philharmonic tries, but can't hold everything, KANA is keen to cooperate within its capabilities, but on its conditions. There's also the Culture Incubator, which is probably the most flexible place, where the average age is no more than

---

196 See e.g. http://www.bryla.pl/bryla/7,85301,21050432,jak-powstawaly-przelomy-historia-architektonicznego-sukcesu.html, http://culture.pl/pl/artykul/centrum-dialogu-przelomy-z-nagroda-glowna-world-architecture-festival, http://archinea.pl/centrum-dialogu-przelomy-zwyciezca-world-architecture-festival-2016-berlinie/ (accessed 31 January 2017).

30–35. That's the only place in the city where you can do something, but they're also very dependent, because the only funds come from the city. That has nothing to do with a lack of infrastructure – the human factor is the most important thing. (SZ06)
There's a kind of myth here, with all the ricketiness of social capital and engagement, in spite of everything there are quite a few artists here, but they work individually, there are a lot of artists, but no community. And secondly, there's also no audience. (SZ02)

There are two main reasons for this: the city's unique history and its spatial character. Szczecin is the second-largest city in Poland in terms of area, with an extremely extended urban fabric, and this has a negative impact on residents' participation in culture.

Szczecin always has this problem with people. Everyone says that Szczecin is an empty place. The reason for that might be that at 4 pm 120,000 people head off to Prawobrzeże, the largest bedroom suburb, and in a city of 390,000 residents that's a very large percentage. (SZ07)

It is worth noting that the problem of urban sprawl described here is not characteristic of Szczecin alone. The majority of Polish cities – in contrast to their counterparts in Western Europe, where one of the most important effects of urban renewal and flourishing of urban culture was slowing the processes of depopulation and sprawl of cities – are losing residents in this way. This has an inexorable negative impact on the operation of the cultural zone in the city, since it is mostly the middle classes, with both cultural and financial capital permitting them to participate in the city's cultural life, who move to the suburbs. This trend is also illustrated by responses from Poznań, one of the cities most affected by the problem:

[. . .] a problem is moving out of the city, as if someone lives outside of Poznań they make use of cultural opportunities less often, or only at weekends. That can be seen in the decline of streets – Św. Marcin [street] nowadays is old and decrepit, and it used to be the showcase of the city. (PO07)
The Zamek Cultural Centre did a lot to help that street [Św. Marcin]. The Castle even became the subject of a process for planning how to stimulate the street, there were a string of discussions about it, and the Castle comes up with such initiatives. For many years there was a kind of thinking, to put it mischievously, that Poznań was supposed to be a kind of bagel with a black hole in the model, capital invested in the peripheries – that was where new property developments and shopping malls were being built, and the city centre was vagrancy and slumming. Św. Marcin was a victim of this process, especially when the new wing of [the shopping and arts centre] Stary Browar [Old Brewery] was opened, there's a widespread view that it sucked commerce out from Św. Marcin. But that's slowly changing, it'll be different, and the Castle has done a lot and I won't say a bad word about their initiatives in that sphere. They were dogged by being a kind of deserted enclave. (PO08)

The problem is compounded by the potential creative class being pushed into peripheral estates, with poor communications with the centre, as our Wrocław respondents noted:

> *There are more such spaces, open-air, open, places where you can meet, there's even a kind of trend that you can go to a debate for a beer and talk about the city. But let's be honest, that lifestyle is shared by a certain proportion of what we might call hipsters, for whom it's possible [. . .]. You also have to remember that apart from those debates about culture and the city there's a world of supermarkets and more ludic events. At the weekends a lot of people go to the supermarket and later to the multiplex [. . .]. It's also a question of transport, where it's easier to get to, and that might be the fault of the cities, that it piles up in one place, the fact that the city develops so chaotically and transport is so deficient. (WR02)*

Wrocław's 'giant': the National Forum of Music

Wrocław's bid for the ECOC 2016 announced the foundation of two new cultural institutions: the Contemporary Museum (Pol. Muzeum Współczesne) and the National Forum of Music (Pol. Narodowe Forum Muzyki – NFM), which, it promised, would fill gaps in Wrocław's "incomplete and inadequate cultural infrastructure".[197] The two institutions, together with other new cultural and educational buildings (i.e. the modernised home of the Capitol Music Theatre, the new library of the University of Wrocław and the cultural-educational infrastructure network), combined to form so-called "new spaces for beauty". Wrocław's Contemporary Museum was established in 2011, starting out in a temporary building – an anti-aircraft bunker modernised for this purpose on Strzegomski Square. Ultimately, the museum will be housed in a modern building located in the city centre, but despite the promises made in the application that the opening of the museum would be "one of the biggest events of the celebration of the European Capital of Culture",[198] it remains at the planning stage. The National Forum of Music, on the other hand, has been completed as anticipated, and today it is one of the most recognisable new cultural institutions in Poland, in no small part thanks to the ECOC.

The Witold Lutosławski National Forum of Music (Pol. Narodowe Forum Muzyki im. Witolda Lutosławskiego we Wrocławiu – NFM) was launched in 2014, following the merger of the International Wratislavia Cantans Festival and

---

197 *Przestrzenie dla piękna. Na nowo rozważone. Aplikacja Wrocławia o tytuł Europejskiej Stolicy Kultury 2016* (Wrocław, 2011), 28.

198 *Przestrzenie dla piękna. Aplikacja Wrocławia o tytuł Europejskiej Stolicy Kultury 2016* (Wrocław, 2010), 171.

the Witold Lutosławski Philharmonic in Wrocław. It is housed in a new multi-functional concert building located at Wolność Square, opened in September 2015. The building was designed by the Kuryłowicz & Associates studio, with an interior based on a design by Towarzystwo Projektowe (the Design Society). The NFM building's shape and colour scheme were inspired by musical instruments: externally, it resembles a huge resonator of a strings instrument, while the black-and-white tones of the interior are reminiscent of a piano keyboard. The acoustics of the concert hall were the responsibility of New York firm Artec Consultants Inc., who have many well-received similar buildings around the world to their name.

The monumental NFM edifice was intended to become a representative building in Wrocław, a place of contemplation of art (music), but also a space where important cultural events would be held – this was the site of the opening ceremony for ECOC 2016 and the European Film Award Gala (December 2016). The building is equipped with four concert venues: the main hall seats 1800 people, while the three chamber rooms have a total capacity of 800. The impetus and size of the investment, considering the narrow specifications of the building (a musical space mainly to be used for holding concerts, recitals and academies of music) led to a number of questions and doubts as to whether it was likely to be filled. And yet, even in its first season (2015/2016) the NFM was declared a success in terms of audience numbers – 450 events had been held, many of them sell-outs. The building itself had been visited by more than 430,000 people.[199]

The fact that the NFM was needed in Wrocław as a new representative cultural institution, especially in the year when the city held the title of European Capital of Culture, is usually beyond dispute. A separate matter, and a more contentious one, is whether the new NFM building plays a city-making role, and thus whether, and how, it influences city life. The reception of the NFM in society indicated by our study is at least ambivalent. Although the institution attracts public attention, in our respondents' view it does not enliven the space, and is closed to the city, failing to resonate to its surroundings.

The NFM doesn't form the city – even its architecture is separated from the city by steps. Designing steps, given the current knowledge of how to design, is a scandal. I hope that the NFM won't appear in any architectural competition apart from as an anti-prize. The fact that it's a beautiful building with its own architectural character doesn't mean that we can't criticise it – there are no services on the ground floor, and I'd say that's a thing that

199 See http://www.radiowroclaw.pl/articles/view/56305/Narodowe-Forum-Muzyki-Podsumowanie-sezonu-2015-16 (accessed 31 January 2017).

shows the urban character of a building and its interactions with its surroundings. The building is closed, the man on the street has no reason to go in, unless they've bought a ticket. Architects nowadays speak first and foremost about functionality and social values, and then about appearance, and this building wasn't designed in that way. But that applies to most buildings, especially a stadium, which is sometimes a cultural arena, but is placed in the middle of nowhere, without any urban context. If you go there on a day when there's no event, it's empty and silent. (WR03)

The NFM is a colossus that cost the most, its upkeep is the most expensive, they probably also employ the most staff of any cultural institution in the city. But it also attracts a lot of interest, many people come there. Tickets are almost always sold out, and you could say that for a lot of people there's a sense of pride that we have this remarkable building, but I'd be careful with such optimism, because in my opinion there's still an effect happening, it's still going on, and we'll see how it is in some time. (WR05)

I think it's slightly taken out of context. There are a huge number of ECOC events going on around it and it's a very lively place, the kind that was missing on Wrocław's map, and it's hugely successful, the concert halls are full the whole time, as they are in the Capitol. But I can't see a close connection between the NFM and its surroundings, just the fact that from time to time they bring Wolność Square to life, but only to a small degree, because there aren't many outside events like that. (WR06)

The biggest problem that has often been cited is the rescaling of the building. The NFM has a usable floor space[200] of 35,300 m² (with a total area of 48,500 m²) and a cubic capacity of 257,000 m³ – in comparison, the total area of the NOSPR building[201] is less than 25,000 m², with a capacity of more than 199,000 m³, and the figures for the Szczecin philharmonic[202] are over 12,000 m² and slightly more than 98,000 m³ respectively.

[. . .] I think there's an excess of supply and not enough integration or innovation initiatives. In my opinion, instead of pumping more money into new spaces, which, incidentally, is typical of all ECOCs, we should be thinking about a sensible system of support for grassroots initiatives, or international collaboration, etc. (WR04)

Let's remember that the previous philharmonic was very inadequate. This hall might be too big, because 1800 seats is really a lot. I remember a study that showed that in this city large and important concerts would be attended by no more than 600 people, and that hasn't changed, or if anything it's even worse. But the philharmonic board are very active in attracting audiences. I know them and their working methods and I'm very impressed by how they manage to employ or use the instrument that the building is to stimulate interest

---

200 See http://www.nfm.wroclaw.pl/budynek-nfm-architektura-i-akustyka (accessed 31 January 2017).

201 See http://www.nospr.org.pl/pl/o-projekcie (accessed 31 January 2017).

202 See http://filharmonia.szczecin.pl/budynek and http://www.warbud.pl/pl/realizacje/d-157-filharmonia-szczecinska-im-mieczyslawa-karlowicza (accessed 31 January 2017).

in music. In my view, though, the hall is too big. And in my opinion too, the proportions between the huge entrance and the main hall are off. (WR08)

A frequent issue that respondents also noted was the high construction costs of the NGM building itself.

A change occurred especially in terms of infrastructure, roads, water supply etc. But it turns out that this money wasn't entirely well spent. It turns out that a symbol of that is the stadium, and for me the second very controversial one is the National Forum of Music, on which vast sums were spent, and today we can see how much is lacking for other fields of art. For me a terrible example, just appalling: two months ago my mum came to Wrocław and I wanted to show her the NFM, and I checked what was happening at the weekend – a month after the opening of the ECOC. In the whole weekend from Thursday to Sunday there was one event, literally one in all the halls in the middle of the ECOC. So either we have too large a venue, or we don't know to use it, but I'd go for the former. I realise that some concerts are sold out, but if today we don't have the money to produce a museum of contemporary art and similar art forms. . . There's a magnificent exhibition, "Wild West", about this actual identity of Wrocław, and it can't be put on anywhere in Wrocław – that's ridiculous, because it's not a gigantic exhibition, it's in Zagreb, in medium-sized cities in the Czech Republic and Slovakia. So there wasn't much thinking before, and now we have a "white elephant". (WR01)

A further fundamental issue is the question of communications and transport, a recurrent problem in most new Polish cultural institutions. The NFM building is equipped with an underground car park with 660 spaces. Its construction absorbed vast funds (around a quarter of the costs of building the NFM went on the car park), which might have been spent differently (better) in order to effectively stimulate the development of creative sectors in the city. Moreover, rather than pushing urban traffic outside of the city centre, in this way the NFM attracts and boosts individual automobile transport.[203]

The Forum is the most awful, because it's anti-urban. OK, a plaza was built by the Forum, but nothing ever happened there, even in German times, apart from German or post-war parades. But below the square for more than 100 million they built a car park that's a generator of car traffic and causes traffic jams in the centre, and encourages people to go there by car, and not to walk around the centre. They say here that to get to the opera you need to drive, because it's not proper to go by foot as it's muddy. Unfortunately that shows what we're like. . . No, we're rustic, one comes to court and leaves one's coach, and doesn't walk. (WR01)

---

203 Kubicki, *Wynajdywanie miejskości*, 274–275.

A positive aspect that our respondents highlighted was the usually well-received way in which the National Forum of Music is managed. This is expressed in its openness to viewers and diverse initiatives aimed at attracting new audiences.

> *Regarding the National Forum of Music, I feel that Director Kosendiak is a person, a good administrator, with a good sense of business and administration, so I have the feeling that this project will be well managed and won't be a burden – it's a state institution, in fact, not a municipal one, but I think it will be well managed. As to whether it will fulfil grassroots, integrating functions, I have my doubts, but I don't want to prejudge, because it's still a young institution.* (WR04)

It is not only the NFM in Wrocław that is affected by this kind of departure from a traditional understanding of a cultural institution, often addressed to a narrow group of recipients, by implementing programmes geared towards stimulating interest in participation in culture among a wider audience. Similar comments also appeared in connection with other new cultural institutions. To a large extent, this is the result of a change in the way in which cultural venues are managed, as a consequence of the more reflective approach introduced by the ECOC effect. The competition contributed to increased implementation in cultural institutions, especially newer ones, of more participatory mechanisms of joint management, which opened them to the city space in the broadest terms.

7. Europeanness and the Europeanisation of Polish Cities

The role of the ECOC competition in the debate on Europeanness and Europeanisation of cities

Bożena Gierat-Bieroń, Paweł Kubicki

The European Capital of Culture, like almost all EU programmes in the field of culture, is clarified in the Lisbon Treaty, putting into practice the European paradigm of being "united in diversity". In the Decision establishing a Community action for the European Capital of Culture event in 2006, with regard to the "European Dimension", Article 4 point 1 states that the programme will: "(a) foster cooperation between cultural operators, artists and cities from the relevant Member States and other Member States in any cultural sector; (b) highlight the richness of cultural diversity in Europe; (c) bring the common aspects of European cultures to the fore".[204] This legal definition is sufficiently broad to leave considerably interpretive discretion in terms of what this "European dimension" is and how it is manifested in practice. Above all, though, it is characterised by features of international and interinstitutional cooperation, searching for the cultural and artistic affinities between nations and societies and pluralism as an axiological value.

Since the "European dimension" was a formal requirement in the competition, recorded explicitly in the Decision from 2006, we also included a question on this issue in our research questionnaire. Responses varied widely, similarly to the interpretation made of Europeanness in the various applications.[205] The question of Europeanisation and Europeanness is not easy to define. The reason for this is that the two terms have interchangeably become keywords of the topic of integration, used in diverse contexts and to mean different things in debates on Europe and the European Union.

---

204 Decision no. 1622/2006/EC of the European Parliament and of the Council of 24 October 2006 establishing a Community action for the European Capital of Culture event for the years 2007 to 2019, Official Journal of the European Union L 304/1, 3 November 2006.

205 More on this in the Appendix.

In academic discourse, the concept of Europeanisation is applied in research on the processes of European integration as well as in certain discursive practices. In most cases, Europeanisation concerns the specific nature of the integration process in its political dimension (internally, i.e. in the EU, and externally, i.e. regarding third countries), and therefore it is usually perceived as the penetration of the political systems of states by processes of adaptation (incrementation).[206] In general terms, Europeanisation is the process of adaptation of member states to EU requirements, meaning the process of adjustment to functioning in new conditions or in a new environment, and, legally speaking, to the adoption of the EU's *acquis communautaire* while preserving the countries' constitutional legislation and principles of sovereignty. Europeanisation is characterised by two stages: 1) formation of the content of European policies, and 2) the actual processes of Europeanisation, entailing the transfer of models and regulations from EU level to member-state level.[207] Europeanisation is a two-track process, meaning that it takes place both bottom-up, via the transfer of competencies to the supranational level, and top-down, when European institutions impact states, and states are open to this impact. It can also be horizontal (cross-loading), when mutual communications and exchange result in a transfer of data and procedures.[208] Europeanisation proves the advancement of integration processes in which a convergence of many factors and a constant flow of data, borrowings and inspirations occurs. The political-institutional point of view is the starting premise of this discussion.

It is important to be mindful of the peculiarities of culture, which therefore undergoes the processes of adaptation to the EU differently. "Cultural

---

206 See Johan P. Olsen, "The Many Faces of Europeanisation", in: *Journal of Common Market Studies* 2002, vol. 14/5, 921–952; Kevin Featherstone, Claudio M. Radaelli, *The Politics of Europeanisation* (Oxford: Oxford University Press, 2003); Alec Stone Sweet, Wayne Sandholtz, *European Integration and Supranational Governance* (Oxford: Oxford University Press, 1998); Krzysztof Wach, "Wymiary europeizacji i jej kontekst", in *Zeszyty Naukowe Uniwersytetu Ekonomicznego w Krakowie*, no. 852 (2011), 29 43.

207 Tomasz G. Grosse, "Europeizacja jako mechanizm władzy: przykład funkcjonowania strefy euro", at: http://ur.edu.pl/pliki/Zeszyt19/01.pdf.

208 Tanja A. Börzel, Thomas Risse, "When Europe Hits Home: Europeanization and Domestic Change", *European Integration Online Papers* (EIoP) 2000, no. 15, pp. 1–20, http://eiop.or.at/eiop/texte/2000-015a.htm, (28 February 2017); Piotr Buras, Karolina Pomorska, "Europeizacja – nowe podejście analityczne w studiach nad polityka zagraniczną", *Stosunki Międzynarodowe* 2008, no. 3–4.

Europeanisation is about transferring ideas, convictions and values which are expected to be internalised by the elites and citizens of member states. The object of the transmission is the ideas, convictions and values deemed in the documents of European institutions to be common to all Europeans".[209] Europeanisation of culture therefore means the supranationalisation of cultural policy, as well as the adaptation of the cultural sector of a given member state to the common cultural space via processes of accommodation and assimilation. As a soft field, culture is not subject to profound legal transformations, and thus the processes controlling it are slow and informal. De facto, they mean producing changes in cultural life resulting from generation of impetuses for integration, importing the logic of integration, and finally transmitting the characteristics typical of Europeans and European culture and countries, or, in the case of third countries, endowing them with European characteristics or exporting the achievements of European culture. As Piotr Burgoński notes, "Cultural Europeanisation also forms the foundations of identification of individuals with the European level".[210] Europeanisation in culture results from the phenomenon of positive integration (as opposed to negative integration), meaning implementation of rules and standards in the name of common values (Bauer, Knill, Pitschel[211]). Since the EU's cultural policy is supplementary to the national policies of member states, the process of Europeanisation of culture is mediated by European Commission guidelines (recommendations, decisions, fact sheets etc.), interinstitutional communication and the open method of coordination (OMC). The communication process enables exchange of information and resources, helps to create networks of connections between actors at various levels, and dynamises cultural contacts. Mutual learning processes stimulate and promote innovative problem-solving methods. As a result of all this, communication in culture taking place between various EU entities furthers community-forming processes tremendously (as well as encouraging networking of culture, as described earlier).

The open method of coordination was adopted as a principle of cooperation and supervision of the cultural sector in the document *European Agenda for*

---

209 Piotr Burgoński, "Europeizacja polskiej polityki równościowej i antydyskryminacyjnej", *Przegląd Europejski* 2012, no. 2, 147.
210 Ibid., 148.
211 Michael W. Bauer, Christoph Knill, Diana Pitschel, "Differential Europeanization in Eastern Europe: the Impact of Diverse EU Regulatory Governance Patterns", *Journal of European Integration* 2007, vol. 29, no. 4.

Culture in a Globalising World from 2007.[212] It is based upon intergovernmental cooperation via the formation of intersectoral platforms in culture, bolstering political independence and professionalisation. These initiatives aspire to implement a similar model for formatting culture without infringing the principles of state sovereignty. Europeanisation of domestic systems can only take place as a direct or indirect effect of the process of communitisation. "Europeanisation" therefore means communitisation,[213] justifying the use of OMC, perceived, as Dorota Jurkiewicz-Eckert suggests, as an "element of soft actions".[214]

It is worth emphasising that "Europeanisation", like "integration", is a process rather than a condition, and that the two factors "motivate" and complement each other. As Johan P. Olsen rightly noted in his now classic work on the issue,[215] Europeanisation is an adaptive processes compelled, so to speak, by integration. In Olsen's division into positive, negative and framework integration, culture belongs to the positive and framework categories, meaning that it enforces very small adaptive changes not subject to normative pressure and taking the form of slow transformation.

As we noted above, the European Commission defined the European dimension in simple terms – as confirmation of the paradigm of unity in diversity and as multi-level cooperation between various entities operating in the cultural sector and public administration. The successive experiences of cities celebrating the title of ECOC have helped to clarify the "European dimension".[216] It has begun to

212 European Commission, *Communication on a European Agenda for Culture in a Globalizing World*, Brussels, 10 May 2007, COM (2007), 242 final version.

213 The concept of "Europeanisation" has been described and studied in conjunction with many phenomena associated with the processes of European integration, including politics and party systems, the principles of democracy in reference to "Europeanisation of democracy", and empirically in the context of changes in legal systems and the judiciary. Researchers particularly emphasise studies on "Europeanisation" of foreign policy with regard to evident common interests outside of Europe. Europeanisation may be geographical, sociological, political legal, institutional, macroeconomic or microeconomic in nature.

214 Dorota Jurkiewicz-Eckert, "Od Traktatu o Unii Europejskiej do Europejskiej Agendy dla Kultury – narodziny i rozwój polityki kulturalnej UE", *Studia Europejskie* 2015, no. 1 (73), 84.

215 Olsen, "The Many Faces".

216 Andrew McCoshan, James Rampton, Neringa Mozuraityte, Nick McAteer, *Ex-Post Evaluation of 2009 European Capital of Culture. Final Report to DG Education and Culture of the European Commission in the context of the Framework Contract for Evaluation Related Services and Support for Impact Assessment EAC/03/06* (Birmingham: ECOTES, 2010).

be defined as a factor stimulating the urban and social development of European cities, as an opportunity to participate in the formation of dynamic metropolises based on knowledge, ecology and engagement of residents in creating a common cultural space. This theme of "space", along with "dialogue" and "intercultural diversity", were the factors that determined the terms of the Commission's 2006 Decision and the *European Agenda for Culture* in 2007. There was an emphasis on the egalitarian nature of festivals, including the highest-possible number of participants searching for values and experiencing community under the prestigious aegis of the European Capital of Culture. The reason for this is that Europeanness generates issues of identity, or that processes of integration led to the formation of a multi-level European identity based on European axiology, comprising human dignity, freedom, solidarity, demos, human rights and the rule of law. The Preamble to the Treaty of Lisbon asks about European identity, referring to the "cultural, religious and humanist inheritance of Europe". These areas are subject to intellectual exploration, to build on their foundations a "space without internal borders" (Tomaszewski, Riedel[217]). A joint catalogue of values is sought in order to turn it into the cement binding nationally and culturally disparate European societies as well as the quintessence of the idea of European identity, which is essential for legitimising the operation of the European Union. The strength of Europeanisation, as well as the semantic core of "Europeanness", is axiological pluralism, deepening the meaning of tolerance, acceptance of difference, and support for cultural differences. And all this comes from the strong symbolic deficit of the processes of integration. "Europeanness" in the context of culture is an interpretation of the civilisational achievements of Europeans in terms of community and shared values, making this sense of community distinct from others and determining the self-perception of the collective entity.[218] "Europeanness" is therefore a community of values, while "Europeanisation" is the process of adaptation to a field of characteristics formed on a bottom-up and top-down basis.

It is important to remember that European culture is not a superimposed, artificially produced ideological construct, but a phenomenon "generated" on the basis of the living cultural traditions of all European nations. This creates the view that there is no European culture without the cultural output of

---

217 Waldemar Tomaszewski, Rafał Riedel, "Europeizacja w wymiarze tożsamościowym", in Anna Pacześniak, Rafał Riedel (eds), *Europeizacja. Mechanizmy, wymiary, efekty* (Toruń: Wyd. Adam Marszałek, 2014), 142.

218 Ibid.

individual societies, and also that there is no national output without European inspirations. We can observe a process of feedback, and in some cases, also a phenomenon of deterritorialisation.[219] The idea of the European Capital of Culture was to emphasise this mechanism as well as to allow it to be discovered in its cultural surroundings. It was aimed both at culture-forming initiatives and at programmes associated with exhibiting and understanding art. It is important to note that this study was targeted at cities that aspired to a prestigious title, i.e. that were seeking to be distinguished from others on the basis of possessing evident elements of "Europeanness" in their cultural tissue. To a large extent, this was also what allowed them to convince international and domestic jurors. This demonstrates their willingness to point to strong cultural ties with Europe in their symbolic layer.

The Europeanness of Polish cities in the light of the ECOC 2016 competition

As we have seen, the concept of the "European dimension" features two main dimensions. The first is mental, resulting from intellectual processes seeking to answer the question of what *Europeanness* is and how it is practised, and what it means to be or not to be a European. This area touches upon axionormative theories, which translate into the creation of standards of legal behaviours, qualitative determinants, including those concerning the values of high culture, belonging to a certain cultural group, linguistic competencies etc. The second dimension is practical. It concerns specific Europeanising processes entailing construction of socio-cultural European standards, delimiting the thresholds of professional administration, design, promotion or cultural diplomacy and international cooperation. When asked about the European dimension of the ECOC competition, the respondents addressed both dimensions (often interchangeably), as the below statements show:

> *This model emerged on the basis of Ancient Greek philosophy and Platonic thought. Beauty and good play a central role in it. (WR08)*
> *This sense of shared roots is the basis of everything we do in Europe, how we think, how we act, regardless of whether we live in Ukraine or in Scotland. There's one common cultural and religious element that bonds everything together. After all, even for atheists the Christian religion is a point of reference. (LU07)*

---

219 Aldona Wiktorska-Święcka, "Europeizacja wartości demokratycznych w procesie kształtowania europejskiej tożsamości", in: Anna Pacześniak, Rafał Riedel, *Europeizacja*, 150–167.

Despite the differences in European countries in terms of languages, culture and customs, there is no doubt that there exists something that means we can talk about European unity. (WR08)

Analysis of the nature of the impact of the ECOC bidding process on the European dimension in Polish cities, however, shows that it is essential to focus on two different European discourses. The first was the one formed in the period of applications for the ECOC (2007–2011), while the second concerned the period when the field research was carried out (February–August 2016). In the course of the bidding process, the European motif, referring to common values and heritage, and after all one of the key elements of the programme, was consigned to the margins. One of the characteristic experiences gained during the interviewing procedure was the fact that respondents spoke at length and enthusiastically about the changes that the ECOC competition had stimulated in their cities. When asked about the European aspect, on the other hand, they noted that it had not been discussed so widely and with such vigour in this period. Three fundamental issues resulting from the broader context influenced this state of affairs.

The first of these was the aforementioned evolution of the ECOC competition itself. At present, the ECOC programme is geared more towards so-called festivalisation and promotion of cities than to strengthening European and local identity. The second was the unique context of the "end of history" – the ECOC contest took place at a time when Poland's Europeanness had been confirmed in public opinion once and for all (EU accession, political domination of pro-European elites, economic growth etc.). Europeanness as a sphere of values was no longer interesting: the potential problem issues associated with the EU and concerning axiology emphasised before Poland's accession to the Union had been marginalised almost entirely. During the bidding process, Poland was the largest beneficiary of the EU budget out of all the new member states within the financial perspective of the time (2007–2013). This gave prominence to subjects concerning the socioeconomic aspects of being in the European Union – the labour markets in other EU countries opening to Poles, EU subsidies and funds, regional development, and development of infrastructure. In short, what become pressing was pragmatic skills associated with attracting EU funds and promotion. Characteristically, though, the pragmatic aspect came to the fore in so-called success cities, as these words by a respondent in Poznań illustrate well:

With the European capital thing, some people were interested in prestige, and others in the budget, because money comes with it. I don't know whether the people preparing the ECOC heard the word "European", if they concentrated on it. (PO05)

In peripheral cities, as we shall see in the next part, a strong European element was present from the beginning of the ECOC application process. The third significant issue was that of discourse. Following the intensive pre-accession debate from around the beginning of the century concerning Polish European identity, post-accession this subject vanished almost completely from public discourse. As a result, in Poland there is a lack of language used to speak about Europe as a common sociocultural space,[220] rather than just an administrative and economic one. In the first decade after accession, the European question was reduced almost exclusively to questions of European funds. One of the authors of Wrocław's winning bid, when asked about the application's European dimension, replied that:

> Well. I'd say it's a problem not just of Wrocław, but of the whole contest, as all the cities struggled with it and hardly anyone coped. The project jurors asked what the European dimension would entail and usually the cities blather something about the subject. But I think that the answer we gave, perhaps it was a little over-philosophical, but still there was one. It was certainly about starting to exist in the consciousness of Europeans, Wrocław existing in Europe, proposing some fresh narrative. Of course, the problems of Wrocłavians are similar to the problems of Europeans, and we wanted to come out with a fresh message and we tried to do that, starting from ideological questions, but that didn't happen and won't happen, because the city insisted on festival. And I'd say it's a certain naivety, that our local politicians think that for example an Italian will be impressed by our opera house, that he'll come specially to see our opera. That won't happen, not because the Wrocław opera isn't any good, but because something like an opera house won't attract people from all over Europe, it'd have to be one of the best operas in the world. And it's similar with other events, like however many thousand people, that won't impress anyone, plus it's a rehash, as that kind of event's already happened in other cities holding the ECOC. So missing this European dimension of the ECOC comes from a certain megalomania and a certain unfamiliarity with realities. The European dimension boiled down to inviting a few stars from abroad. Whereas it ought to be about developing long-term, but balanced collaboration with various entities from abroad, at various levels and at the level of citizens with citizens. That's hard, of course, and time-consuming. (WR04)

Similar responses were also given in other cities:

---

220 Conclusions formed on the basis of research grant "Polska lokalna wobec integracji europejskiej – dekada doświadczeń", financed by Polish National Science Centre funds awarded on the basis of decision number DEC-2011/03/B/HS6/01163. Project implemented in 2012–2015 by a team of researchers from the Institute of European Studies of the Jagiellonian University. For more on this subject, see Dariusz Niedźwiedzki, Paweł Kubicki (eds), *Dylematy i kontrowersje wokół integracji europejskiej*, *Politeja* 2015, no. 33.

Europeanness is understood in a simple way. We'll make a programme that will attract crowds of people from Europe. I pay a lot of attention to that kind of projects. I believe that they've changed something in the local significance of the city, or thinking about culture. But in actual fact they don't break through to the European consciousness at all. Who knows about the Wrocław ECOC in Poland? Those who listen to TOK FM, Radio Three, or watch TV Kultura? If you ask people what the ECOC is, in the cities that applied for it quite a few people will know, but in other cities no one knows what it's about. (GD06)

The owl of Minerva, of course, spreads its wings only with dusk. Identity becomes "visible" (discussed and reinterpreted) when it becomes a problem. For this reason too, the context in which the interviews took place (February–August 2016) had a major impact on the perception of the European dimension of Polish cities. Firstly, it turned out that Poland's history had by no means come to an end; on the contrary, it had accelerated substantially. Secondly, at a time when both the EU itself and the individual member states are riven by major decentralising conflicts, EU funds are put to the side, and questions about the ideas that could be used to reunite Europe assume a key role.

In some respects, the contemporary discussion on the EU resembles that from prior to accession. Increasingly today, as was the case previously, Europe is spoken about in terms of an axiological space. Both the internal situation and political moods in Poland and events in Europe have led to a return in the public debate of questions about the country's place in the EU. Before the accession referendum, the Polish public discourse was dominated by two narratives: one (supported by advocates of Poland's EU membership) in which the Union was to be an opportunity for Poland, a symbol of civilisation, development, progress, democracy and freedom, and the other presenting the EU as a threat to traditional Polish national values, and especially religion (the Union as a secularising "force"). If we treat the results of the accession referendum as a barometer of Polish moods regarding the European Union, we can assume that in general it was perceived as a chance for Poland's civilisational development. This correlates with the results of a public opinion poll from 2004, stating that more than half of Poles considered membership in the EU to be beneficial to Poland on the whole.[221] In the current debate on the EU, certain topics that until recently seemed to have vanished entirely from the discursive mainstream are recurring. These include such issues as sovereignty, national interest, national identity, and national values. These are becoming axes, with Poland and everything Polish (sovereignty, national interest, Polish identity, national values) on

---

221 Data based on: Eurobarometer 62, European Commission, May 2005.

the one side and Europe and everything European (shared sovereignty or post-sovereignty, European interest, European identity and values) on the other. Until a few years ago, these were generally treated as coherent, in keeping with the premise that the Polish interest is pursued through being in the EU, and Polish national identity is consistent with European identity. In today's public discourse, however, there are increasingly vociferous challenges to these premises, despite the fact that Polish society has been, and continues to be, firmly pro-European.[222] Questions over what Europe is like, what it is and what Poland's place in Europe is have again returned to mainstream debate.

This new context gives new significance to the famous maxim *Stadtluft macht frei*, which stems from the times of medieval integration based on urban networks. The "city air" assuring freedom turned out to be a precious resource permitting the development of cities within a post-Fordist economy and providing the foundations for innovation and creativity. These particular attributes of a city are also exceptionally valuable in the context of a contemporary Europe plagued by nationalisms and xenophobia. Our respondents noted this characteristic:

> And now perhaps a Coalition (of Cities) makes more sense in the current political situation, because cities have autonomy. In fact I have a vision of a country as a federation of cities – the nation state is sick, and what's happening now confirms that. In the realm of culture, it might be an opportunity for autonomy of culture in a time when nationalism and xenophobia are dominant. They also call Poznań "Free City Poznań", to a large extent in opposition to the God-Fatherland message [. . .]. Here in this sense the status of such initiatives is growing, to preserve the autonomy of the city, I don't want to use the word "liberal", because it has certain connotations, but freedom from the pressure, the domination of the state. (PO08)

Thirdly and finally, a new language of debate on the European dimension of Polish cities has started to penetrate public discourse, mainly as a result of the growing power of urban movements. Although they have been developing for more than a decade, not until after 2011 – following the conclusion of the ECOC competition – did urban movements make a mark in public discourse, with the formation of the Congress of Urban Movements. This change in the discourse is conveyed well by the following responses from individuals representing various communities:

---

222 For more on the EU discourse on the Polish political scene, see Natasza Styczyńska, "Does Europe Matter at All? European Issues in the Discourse of Polish Political Parties", in Gilles Rouet, Radovan Gura (eds), *Les citoyens et l'intégration européenne* (Paris: L'Harmattan, 2016).

For me it was a big social experiment, I observed how the city can change, hoping that Katowice would become a European city, meaning that it would be sexy to go into town, not to drive around it, that Katowice's pro-car policy would end. It's a tragedy what they've done to the city in terms of transport. Hoping that the way pedestrians were treated would end. But it didn't. (KA01)
For me, the Europeanisation process is one of general Europeanisation in terms of mentality and urban planning, because at present Europe is moving towards ecological administration of cities, sustainable transport, and also a participatory model in city administration. In the former respect, I think we're very much behind, and in the latter we're more or less in the second wave. So for me a European city is an ecological and sustainable city on the one hand, and a participatory and openly managed one on the other. (WR03)
A European city has to be comfortable to live in, accessible, we're still missing various things. . ., such as with various infrastructure – both sporting and cultural, so that people can spend their free time in many different ways. A city should be green, friendly, open, a marketplace buzzing with life – that gives a sense of energy. We're trying to build local centres in areas far from Wrocław – perhaps we'll manage to do that. It's important. And ideologically, certainly open and democratic. . . (WR09)

In response to a question on the European dimension of his city, the leader of an urban movement in Poznań said the following:

One time we [the movement My Poznaniacy – "Us Poznanians"] went to the local elections with the slogan "European Poznań" – with a wide-ranging meaning, from road issues to the equality march. That might be taking on a new meaning now. In culture we have dimensions like universalism, and now it will be this God-Fatherland bludgeoning, which damn well isn't universal. Localness becomes universal when you don't have the same rigidity. Take [the writer Witold] Gombrowicz, for example, who was Polish through and through, but at the same time universal, or [the artist and theatre director Tadeusz] Kantor. So when localness is real and has the depth of truth, it's European, because it's original, it's something unique. And now I have the impression that what's dominant is a kind of Polish People's Republic Part II, but with more of the God-Fatherland element. Our Poznań, if it is itself, it will be European, that's the way I see it, to European universalism through its own localness, its own identity. (PO08)

Respondents from the institutional sphere also presented a similar perspective:

For me, something very local or regional is also a marker of Europeanness. Silesia has a local culture that it nurtures, which for centuries has been firmly rooted in people. (KA05)

The mechanisms described above accompanying the ECOC bidding process have led to greater importance in the public discourse of the new generation, whose social and cultural capital have allowed them to contribute to a new European discourse in Polish cities:

Łódź is returning to the European network in which it once was. It was also a kind of thinking that we already have cultural managers here who are in the international network – that was a new category that wasn't there before – cultural manager, those are people who have contacts, know how to get hold of people, obtain funds, they have a kind of knowledge that the directors of cultural institutions waiting for specific grants are lacking. (ŁÓ06)

Regarding the European dimension of Polish cities, the respondents emphasised a comparative perspective: Poland vs Europe, national culture vs European culture, Polish culture vs regional culture. These dichotomies sometimes had strong negative connotations for one of the sides (e.g. peripherality vs worldliness, localness vs universalism):

Showing the uniqueness of Wrocław and the abundance of Europe in Wrocław. It's important what Wrocław is like in comparison to the abundance of European culture, where its place is and what we are like in Wrocław, here and now. (WR07)

Europeanness is our place in Europe and our response to how we see ourselves in Europe's cultural landscape. The Silesian tradition, perceived as local and regional, is important in the European context. In actual fact every culture has a regional identification. Every sensible European doesn't think about absolute unification, but thinks about collaboration while maintaining some kind of distinctness, which is an expression and sign of a certain culture and a certain European area. (KA05)

Europeanness is a process of leaving behind complexes of inferiority, localness, peripherality. It's a process from "closure" (a focus on tradition) to "openness" (the will to build a culture based on elements coming from outside) while maintaining a healthy balance. (LU06)

Incorporation into the European city network as a result of accession to the EU also changed relations in the sphere of symbolic power. Traditionally, the Polish cultural and opinion-forming discourse has been designated by two dominant centres: Krakow and Warsaw. The Europeanisation and networking process has meant that these relations have begun to change, lending increased value to cities that were previously seen as peripheral. As an example, we can cite this statement by a respondent from Szczecin:

A large percentage of people here, when thinking about their development and career, don't take other Polish cities into account, just Europe. [. . .] Artists who make use of it [the local identity] came up with the idea of promoting themselves in Poland – they go to design fairs, in Warsaw or wherever, and there they've run up against a wall. But when they've gone to Europe, to Berlin, Amsterdam, there was a large amount of interest, as it's something original, something different. (SZ01)

The importance of participation in the ECOC competition, in terms of what the European dimension means, had a major practical dimension for our respondents, for instance allowing them to gain experience in administering European projects. The following response is a good example of this:

> In Lublin people started to think about Europe, and suddenly it turned out that Lublin could have "European Capital of Culture" by its name. When I said that, people laughed. When they saw the billboards, advertising banners and the note "Lublin – European Capital of Culture", they couldn't believe it. Culture OK, but European? Capital?! Where? The eastern provinces, a squalid, hard-to-reach town. . . That was completely unimaginable in Lublin! There were huge complexes and insularity here. I'm talking about the mentality of the normal resident, but also the mentality of officials and decision makers. Absolutely the best thing that happened for Lublin, and Europeanised thinking, was inviting external experts. They were Europeans down to the ground (Dragan Klaić, Czyżewski, Ruth. . .). They taught us how to act, the philosophy of the project, finances. Suddenly there were people from Europe here who believed in Lublin, and showed us how we could develop it, how we could work together and what's important in Europe. How to network. They started to push us into networks. We had no idea how to get into them. And suddenly Dragan says: here's an email, go ahead and send it, I'll support you, but you need to do this and that. And we did. Then we started to travel, meet people and bring knowledge back. Suddenly we started to be in contact with Europe. Later we started reading about it, and then we started to design something. Now European projects have become the norm for us. It's not some mythical sphere now, it's real. That was a fast acceleration. (LU08)

Since Europeanisation also means stimulating European cooperation networks, the bidding process also permitted the formation of a new platform of exchange of information as well as learning Europe, as most respondents noted:

> Poland is not networked at all. We don't have big European contacts, sorry. Local authorities haven't created any grand narratives with Europe, interesting projects, challenges. We don't have that. Producers, managers, artists, we don't know what the musical situation is in Nuremberg, for example. If we want to start working together with Germany, we don't know much. In local authorities it's pure artistic management. You could have an artist coming, taking the children from a neighbourhood, doing some project, good or bad, there'd be a show or a concert. It's not that. You need to have an understanding of the mechanisms of operating in both Poland and Europe; what's going on there, in those cultures, to be able to network, get an overview of development trends, what can be done together – what we have to show and then we learn what's interesting for them. We see it in a network: ah, that's interesting. . . it turns out we have a completely different perspective. In local authorities now we just have artistic management, without any in-depth knowledge. Europeanisation for me means being there a little bit, getting to know them, they get to know us. Only after about two years of the networking process do we begin to understand what we can do together, what we actually need. For example look at Wrocław. There's the Grotowski Institute, New Horizons, but the entire cultural reality of the city, alternative bands, in-depth things are not understood. And now why should they get to know what, what for? If there isn't any European grant earmarked for collaboration with partner cities, then there isn't any! And then suddenly from the network some problematic

situations come out. For example problems in the districts that were revitalised, we find out
that certain things can't be done, they say do it differently, because it's not working out. . .
A completely different level of discussion. (LU08)
I think that the candidacy alone raised certain standards – e.g. in galleries English-
language materials appeared, things to do for foreign tourists, international projects and
residences. Two processes coincided. On the one hand the ECOC candidacy. And on the
other new programmes and initiatives (Creative Europe, Erasmus+) – real tools appeared.
Most festivals and events have a European element now. We used to talk about "Poland-
wide" events. . . I can't think of any Poland-wide event in Łódź now – they're all interna-
tional and European. (ŁÓ07)

The Europeanisation of a city also entailed its contextualisation, i.e. recognition
of its accomplishments and ongoing changes against the backdrop of European
culture in the broadest terms as well as the culture of other European cities. This
is illustrated by the following response from Wrocław:

I was interested, for example, in attempts to translate into contemporary language the
multicultural, and specifically European, aspects of the culture of Lower Silesia. I tried,
although this wasn't in the application, to have the Book of Henryków *inscribed on*
the UNESCO List. That was successful. I wanted to have it for the ECOC. The Book
of Henryków is doubly appealing. Firstly, it contains the first sentence in the Polish
language, and secondly, it is extremely clear evidence of the multicultural character of
this region in historical terms, but it translates into modern times. It's written in Latin
by a German monk, who quotes the first sentence that a Czech speaks to his Polish wife.
That's absolutely remarkable. The second example of European thinking is the figure
of Cardinal [Bolesław] Kominek. In the introduction to one application I write about
the process of population exchange in Wrocław, how Wrocław's identity developed and
what is worth remembering, especially with the European Union undergoing a crisis.
Cardinal Kominek is the father of Polish-German reconciliation. In order to achieve
an effect of conciliation, he uses this famous and beautiful sentence in the Letter of the
Polish Bishops to German Bishops: "We forgive and ask for forgiveness". In 1966, asked
why he was interested in Polish-German reconciliation, he said, "The only path for our
continent that will allow us to live together in peace and develop is to look for a federa-
tive solution in which we will have to abandon part of our sovereignty in the economic
sense and the defensive sense". (WR10)

It is important to note that the respondents were aware that the Europeanisation
process was not the sole result of the ECOC applications. It is a process that has
taken place at many levels, and the competition was an important mechanism
stimulating Europeanisation, but not the only one.

I don't know if Łódź has become more Europeanised. Has Łódź become more open to
Europe, or have its residents become more aware of it. . .? It's happening in many countries.
I don't see a particular correlation. Foreign artists always came here. The industrial ele-
ment was very attractive for artists. Perhaps the nature of visits has changed. I remember

alternative Łódź, the first techno party in Poland, the Łodź Kaliska group. Still everyone was coming, just the scale and access to funds was different. (ŁÓ08)

In summary, we can point to certain patterns. According to the respondents, what the "European dimension" means above all is a European city not defined by culture in the sense of the number of monuments, abundance of cultural and national heritage or the contemporary potential of artistic communities. Rather, they saw a European city as being a sustainable one, meaning pro-social, ecological, and clean, with pedestrians and not cars in the foreground. A city in which alongside good and inspirational work there are also good residential and recreational spaces. This issue was often raised in the context of the increasing decapitalisation of housing stock, especially from the communist era, as well as destruction of the spatial order and natural resources, by market forces, ruthlessly exploring city spaces.

The desire for an ideal European city appeared in the ECOC bids.[223] For example, the proposals of Lublin and Szczecin contained in the application forms and addressing the "European dimension" criterion were particularly significant in the post-factum reflections provided by respondents. Calls for democratic management of the city and implementation of deliberative and participatory democracy as characteristics of Europeanness, in fact, became more significant in the course of the competition process. The authors of the applications, as well as those working with them on the projects, believed that participation is practically a guarantee of a well-functioning urban community. Calls for a "European dimension" of other cities applying in the ECOC process went hand in hand with the spirit of integration. Szczecin placed the emphasis on trans-border collaboration, Lublin on neighbourly cooperation, and Wrocław on multicultural dialogue, open to the return of Polish immigrants from the West. There was a general consensus that cities need to function in networks and associations of cities, forming partner relationships and deepening cooperation. International relations were also expected to intensify and achieve a process of abidance by shared European values such as freedom (an important point in Gdańsk's interpretation of the "European dimension") or the local and regional factor (in Katowice's case).

The very fact of entering the competition to become European Capital of Culture should be seen as part of the Europeanisation process. In so doing, and particularly by fulfilling the formal requirements, the cities were involved in a process of familiarising themselves with the ideas of Europe in the everyday

---

223 These are analysed in depth in the Appendix.

professional practice of cultural institutions and creative people. From a domestic level of discourse on the subject of urbanity, they began to progress to the level of urban international discourse; the cities no longer compared themselves to each other, but rather joined a broader perspective, comparing themselves to their European counterparts. The process of self-reflection in the idea of the city, essential for defining the "European dimension", also entailed working through traumatic historical experiences and peripherality complexes. Introspection allowed them to redefine old, well-worn ways of thinking, showing that the situation of periphery is not defined once and for all and that local characteristics can be turned into assets.

8. Summary of Research

The European Capital of Culture 2016 competition in Poland served as an impetus for many changes to take place in the participant cities. These particularly applied to the sociocultural sphere, encompassing such issues as a city's identity and social capital. Consequently, it became possible to create new urban narratives which also contributed to changes regarding the cities' images. In some cases, this could even be described as a real revolution which was able to take place as a result of unprecedented social mobilisation. Yet the scale of this mobilisation varied. Its highest level could be seen particularly in those cities for which the process of system transformation had been painful, causing traumatic social change. In this case, in certain respects the ECOC bidding process became something of an origin myth, the moment from which new urban narratives began to be shaped. The process enabled cities to discover their own resources, "opening the eyes" of residents and encouraging them to reflect on local communities. This was particularly important for cities struggling with negative stereotypes imposed from outside. In such cases, it was evident that the "misrecognition" syndrome was being overcome. This process was most intensive in Lublin, Łódź and Katowice. It was in these cities that the ECOC bidding process had the most positive impact on their image, and according to their residents, they also gained in the external perspective. It is crucial to note, however, that the evaluations of cities' images were conducted from an internal perspective, as a consequence of the research methodology we adopted. Whether and to what extent the external view of the cities (judged by outside actors) changed is an interesting subject in itself, which could become the subject of further in-depth research.

The ECOC effect also means an intensive process of shaping new urban narratives, empathetic stories about the city. This stemmed from the fact that the bidding process altered the perception of the role of culture in cities. It was taken from the "temples" of culture to the public sphere, available to the average citizen. Participation in culture ceased to be seen as something sanctified, reserved solely for the elites, becoming an everyday practice and an important element of urban reality. This was an experience common to all the cities we investigated, resulting both from a self-reflective approach to the role of urban culture (accompanying the ECOC application process) and bringing various entities from the artistic and social world into this process. This in turn helped to break down the previous discourse on culture as a field of high culture. Consequently, on the one hand city residents' cultural aspirations grew in comparison to the activities on offer as well as spatial development and opportunities for spending free time ("awareness of place"). On the other hand, residents clearly began to identify more with the city and to feel a greater sense of agency.

In the majority of the cities, the social capital unleashed in the course of the competition was preserved, and with varying degrees of effectiveness is being used in a broad range of development processes there. With few exceptions, however, this capital is being used outside of local government institutions – which is not to say that it does not work for the cities. It is usually expressed in non-institutional forms and social activity on behalf of local communities. The stimulated interest in the city did not vanish when the bidding process came to a close, and one reason for this was the parallel development of urban movements, in many aspects drawing from the experiences of this process. An important and unprecedented factor in this case in the history of national ECOC bidding was the formation of coalitions of cities for culture. The initial spirit of rivalry transformed into networking collaboration and exchange of experiences. Furthermore, the interpersonal and professional relations forged during the competition have lasted to this day, translating into collaboration on various levels. The race to be European Capital of Culture, therefore, rather than engendering ambitious rivalry, contributed to the development of a city network that has an impact on the change in the urban discourse in Poland.

In the case of the institutional sphere, it is difficult to generalise, since change depended above all on local factors. Certain patterns could be observed, however. In the institutional sphere, the applications for the title of ECOC did not lead to a radical system change, although in certain cases they did contribute to certain adjustments such as the aforementioned "hacking of the system", entailing bringing people with experience in NGO work into local authority bodies. This also applied to cities' development strategies, in which culture began to occupy an important place. This lack of profound changes at the institutional level resulted both from the contradictions inherent in the European Capital of Culture bidding procedure and from the lack of coherent urban policies providing a framework and ensuring systemic support for the social processes unleashed by the whole process.

In the cities we studied, a major role was played by investments in cultural infrastructure. The ECOC competition coincided with an enormous financial injection given to Polish cities in the shape of EU funds. A large proportion of these was invested in infrastructure in the cultural sphere. The contest for the title of ECOC was significant in this respect in two ways. First, the huge interest in urbanity and urban culture that it stimulated translated into increased participation in culture, with new audiences filling the newly opened buildings. Second, the teams managing the new institutions were recruited largely from among people who brought their experiences from working on the ECOC. This had an impact on the ways in which these places were administered, as more participatory mechanisms of co-determination began to be implemented and institutions were opened to residents and to the city space in the broadest terms. In this case too, however, factors beyond the control of the ECOC competition, such as the primacy of the market over the common good (city spaces) meant that the new institutions were scarcely able to become new driving forces of development, leaving a so-called Bilbao effect out of reach. At the same time, though, largely thanks to the ECOC effect, we can hardly speak of a Valencia syndrome either, and at least the majority of these investments will not become "white elephants".

There is also no doubt that the bidding process played a major role in terms of Europeanisation of the cities. By stimulating the circulation of community ideas, it encouraged Polish cities to leave behind their inferiority complexes regarding the cities of Western Europe and programme their sociocultural and image-related activities in accordance with European standards. This resulted in the people responsible for administering urban culture acquiring managerial and organisational competencies, as well as professionalisation of the evaluation processes operating in this field. The Europeanisation of culture had a signifi-cant effect on dynamising informal communication channels, resulting in closer cooperation and tighter bonds in Europe's "borderless" cultural space. We can argue that the ECOC competition had an inspirational impact on the formation of extra-political interactions in the field of institutional, social and artistic cul-ture, creating a horizontal "exchange of approaches, models, and strategies with the objective of learning from each other".[224]

Finally, among the most important effects of the ECOC competition in Poland is internationalisation of interpersonal and interinstitutional relations, as well as an unprecedented opening of Polish urban communities to the transfer of European ideas, know-how or inspirations, flowing both from information exchange within the country (between cities) and from outside. It seems that most of the people participating (in various ways) in the bidding process were aware of the "new cultural geography" in which Polish cities found themselves. We would describe this "geography" as eschewing concentration on one's own

---

224 Dragan Klaić, *Mobilność wyobraźni, Międzynarodowa współpraca kulturalna. Przewodnik* (Warszawa: NINA, 2011), 74.

city and its success in terms of social issues, urban planning and image in favour of discovering it on the map of Poland and of Europe in the context of common city-making processes jointly creating an urban cultural policy. Most important in this context is suitably mature human capital secured in the process of transformation of the city, along with intelligent use of cultural resources. The ECOC competition in Poland resulted in cities laying the groundwork for building lasting supranational connections, with the Coalition of Cities being the best example. If it successfully negotiates the stage of forming structures and tasks, it has every chance to become a partner in all "eurocities" networks existing in Europe today, producing a polyphonic space for cultural exchange.

9. Appendix

Analysis of the applications of Polish cities bidding for the title of European Capital of Culture 2016

Bożena Gierat-Bieroń

Analysis of the initial programme briefs

1. Gdańsk: "Freedom of Culture. Culture of Freedom"

Perhaps no other city in Poland is associated so unequivocally with the subject of freedom as Gdańsk. The need for freedom triggered solidarity and power among the workers of the city. Freedom in Gdańsk erupted for the first time in December 1970, only to be bloodily suppressed. In 1980, it erupted again, with redoubled power and a peaceful conclusion. And this was possible thanks to human solidarity and the shared conviction that humans are made to live in freedom and culture. At this time, freedom came with the face of Lech Wałęsa, and symbolised the desire of almost 40 million Poles to be free. This fundamental longing proved so strong that it led to the dismantling of the political system and the disintegration of the communist bloc, an event that today has become a crucial lesson from history. It showed that our European culture cannot erase human dignity, founded on the sense of freedom and bonds between people. The ECOC application form asked about the capacity to draw from freedom and the possibility of using it for democratic purposes. The question was asked whether today's unfettered freedom of speech and imagination might not harbour a danger of which we are not aware, and which could prove an equal threat to the state interventionism of yesteryear. Are we able to put freedom to good use? How does today's young generation make use of its liberty? Gdańsk intended to pose all these questions to Europe in 2016 as part of a series of debates on freedom. As a city of rebellion and revolt that broke the impasse of the Iron Curtain, it saw itself as symbolically predestined to a philosophical discussion on the subject "What kind of culture do we create when we are free?" A number of European artists and intellectuals accepted Gdańsk's invitation to participate in the debate, becoming ambassadors for the city in the ECOC competition.

2. Katowice: "City of Gardens"

Katowice's slogan for the ECOC 2016, "City of Gardens", came as a surprise to the public. It was expected that the capital of Upper Silesia would be more likely to allude to its post-industrial heritage, steel industry or barren post-mining land-scape. Instead, the city opted to stress life alongside nature, and greenery, which constitutes some 42 % of the voivodeship's administrative area, making it one of the most forested regions in Poland. References were also made to the local tra-dition, meaning the urban and architectural plans of Giszowiec – once a small mining settlement, and today a district of Katowice. The "City of Gardens" had an unforgettable history in Silesia. The "garden city" was conceived by the English urban planner Ebenezer Howard in the early twentieth century, as an alternative approach to use of urban space in response to the declining industrial behemoths of Glasgow, Leeds and Manchester. The planning he proposed favoured a garden style, with large amounts of greenery, areas for walking, and town parks, as a stark contrast to the dirty cities of Scotland and Northern England, struggling with de-urbanisation and fragmentation of the public space as well as the disintegration of interpersonal connections. The result of this conception was to be an attempt to "humanise" mining cities by introducing gardens to the cityscape to neutralise the atmosphere of slums and poverty. Howard's ideas were applied in Giszowiec, built in 1907–1919 and conceived as a "green island" for work-weary miners.

The image of the garden city, i.e. the transformation of Katowice into a vast green meadow, launched the conception of a number of artistic and para-artistic projects that were described in the 2016 application form. One of the most impor-tant aspects of the implementation of the project was to alert the local authorities to the development of green spaces and the need to care for them. Exhibiting reju-venated parks, restored to the population, was to play an important role in building a new identity and forming a good neighbourhood. The atmosphere of tidying up, decorating and planting flowers in the city also stimulated cultural initiatives. A garden represents peace, quiet and meditation. It is a place of relaxation and Arcadian discussions on the world. Katowice wanted to suggest that Europe meet with it in the garden, not in a public building. This was to be in keeping with European tradition, in which philosophical debates or disputes in ancient Greece took place amid palms and flowers, forging Europe's intellectual history.

3. Lublin: "City in Dialogue"

Lublin's proposal for the European Capital of Culture 2016 was built around the concept of "dialogue" at various levels, with many people and institutions and particular attention paid to the Eastern borderlands. The city aspired to be able to present itself as the European Capital of the Eastern Frontier. The organisers were aware of the drawbacks of their geographical location: in Eastern Poland, in the more deprived so-called "Poland B", far removed from the cultural mainstream. They understood their locality and isolation in terms of communications (at the time, there were no motorways or airport, for example). Yet they turned this Eastern location into an asset of the bid. As the largest city in the Eastern borderlands, Lublin wanted to conduct a "dialogue" on the possibility of developing a new cultural and political for the region. It proposed harnessing its geopolitical conditions to gradually transform the city into a centre of cultural contacts, going beyond the administrative border of the Schengen area and ultimately becoming a major advocate of the EU's "Eastern Partnership" project. The second important element that Lublin emphasised for the ECOC 2016 was local culture and indigenous tradition. Starting from the premise that provincialism also means reference to original sources, beliefs and ideas about the world, assembling information about local culture can constitute a treasure chest providing all kinds of creative inspirations for contemporary, cosmopolitan artists. Dialogue is a dynamic phenomenon. It evokes activity, and even activism, which Lublin included in the application form as a key driving force of action, igniting energy for the coming years.

4. Łódź: "(R)evolution of Imagination"

Łódź's conception for the ECOC was based upon two premises, each with two fields of application. The first, "From the Promised Land" via "the Awakened Land" to "the Renewed Land", alluded to Polish literary tradition and the famous novel *The Promised Land* by Nobel Prize winner Władysław Stanisław Reymont. It envisaged a narrative of development. The second mainstay of the conception, "(R)evolution in Process", was a record of specific tasks that Łódź set itself in 2010–2015 with the goal of turning the city into a buzzing modern artistic and investment centre for the twenty-first century. Here the emphasis was on practice. It produced the campaign slogan, "(R)evolution of Imagination".

Łódź is a city with an industrial past, an important hub in the Kingdom of Poland, centre of weaving and the textile industry. It is a multicultural and multiethnic city in which Poles, Germans, Jews and Russians once lived side by side. For decades, Łódź saw itself as a needed city. Associated with the Industrial Revolution of the Positivist era, it was a mecca for entrepreneurs and traders. The city produced the leading class of Polish capitalists. Built on a chessboard plan resembling New York, it possesses many unique monuments. At the time of the Polish People's Republic, it was a communist textile empire in which the proletariat was the foreman. Today, in the post-industrial age, Łódź is facing major dilemmas as it shrinks and deals with depopulation. The slogan "the Awakened Land" was supposed to give residents an impetus to act, "arousing" them from their slumber and encouraging them to take steps to rescue this once dynamic conurbation, the second largest in central Poland. The beginning of the process of leaving the lethargy behind was to be marked by steps which provided a logical continuation of Łódź's industrial tradition. Emphasis was therefore placed on developing technology and business. The idea was to encourage investors, demonstrating the opportunities for entrepreneurs to set up companies and international corporations to establish bases. Afterwards, the concentration was on culture. Important names from the city were introduced, along with avant-garde musical and artistic traditions, and the textile image was seen as a perfect fit for use in the modern fashion and design world. The campaign also returned to the memory of Łódź's famous film school and the history of pre-war cinemas. Culture was supposed to bring about a symbolic rejuvenation of the city, seen as a hotbed of design, comics, fringe culture and the creative industry, including cinema. Many social groups were invited to participate in piecing together the ECOC 2016 programme. The period of operationalisation of tasks and objectives was to be a step in building a modern cultural policy for the city unique in Europe. The preparations for the ECOC in Łódź assumed the dimensions of a massive artistic and social revolution planned for the years 2010–2015, to culminate with the Renewed Land in 2016.

5. Poznań: "Poznań Cultural Storm"

Poznań built its ideas for the European Capital of Culture 2016 around the notion of "change". This was defined as an essential condition for producing work for cultural development. As a city founded on the principles of economic solidity and ideological conservatism, on the one hand it wanted to protect the good traditions of the past, but on the other it was aware of the need to redefine the values on which for years the professional ethics and morality of its citizens had been based. These values included efficiency, solidity, defiance, persistence, fight, and organic work. Owing to these traits, in a sense specific to the Poznań people, and the city's economic accomplishments, it could be seen as the most Western city of the East. It stood out from other Polish cities in terms of its high business and administrative culture. Poznań also understood "change" through culture as a bridge to building a metropolis, which is more capable than a single city of creating partnership links and forces of support. Poznań's "change" also means a transition from an industrial economy to one based upon knowledge and intellect. The city intended to use culture to develop the cultural services sector. By supporting culture, it hoped to secure investments in social capital, which would in turn stimulate creative forces. "Change" is a large-scale process, planned for several years. For this reason, the authors of the application form believed, it made sense to allude to the Shakespearean "tempest", the storm that cast its protagonists onto new lands and had them discover new territories as proof of the unending nature of the world and its cultural diversity.

6. Szczecin: "Power to Join"

Szczecin's slogan for the ECOC 2016, "Power to Join", speaks for itself. Szczecin lies almost on the Polish-German border, a city in the so-called Recovered Territories, where an unprecedented complete exchange of population took place after the end of the Second World War. The idea of "joining" was taken to mean the act of "putting together that which seemed disconnected", "stitching together" with Europe, and coming together. The stylistic device of "joining" or "cementing" is used widely. Apart from the idea of joining Europe, it also concerns the internal fusion and integration of a city that for years has had problems with specifying its own cultural identity, and, at a trans-border level, leads to the formation of a Common Cultural Space, meaning agreement and collaboration taking place across territorial and mental divisions. For its ECOC concept, Szczecin cited Churchill's famous words spoken in Fulton, Missouri in 1946: "From Stettin in the Baltic to Trieste in the Adriatic, an iron curtain has descended across the Continent". The organisers from the first of these cities – Stettin, or Szczecin – decided to go the other way, resolving that it was high time to raise the curtain, disenchant history and rebuild inter-territorial ties. "Joining" Europe meant linking the continent's old residents with its new ones, regulating the critical points on the border between East and West. Szczecin's programme emphasised the related themes of borderlands, minimising barriers and contemporary migration. It proposed establishing a common, cross-border cultural policy to permit thorough development of the neighbouring areas. Regarding the city itself, the organisers focused on redefining cultural identity, which was to be rebuilt on the basis of the process of recovering memory, reconstructing collective memory, and rehabilitating difficult issues from the past in order to forge a wise and prudent future. As a city lying in the Odra river basin, close to the sea, surrounded by water and lakes, Szczecin's ECOC conception proposed a large-scale pact with the natural environment, directing residents' attention to the nature surrounding them. It emphasised the city's links with the water, harnessing canals and rivers to create a new city space. Residents were encouraged to participate in work for ecological purposes and to popularise water sports.

7. Wrocław: "Spaces for Beauty"

"Spaces for Beauty", the main slogan of Wrocław's campaign, has a wide philosophical and anthropological context and traces its ideological source to classical aesthetic tradition. It refers first of all to the urban area and city space. A city, after all, is to a great extent a space. And yet, the organisers stressed, it is hard to imagine an urban space without people, unless we are talking about a travesty of an artistic idea or fantastical concept. In addition to its physicality, an urban space also possesses a human dimension. It exists for and with people. The quest for beauty in Wrocław suggested by the slogan was therefore to take place by joining together two elements: the physical and the humanistic. It thereby designated the direction in which the city was to transform. The plural indicates that it is not one space that is at stake here, but a multitude of overlapping and complementary areas in which transformation could take place. These phases of change are: "Space for beauty", "Space of human life", "Dynamic of space", "Nulla ethica sine aesthetica", and "Beauty of freedom – freedom of beauty".

The Wrocław team intended to search for beauty in the spiritual space and sphere of interpersonal interactions, assimilating the reality that surrounded them as a friendly area and one that is good to live in. The task of the space was to appreciate people, convincing them that a city square or street can become a place in which beauty is presented, permanently etching itself into the environment. A space was to be subject to dynamic changes on the basis of the principle that nothing stands still and that people fill the space with their energy. The central component, "Space of human life", occupied the key role in the initial description of the slogan. It was divided into six levels: the sphere of intimacy, the sphere of privacy, the public sphere, the social sphere, the sphere of nation and the cyberspace. All these spaces pointed to the integral link between the factor of culture and nature and the correlation between the world of the individual's internal sensations and the external world of physical phenomena, including the accomplishments of the technological revolution.

In the application form, the allusion to the ancient maxim that beauty is a derivative of good (*nulla ethica sine aesthetica*) formed the basis of construction of large-scale educational programmes aimed at various age groups, as well as establishing the foundations of knowledge on European culture. The Wrocław team wanted to bring about the cultural transformation of the city by pursuing the conviction that beautiful things cannot be created without noble intentions and a disinterested attitude. In this respect, the city's bid referred to the urban ugliness of Polish cities as an unwanted communist legacy that had not gained public acceptance as it was created against people, rather than for them. The ideological oppressiveness of the world continues to appear today, symbolised by mass culture, globalisation and consumerism. The Wrocław bid aimed to use the transformational process of the ECOC to learn to differentiate good art from the kitsch products of mass culture, which often assume the form of attractive works and are fundamentally lacking in depth and value. Since liberal democracy assumes freedom of good and services, speech, expression, religion, customs and morals, it is important to consider the role of beauty in all of this. It is assumed that today there is no single model of beauty, as pluralism exists in the definition of the concept. For this reason, the organisers of ECOC 2016 in Wrocław concluded that in the chaotic world of today's aesthetics it makes sense to give attention to the dualistic conception of the ancients in order to be able to maintain an Aristotelian "appropriateness".

Cities in a process of change: redefining identity, re-evaluating the function of the city, metamorphosis of the image

The ECOC 2016 slogans and logos were just a prelude to the proposition of using culture to undertake a comprehensive metamorphosis of a city. What was significant was the question of the way in which local authorities, decision makers, organisers and artistic communities intended to face up to the major project of cultural transformation of the city, planned for 2011–2016, constituting a milestone in shaping its new image and establishing a cultural brand. The following descriptions provide an introduction to the various approaches they took to the cultural deconstruction and reconstruction of Polish cities, indicating the effectiveness of their objectives and the adaptive competencies of people and places to new ideas.

These analyses are cross-sectional and interdisciplinary. They contain historical elements, an outline of the city's image and a diagnosis of the biggest problems – social, political, geographical and mental – that the organisers faced when conceptualising their proposals for ECOC 2016. The analyses focus particularly on a detailed discussion of the initial premises adopted in the ECOC programmes, which acted as a template for generating artistic projects and preparing logistical/infrastructural plans that were part of the complicated process of transforming cities into modern and creative metropolises aware of their role in creating culture.

1. Gdańsk – an axiological discourse on freedom

In the transformation process for ECOC 2016, Gdańsk set itself six main object-ives. The first was "Promotion of European debates on freedom and solidarity". Gdańsk aimed to use this project to join Europe's axiological discourse. Debates were to concentrate particularly on issues of culture in captive societies, which generated an array of secondary topics, including the principles of censor-ship, resistance to oppressions and restrictions on freedom of expression. The city's second objective was "Adaptation to the post-industrial economic model". The capital of Pomerania, apart from its magnificent Old Town, also possesses degraded post-shipyard areas, which the organisers identified as potential sites to incorporate into cultural initiatives, including developing the shipyards as part of development of creative industries. This was possible as a result of the emer-gence of an IT sector cluster in the Tri-City area, as well as innovative research projects pursued by scientists from Gdańsk University of Technology. Culture and new technologies were designated as integrated action areas in Gdańsk. The city's third objective was "Strengthening civil society", referring to the city's residents learning to make use of their freedom and democracy, harnessing the ECOC 2016 celebrations as an event to integrate citizens.

The history of Gdańsk is a difficult and long one. The conflict over the Gdańsk corridor is regarded as the beginning of the Polish-German dispute that brought about the Second World War. The former Hanseatic city, buzzing with com-merce and open to different cultures, was destroyed by wartime activities. In the communist era, nobody cared to remember that Gdańsk had once been home to sailors from England, Holland and France. Polish was spoken here, but also German in its local form, as well as Kashubian, Dutch, Latin and Yiddish. This was a place where the Europe of freedom and the Europe of serfdom met. Today's Gdańsk is a restored and resettled city. This is why the fourth objective of the city's application proposed "Strengthening local and regional identities" – in the conviction that Gdańsk's citizens are trying to define their culture and their place on Poland's cultural map. This definition was to take place at local level (in their own neighbourhoods) as well as within the Tri-City conurbation and the voivodeship, with particular emphasis attached to the cultural and linguistic uniqueness of the Kashubians. In reference to the Hanseatic traditions of the city, once the most "international" in Poland, the fifth objective is "Development of links with Poland and Europe". A prosperous trading centre lying at the inter-section of communication routes from West to East and North to South, and a port of call on the Baltic Amber Road, Gdańsk is a symbol of defiance, but also of rational, commercial thinking. The cradle of Solidarity and nursery of many

Polish politicians, aware of the pride of its inhabitants, the city aspired to become an ambassador of rapprochement between Poland and Europe. The final, sixth objective – "Stimulating cultural life", foresaw Gdańsk transforming on the path to 2016 into a city of year-round artistic festivals and events that would accustom its residents to making art part of their lives and teach them active participation.

2. Katowice: from industrial city to garden city

Silesia has seemingly forever been associated with factory chimneys, mineshafts, water towers, power stations, domestic and international rail networks, breweries, cotton mills and weaving plants. It is a huge urban-industrial agglomeration. This industrial image of Katowice is the most enduring in Polish popular consciousness, but it also stereotypes Upper Silesia strongly as an area of natural riches, rather than cultural ones. The general view of Silesia is unfavourable, as it is connoted with the negative consequences of industrialisation. Regardless of any changes that might be made for Katowice, industry retains the lion's share of the economy in Silesia.

The urban planning of the Giszowiec "garden city" produced a contrast to this picture. Giszowiec, designed by architects from Charlottenburg, was to be a colony of one- and two-family workers' houses with a garden and utility buildings, green belts and pavements. It was sketched according to a classic square plan with sacred and restaurant buildings. The residents of the district, around 600 families of miners and 40 of clerical staff, worked in the Giesche mine, today known as Wieczorek. After work, they were to rest in the shade of trees. A significant element of the new estate was that the designers alluded to the traditions of Silesian urban planning. The shape of the miners' houses was supposed to allude to Upper Silesian cottages, corresponding to the local tradition of folk architecture. The history of Giszowiec as a mini-project for the arch-European Katowice was all the more interesting as it met with resistance at the destruction of tradition and Silesian heritage, as Kazimierz Kutz, one of the Polish well known film-director, depicted in the film *The Beads of One Rosary*. In the early 1970s, the communist authorities decided to demolish the German buildings of Giszowiec and erect prefabricated tower blocks in their place. The dealings encountered resistance from the mining community, who defended their neighbourhood from the barbaric demolition. The topic reared up again in 2007, with the publication of Małgorzata Szejnert's volume of reportage from Giszowiec, *Czarny Ogród* ("Black Garden"). The book led to reflection on the regular destruction of a city's green tissue, with time turning into post-industrial dust and dirt, despite having been intended as an antidote to the sombre landscape of mineshafts.

The historical subject of the garden(s) showed the city a wide-ranging vision for a future, almost Arcadian conception of development. Firstly, it allowed the revitalisation processes of the recreational areas of the Katowice agglomeration to be defined: parks, greens, and former pre-war public gardens. Secondly, it triggered mechanisms that are crucial in Poland today, of care for one's immediate surroundings (private gardens, public squares and greens, and lawns), which for years were looked after by the state, rather than the individual citizen. Thirdly, it represented an end to looking at people from large agglomerations as cogwheels in the capitalist machine, revealing the individuality that is part of nature. The meaning of human life in twenty-first-century big cities is no longer murderous physical labour or the huge stress of corporate life, and can instead become the need for rest, recreation, self-understanding and the resultant openness to ecological processes, climate changes, recycling and keeping the world clean in general. Katowice's celebration of ECOC 2016 was supposed to make it a modern, environmentally aware and cybernetic metropolis of Southern Poland.

3. Lublin: generating local culture and aiming eastwards

By choosing the word "dialogue" in its ECOC 2016 slogan, Lublin showed that its approach to problems would be based on compromise. Dialogue is a joint search for understanding. It assumes collaboration, rather than competition, in contrast to discussion, which entails victory. It means listening to the arguments others, finding agreement, and reaching a consensus. "Dialogue" is also one of the key components of the European Union's cultural policy, and this is also important in the ECOC competition. "Dialogue" at European level presupposes reaching an agreement across national, political and cultural divides, in spite of linguistic differences, conflicts of interest and economic rivalry. Lublin sought to operationalise this European aspect of "dialogicality" in its application form.

The idea of "Lublin – City in Dialogue" was to be implemented through four thematic axes, three areas and four principles – "4 x E". Let us begin with the thematic axes. The first, "City and region", established a dialogue between urban and rural culture, assuming that these areas always correspond. The clash between rural and urban culture was deemed to be relevant to Lublin's residents, who often come from rural areas. The second thematic axis, "Remembering and anticipation", pointed to a kind of dialogue between past and future and the use of memory for future needs and cultural phenomena. The third axis, "Towards the East", was designated as the ideological message of the entire 2016 programme. It emphasised the need to clarify the city's new function, by strengthening and expanding Lublin's cooperation with neighbouring countries, especially Ukraine,

Belarus and Russia. This thinking about the East also led to the appearance of the natural need to participate in the formation of the "Eastern Partnership" programme, meaning intensified collaboration with Moldova and the Caucasus states. Lublin assumed a permanent position in the role of ambassador of the Eastern Partnership in Poland. The fourth thematic axis proposed by the application authors, "Culture of knowledge", initiated a dialogue on harnessing the city's intellectual potential for future creativity and innovation. The authors pointed to the need for artistic initiatives to fuse with social ideas in the belief that this would generate projects stemming from the imagination and needs of citizens. Three of these areas of cultural activities were supposed to refer to production of culture (in exchange for import of external "products"), greater participation in culture and increase in competencies. The four "E" words, meanwhile, aimed to help with appropriate selection of projects. The first was "Empathy", meaning sensitivity to the closeness of the other, and on the cultural level, acquisition of the skills of discovering indigenous and archaic culture as that intrinsic to the region's DNA. Second, "Efficiency", resulted from the conviction that culture has agency and can be used to change reality. The "Ecology" of culture focused on care for the environment in which culture is produced. Finally, "Experiment", an attempt to restore appropriate magnitude to subversive, alternative art, which constituted the essence of Lublin's artistic movements.

Lublin's "dialogicality" means a symbolic orientation towards discussion, i.e. listening to the voices of artistic communities, consumers of art, and citizens. The authors assumed that, in order to clarify the authentic needs of residents and artists, it is essential to initiate a conversation. The contemporary person is one of communication, an operator in the world of media and interpersonal relations.

4. Łódź: revolution versus evolution

The city of Łódź divided the implementation of its main slogan, "(R)evolution of Imagination", into two main action areas. The first was to be tasks put into practice in the years preceding the date of the festival, proper, between 2010 and 2015, while the second was for all the initiatives of the ECOC 2016 programme (in 2016). The first five years were dubbed "(R)evolution in process", while the year 2016 itself received the same name as the ECOC slogan, "(R)evolution of imagination". All the activities, irrespective of the time, employed the same methods. They analysed the potential of the city in a specific area, designated the objectives within the framework of the ECOC, then elaborated instruments and a plan for action implementation, prior to the realisation and evaluation of the whole idea. These activities were expected to change the culture of Łódź and revolutionise the lives of its inhabitants – all social groups, artists, and local politicians – as well as residents of the voivodeship. The intention was to turn the city into a modern laboratory of creative ideas and solutions for Łódź and many other towns in the region.

The revolution was to take place in a specific geographical area, in a layer of interpersonal relations and at the level of international cooperation. It was to be both horizontal and vertical. The intervention areas for 2010–2015 were: Revolution in the city, Social revolution, Revolution in business, Revolution in culture, Revolution of international cooperation, and Creative revolution. These concerned such issues as revitalisation and the urban space, business and culture, and the creative sector. The slogan "(R)evolution of the imagination" itself comprised five categories of activities: "(R)eflections", ("R)elations", "(R) econstructions", "(R)ecreations", and "(R)evelations". "Reflections" refers to an exchange of ideas in the broadest sense, meaning discussions, consultations, workshops, symposia, meetings, and conferences. This concerned five further subjects: 1. the creative sector, 2. the economic and urban planning situation of the city and the region, 3. the city and region's identity, 4. the history of Łódź's four-culture tradition, and 5. the situation in Europe, with a particular emphasis on Eastern Europe.

The next thematic axis grouped together a series of activities, with "(R) elations" as the leitmotif, referring to the generation and construction of good social bonds and formation of trust. Here, the authors of the application pro-duced a set of socio-artistic projects intended to change interpersonal relations, influencing relations between people and art, the city and the community. The next projects engaged residents of the city and the regions, and the final ones strengthened ties between artists and society. "(R)econstructions" referred to rebuilding the character of the city and its historical fabric. It aimed to restore the beauty of industrial architecture, rediscover the artistic character of the city, and create a multicultural atmosphere. The following priorities appeared in this area: 1. Revitalisation, 2. Ecology, 3. Art in the urban space, and 4. Attention to image. The next project, "(R)ecreations, incorporated contact with others people, contact with nature, and contact with the voivodeship's spiritual culture. "(R)ecreations also includes "Łódź by bike", free time, open-air meetings, cul-tural tourism, and workshops in spiritual development using culture and Eastern philosophy. "(R)evelation" covered series of meetings distinguished within the ECOC, major events, and large-scale festivals. Łódź opted to promote itself as a centre of big, modern, international festivals, intended to become the city's show-case in 2016 and to stick permanently to its domestic and international image.

5. Poznań: between economics and culture

Poznań is the affluent and sedate capital of Wielkopolska, or Greater Poland. Once an important centre of the resistant movement to the partitioning powers and Germanisation, and then to the German state, it is the former capital of Poland, with a history stretching back more than a thousand years. Poznanians have always been accustomed to independent organisation of public structures, renowned for their organisational work, implementation of positivist ideas and economy. They were responsible for some of the groundbreaking socio-political events of Poland's twentieth-century history, such as the Wielkopolska Uprising and the workers' revolt of 1956, which paved the way for the Hungarian Revolution. Poznań today describes itself as the westernmost city of the East. The reasons for this are the city's organisational competencies, its residents' spirit of enterprise, and the fact that, with its International Fair, it is a major trading and congress centre. Consequently, the task for Poznań ECOC 2016 was to be to attempt to redefine its residents' needs: from a serene life to needs for active participation in culture. The people of the city are known for conservatism, and this creates a certain distance towards artistic novelties. The organisers wanted to direct Poznanians' high level of social sensitivity towards nurturing a jointly created, long-term cultural policy for the city, greater engagement in group activity, and making use of the ability to easily adapt to modernisation processes for cultural purposes. Poznań asked itself whether it was an optimal city, and replied in the negative. The city could become "optimal" in future by engaging in dialogue in culture, harnessing its people's creative capacity and creating mechanisms stimulating the development of culture in 2016.

6. Szczecin: cultural crossing of borders

Szczecin's "power to join" concerned areas, places, territories and a tangled history. Joining is a counterweight to division and dispersal. Since the Iron Curtain divided Europe into two separate political and ideological worlds, the Szczecin team wanted to use the ECOC programme to propose initiatives with the opposite effect. The "joining" was therefore to take place in three subject areas: "Connecting Europe", "Szczecin: redefinition" and "Flows, waves, currents". The first thematic node referred to the specific geographical area. Since Szczecin lies at the sensitive point of contact between East and West and between the old inhabitants of the continent and the new ones, the authors stressed the creation of a programme developing the common Polish-German space. ECOC 2016 was intended to contribute to forming this space based upon trans-border cooperation, exchange of experiences and learning about one another. Szczecinians were supposed to grasp the fact that the borderland need not be a "cursed" place and be synonymous with transfer of goods and transport routes, but that it could become a place of celebration of shared traditions or a language laboratory. The organisers aspired to create a uniform cultural policy in which the interests of border towns would be incorporated into the broader perspective of the region's cultural development. In this thematic area, therefore, they were concerned with minimising the barriers that post-war migrations had erected, consigning the region to unwanted neighbourhood and mutual hostility. Since Pomerania was the site of a huge population exchange, it is worth today reflecting upon the consequences of migration of contemporary Europeans and its influence on construction of the identity of today's multicultural Europe.

The next core subject area, "Szczecin: redefinition" was an attempt to search for the city's cultural identity on the basis of reflection on the past and the future. According to the authors, memory of where Szczecinians came from needed to be reconstructed, after successive destruction during the communist era. In order to do this, they wanted to create a collective picture of the memory of residents: Poles from the East as well as Germans expelled from the city. An additional element of this thematic module was the question of residents' participation in forming a new cultural policy for Szczecin. This issue was emphasised because creators of culture and administrators of cultural institutions were painfully aware of the lack of such a policy. It was decided that a participatory model of democracy should be put in place in the city, permitting residents to take part in drawing up the cultural policy and squaring it with other regulations governing the sector.

The last module, "Flows, waves, currents", intentionally included aquatic metaphors. The organisers underlined "Szczecin's unique location as a city lying close to water and to the sea". It was crucial, they stressed, to integrate the reservoirs, rivers and lakes into the city's cultural life and use them for open-air events and meetings with residents. Szczecin's "Middle Oder area" (Śródodrze) was treated as a major environmental challenge, as endangered species of birds live there. The "flow of ideas" is a metaphorical buzzword for the city's opening to new artistic possibilities, designed to target the aquatic surroundings.

7. Wrocław: mental metamorphoses

Wrocław is a city that has been characterised by cultural exchange for centuries. Suffice it to say that German Breslau transformed into Polish Wrocław; this statement alone conceals an array of transformational phenomena. It is a city of sociocultural metamorphoses, a symbolic example of evolving

Europe. And Europe's history as it is would not exist if Wrocław's were different, with its resettlements and expulsions, forcing people to adapt to new conditions and to redefine their affiliation to nation, society, culture and religion. It is this historical complexity and genealogy that is the source of the enigmatic character of Wrocław to which the organisers refer. The belonging to various culture and nations, and diverse nomenclature (Presslaw, Wretslaw, Wrocław), means that the city's inhabitants construct an image founded upon multiplicity, which in socio-anthropological terms is called "multiple identities". As the city of the historical and dramatic experiment of resettlements, Wrocław holds a dialogue with itself. The city's new residents, who came to the regained lands from the East, have been asking themselves about the value and meaning of their new home for 60 years. They were open to multicultural dialogue. Indeed, one could say that the identity of Wrocławians, shaped over the decades, has become a dynamic identity, and as such can now meet the challenges of forming a European identity, which is inherently a conglomerate of cultural flows.

Wrocław possesses tremendous cultural potential in terms of the cultural heritage of the city and Lower Silesia and the tradition of avant-garde art. Here, alongside the Centennial Hall, listed as a UNESCO World Heritage Site, the "salvaged" Old Town, and the unique Racławice Panorama, one can find a number of monuments to contemporary culture testifying to the power of resistance to the communist authorities and manifested through art. Here, respect for tradition clashed with the energy of avant-garde rebellion, expressed in original theatrical and artistic concepts. It was here that the Lower Silesian arm of the Solidarity movement emerged, demonstrating civil dissension towards the regime and compromise with the authorities. As a city functioning in a paradigm of discord, Wrocław is able to connect contradictory characteristics to form a new quality from this contradiction. A city of supranational aspirations, forger of good neighbourly relations between Lower Silesia and the Czech Republic and Germany, and former host of the World Congress of Intellectuals in Defense of Peace and the European Cultural Congress, it wanted to use ECOC 2016 to once again prove that it was capable of working with international organisations and building an international brand.

Adaptation of European ideas (selected examples)

1. The "European dimension" criterion

For **Gdańsk**, the most important task at European level was the attempt to inspire Europeans to participate in the culture of freedom. A large-scale,

European debate entitled "Freedom of Culture. Culture of Freedom" was proposed, to tackle freedom and solidarity as axioms of the continent's civilisational development and the common features of European culture, essential for survival and development. The plan was to discuss the cultural state of Poland and Europe in the context of development of new technologies. The proposal was to strengthen international cooperation in every sector, or rather to strengthen the cooperation that Gdańsk already has, especially in the framework of partner cities, networks, collaboration of Hanseatic and Baltic cities and in the context of the Amber Road. What was new was a focus on orientation towards the East. Gdańsk wanted to restore Kashubian culture to Europe, promoting its presence throughout the entire ECOC 2016 process. Since Poland is a culturally homogeneous country that does not value intercultural dialogue, the city decided to explore issues of migration, thereby focusing attention on intercultural and intergenerational ties.

The problem of migration, in its contemporary dimension, was also a focus for **Wrocław**. In 2006 the capital of Lower Silesia became the only city in Poland to embark on a full-scale campaign targeted at Polish emigrants after 2004 encouraging them to return. Wrocław is a city that is familiar with the subject of migration, as its social fabric was formed by the process of resettlements. It is aware of the moral and material costs that migration brings. Wrocław is particularly sensitive to the "peregrination" of Europeans. Milan Kundera described the city as a miniature model of Europe, and Homo wratislaviensis as a multicultural, tolerant and cosmopolitan figure open to otherness. Wrocław has continually experienced fusion of cultural horizons, and thus the city lives in the awareness of the need for dialogue, in spite of and in defiance of differences. Wrocław's experience in this respect (on a micro scale) can be very useful for solving the problems of Europe as a whole (i.e. on a macro scale). The city's main slogan for 2016, "Spaces for Beauty", was intended as an invitation to fill these spaces with diverse works and ideas of European artists and foreign guests. It was supposed to encourage the formation of direct relations between Wrocławians and other Europeans, serving as an incentive for learning about culturally different models of beauty and for searching for how, despite the diversity, these models are linked, and what they have in common. And what Europeans have in common is knowledge based upon Greek philosophy, Roman law and Judaeo-Christian ideas. To cite the reflections of Hans-Georg Gadamer, Wrocław highlighted the fact that European unity and identity are a result of negotiation and constant renegotiation of compromise, rather than imposed dogma. According to the authors of the application, therefore, Europe's powers of development lie in the capacity to appreciate diversity, and not in suppressing it. The diversity of the European continent is its great aptitude.

In the European dimension, **Szczecin** put the emphasis on strengthening cooperation in its geographical neighbourhood, in which Polish, German, Danish and Swedish influences meet. The city proposed the formation of a Common Cultural Space comprising three projects: common circulation of culture, common public opinion, and trans-border democracy. Common circulation of culture would concern strictly artistic initiatives, common public opinion would mean creation of an information platform about the region, and trans-border democracy was intended to encourage the formation of a cultural policy for the whole area based on neighbouring conceptions: Danish, Swedish and German. Even now, this border region boasts a number of initiatives. The scientific and artistic project entitled "Culture Collider" planned for 2010–2016 sounded particularly interesting. Its main subject was to be a discussion of the problems of globalisation and cultural differences, held at three major conferences: "Critical Raw Materials in the Possession of Civilisation", "What Multiculturalism for the Cities of Europe?", and "Clash of Civilisations or a Great Culture Collider?". These meetings were to seek to answer the question of how to function in a border region, how to respond to the clashing of cultures, which is an intrinsic characteristic of civilisation. Szczecin, founded by the Pomeranians, is a multicultural site, and therefore, in the framework of European contexts, it proposed specific multicultural narrative projects to discover this area. These were to be "A walk around. . .", "A melting pot of cultures", and "Euro-Arabia". The objective was to unearth the spirit of the place and time, challenge the stereotypical image of the Arab in Europe and discover the cultural connection between European and Arab culture. Common heritage, the idea of democracy and rehabilitation of the cultural landscape were dominant themes of the European dimension in the programme. The idea of democracy, linking all European nations, is a unique phenomenon in world history. The idea of democracy according to Szczecin's application in its deliberative version was supposed to contribute to creating the new premises of the city's cultural policy. Yet Szczecin also means large bodies of water and greenery, and the natural values of cities can help residents to understand nature, as well as shaping their cultural sensitivity.

Lublin focused on creation of partnership networks in its approach to the European context. The intention was for the city to become known as a partnership city from East to West and from North to South, as well as a city of mobility, paving the way to getting to know others, learning from one another and sharing experiences. Lublin concluded, based on sad reflection on recent times, that the multicultural project was coming to an end in Europe, and asked

itself the question before ECOC 2016 of how to meet this challenge and to rein-
terpret the project. The city's programme suggests several solutions. One is to
focus on regional trans-border cooperation of a lasting character and providing a
guarantee of a good agreement. As an example, Lublin gives its long-time collaboration with Lviv, which is neither in the European Union nor in the Schengen
Area, and yet whose residents have found a common language with those of
Lublin. Such multifaceted borderland initiatives can offer new value to European
identity, strengthening it in the face of other threats. Neighbourly inspirations
can counteract the cultural unification of Europe. Lublin called for a multicultural Europe, broadened by cultural cooperation with the states of the Eastern
Partnership and Russia; this was its proposed contribution to the "European
added value". This was why the city's programme underlined the function of the
Europe's Eastern neighbourhood so clearly. In its authors' view, a key focus of the
EU's Common Foreign and Security Policy should be expanding the sphere of
influence to the countries of the Eastern Partnership.

Łódź was founded on the mobility of nineteenth-century entrepreneurs, and
it was this tradition that it wanted to emphasise as the city's power to create and
form culture. In the Łódź application form, the question of the European dimension was broken down into operational tasks. This was not a list of ideas, but of
concrete actions and initiatives. The city's European perspective aimed to take
a place in the latest trends of global culture. Rather than forming a specific ideology for the European celebrations, therefore, it wanted to use them to create a
modern city, based on other prosperous metropolises founded on enterprise and
creative industries. The authors tried to show that, although Łódź is a city from
Central and Eastern Europe – a region that is behind the rest of the continent
in many respects – it had a modern team of culture professionals. They invited
not only residents, but also world-renowned curators, artists, heads of major
art galleries and directors of international festivals to participate in writing the
application. The "European dimension" in this case was therefore achieved even
at administrative level. As part of attempts to build an international platform for
artistic cooperation, the Polish Comics Centre and the Dialogue Centre were
invited to form contacts with professionals from other countries in order to be
able to share their knowledge and experience. The aim of this cooperation was to
make it possible for Łódź to be home to programmes developing competition in
culture at the system level and bolstering enterprise. The platform raising these
initiatives to European level was to consist of a series of training programmes,
seminars, bilateral study visits and networking opportunities. Łódź wanted
to become a city active in networks. It proposed mapping its residents' cultural needs and passing this information on to networks. Following the path of

post-industrial heritage, Łódź aimed to be present in cities with a similar urban image and to be seen at international thematic fairs. The city aspired to collaborate closely with partners in the USA and Israel, as well as proposing cooperation with Russia, with which it had previously nurtured cultural contacts. As the centre of the Polish avant-garde, Łódź planned to present its best products in this field in 2016 in the form of an exhibition on aspects of the avant-garde and by becoming the fashion centre of Central and Eastern Europe, as well as a centre of world design and a hub of comics and games, film, and creative industries.

Poznań, as a city of the "worse" part of Europe, proposed joining the area known as the heart of European culture. In this context, the application form emphasised the question of a "return" home and becoming a fullyfledged member of the European "household". The Poznanians asked whether the "old" part of Europe needed the "new" one, and whether Europe was curious about itself. This question was to be the focus of numerous debates and discussions. The main idea in the European dimension was to be that of exchange between Poznań and the rest of Poland and between "old" and "new" Europe. Poznań also wanted to use the ECOC as a means for entering the global network of exchange and cooperation.

Katowice's "City of Gardens" was a voice in the discussion about the shape of Europe. The authors of the application proposed a new narrative for Europe, writing, "Just as Katowice's garden is a city, and not a garden in a city, Katowice is Europe, and not just a city in Europe. A voice about the city is therefore always a statement on the question of Europe". This new narrative was supposed to entail reaching Europe via an educational system that would first develop Europeans' cultural competencies. They proposed several solutions in this respect. One was *Baroque Factory*, a scholarship programme for young musicians from Europe. Another was to work with the Silesian University and international partners to develop the structures of the University of the Third Age, and a third was an exchange programme as part of the "Cultural Townhouse" project. As part of the process of discovering folk culture and the contents of original culture, Katowice proposed recycling of ideas, i.e. creating an online database of cultural ideas and skills that are dying out in the era of globalisation and mass culture. One of the more interesting proposals was the "Hyperbook for Kids", full of European tropes and myths, a treasure trove of knowledge about the European's fairy-tale world. Children from diverse cultural circles within Europe would have the opportunity to gain an insight into the imagination and fantasy of other literary cultures. The final idea in response to the "European dimension" was the concept of creating European neighbourhood gardens – which in practice would mean designating areas to be cultivated as French, English or Dutch gardens as examples of various agrarian and recreational conceptions.

2. The "City and residents" criterion

The "City and residents" idea in **Wrocław** aimed to overcome the notion of the city's enigmatic character with the idea of "shareholders", institutions launch initiatives: the Wrocław Culture Shareholder and the Children's Culture Shareholder. In the former case, this entailed an exchange of ideas between independent groups and associations concerning what kind of city Wrocław was to be today. In the latter case, the shareholder was to collect children's ideas on the same subject. This was about establishing a consensus and shaping a civic approach. The "Cultural Bond" initiative was supposed to incorporate districts into the ECOC programme. Staff from the ECOC office were to be part of neighbourhood council meetings to allow them to influence the synergy of local plans with the overall premises of ECOC Wrocław 2016. The next step was in response to the city's artistic community. The idea was to invite numerous experts and representatives of cultural institutions from Wrocław and Lower Silesia, the world of science and education to participate, in response to statistics showing that Wrocław's students comprise around 20 % of its population. Schools superintendents and representatives of NGOs were also included. There were also plans to tap the world of business by collaborating with the Lower Silesian Chamber of Commerce. These initiatives were supposed to combine to contribute to a major increase in participation in culture. Yet their main objective was to create an appetite for culture, and, in the long run, equalise access to culture as well as increasing participation.

The idea of civic **Lublin** was derived from Socratic ideas, cited by Zygmunt Bauman, which was a focus of the city's application form. Bauman wrote that "the meaning of living one's life 'the Socratic way was self-definition and self-assertion and a readiness to accept that life cannot be other than a work of art for whose merits and shortcomings the 'auctor' (actor and author rolled into one; the designer and simultaneously the executor of the design) bears full and sole responsibility".[225] Creating a civic Lublin became one of the key goals for the city's ECOC 2016 team. The application authors thought that, as in a Greek *polis*, a city is formed above all by its citizens, who make joint decisions in an agora, rather than the enigmatic authorities with a monopoly on knowledge of self-organisation. The notion of "auctor" took a firm hold in the glossary of terms

---

225 Zygmunt Bauman, *The Art of Life* (Cambridge–Malden, MA: Polity Press, 2008), 79.

defining modern Lublin. What did it mean? The fact, for instance, that even in the initial phase the residents assimilated the task that the ECOC 2016 office had outlined for the city. This was the idea, stemming from Socrates, that citizenship is a complicated process of forming a self-aware person who knows that his or her life, and that of the surroundings, depends above all on him or herself (the auctor). This is a very sophisticated concept. Furthermore, the authors noted that Lublin's local community should be composed of citizens aware of their lives, for whom the city is not an alien space, but an agora over which they hold power. This was the source of the slogan "City in Dialogue". The civic ethos thus became an element of the whole application process for Lublin 2016. From the outset, citizens were expected to be engaged in the process of defining and appropriating the city. Civic Lublin is characteristic of the Socratic myth, and the city's life is understood as a work of art that develops in time. Lublin was to become a work made by its own residents. This process took place in several stages: integration, constant activity, self-organisation, self-study, creativity, volunteering and cultural education. "Integration" in Lublin meant including everybody in this understanding of the process of building the new city.

The process of shaping active citizens also included "constant activity", i.e. stimulating action via various types of initiatives with the aim of unleashing the city's creative potential. The leader here was an "alternative city council", the "Social Organising Committee (*Społeczny Komitet Organizacyjny*, or SPOKO, meaning "cool"). Public discussions and debates, task forces, and the most active members then set up the *Kultura 2016* team. The city's "self-organisation" was not confined to a uniform movement, but was rather a dynamic self-definition and self-organisation campaign. The self-organisation activities led to the emergence of further groups: Citizen Students and Citizen Entrepreneurs. These were followed by Self-Education, a permanent, informal education initiative organised by residents. The "creativity" of the civic idea of Lublin 2016 was about "generating culture" in return for mass provision of ready-made products. The "wide culture" idea entailed incorporating initiatives from outside the mainstream into the city's civic activity: punk, street art, folk culture, tourism, ecology, and even extreme sports; in short, everything that city life creates, including niche cultures. Informal culture was to come out of the shadows. "This culture represents the social 'capital of risk', investing in something that sometimes does not yet have a name but already generates creative social energy. It is based upon capacities and participation that are within the reach of every resident".

Szczecin divided its projects into those targeted at a wide audience (a 100-day summer festival) and those aimed at narrow, profiled target groups. From the outset, the programme was an emphatically civic one, since it was initiated by one person. The organisers proposed several projects seeking to promote civic knowledge. The "Hospitality" project was about creating links between residents and artists coming to Szczecin. One of the task areas included guiding visitors around places of interest in the city. Knowledge of foreign languages was therefore essential in this project. The next project from this subject field, "A Walk Around...", was an initiative appointing local guides and routes to introduce less well-known areas of Szczecin and create a new map of the city. Other projects mentioned in the application form were "Cultural Labyrinth", "Cultural Laboratory", "Cultural Incubator" and "Micro-support". An important, long-term venture was the creation of "Cultural Democracy", which entailed participatory formation of a cultural development plan for Szczecin. The concept of "Integrity" was understood as joint, considered planning. The result of all these initiatives in Szczecin was to be a lasting change in residents' attitudes, becoming more active and engaged. This was possible above all thanks to projects geared towards creating social ties, with a particular emphasis on inclusion of people threatened by exclusion or marginalisation. This was to be the role of the "First contact with culture points". The authors of the application thought that when a certain stage of democratisation was realised, it would be necessary to use more advanced instruments in order to complete the process.

Gdańsk promoted civic ideas not only within the city itself, but also in the potential metropolitan area, creating the first "metropolitan volunteer service" in Poland to help realise this aim. The city's main focus was on harnessing all its forces, opportunities and means to exact a comprehensive transformation at many levels of activity, from changes in transport and infrastructure to changes in residents' mentality. The Gdańsk Shipyard was to be rebuilt, while the city's waterways and canals were to be turned towards the sea. Volunteers were to have the task of working to revive Gdańsk's neighbourhoods. It was planned that by 2016 Gdańsk would become a city friendly to both residents and tourists, using sustainable development and a rational development plan. Cultural hubs were also to open by this time. The city space was to be subject to the processes of democratisation. Various campaigns were planned to encourage tighter neighbourhood relations: "My district is the capital too", "Neighbour days", "Parking 2016", and "Urban signs of the times". Creative tourism initiatives were also launched, with the aim of presenting less well-known places. The city's spaces were also to be freed up for artists: from huge housing blocks in the Zaspa district to the shipyards. The idea was to show "hidden" places. There were also plans to evaluate the work of cultural institutions and supervise the city's culture policy in order to redefine Gdańsk.

Its citizens were to be auditors of the authorities, who in return had to learn to work together with the citizens.

Katowice inaugurated its bid to gain the title of ECOC 2016 by giving several thousand sunflower seedlings to residents. In 2016 the whole city was supposed to become home to new so-called Private Gardens, created in private courtyards, allotments, greens and squares, as well as on balconies and terraces. The city was to be immersed in flowers. In 2016, when the organisers' intentions came to fruition, this would prove that the residents had truly understood them. It is also important to remember that the very idea of Katowice bidding for the title came from the initiative of one person, who asked friends on Facebook whether it might not be an important exercise for the city. This, of course, reveals the power of social networking sites, and how they are capable of mobilising people to act. The aim was to activate whole districts. Each year, a different one was to present an original narrative. Campaigns such as "Go out onto the Square" were to inspire residents to shape a new complexion of their surroundings, and in future also of the cultural landscape. An important element was the idea of making music together, alluding to the musical tradition of Upper Silesia. The "musical potlatch" was expected to become a meeting place for local musicians and composers and somewhere to exchange various musical genres. At the educational level, Katowice presented two very interesting ideas: school and sport. In the former case, the city launched a competition (together with Spain) to win the title of School Cultural Capital. The Centre of Art project, meanwhile, was supposed to focus the attention Europe's attention upon promotion of sport not in terms of racing and competition, but as an art form. Other aspects included the initiation of completely new forms of collaboration between communities to support Katowice's culture. The Cultural Townhouse was to play an important role as a place of contact for cultural operators and businesspeople to meet.

From the outset, **Łódź** encouraged everybody to participate in creating its programme and shaping the city's cultural policy. Participants also included Polish and international representatives of business and the designers who created the logo. Studies on the development of audiences were among the most important that Łódź intended to carry out in the period prior to the ECOC. The organisers invited all qualified people, including foreigners, to participate and help to create a programme and brand for the city. Nobody was excluded from taking part in the revolutionary process of changing the city.

Innovativeness of the project (best examples)

In terms of innovativeness, Katowice's "garden city" idea contributed to improved communication on the basis of the conviction that if a city can turn itself into a garden, then discussion is a simpler operation. As the capital of the Silesian Agglomeration, Katowice was accustomed to partner-based discourse, and naturally worked together with the surrounding municipalities and administrative districts. The city's "new narrative" proposed to Europe was therefore a model of dynamic co-existence of a large economic and urban hub, the key to which was balanced discussion on responsibility for issues that affect us. As the authors of the application wrote, "in a garden city there is no division into civilisation and nature; ecology is not an empty word or the city an empty place". The new narrative also signified the city as the space and language of Europeans about their own identity and future, as well as about openness to the world of nature that surrounds us.

In **Szczecin**, the authors of the application stressed that bidding for the ECOC title had begun with NGOs, and not with decision makers, noting that every city in Poland has the capacity to democratise its public life and that the participation of the people in shaping its cultural life has become an irreversible phenomenon in Poland. Culture was therefore to be used as a laboratory of good practices and solutions that could also be applied in other spheres of public life. The organisers saw the introduction of deliberative and participatory democracy as a good start for the promotion of trans-border democracy. As an innovative exercise on a national scale, Szczecin proposed testing the city's budget in terms of its impact on equality of opportunities and gender, as well as making amendments.

Innovative **Poznań** meant supporting the activity of medium and small enterprises working in culture, artistic agencies and other companies. The assumption was that if the city prospered economically, this could stimulate its cultural development. The importance of modern technology and knowledge was emphasised. The project was rooted in building a suitably large and professional economic base for intensified future cultural initiatives.

Wrocław's "Spaces for Beauty" project was envisaged as a comprehensive process of stimulating the cultural life of the city and the region. The concept of "beauty" itself was an innovative element. This was to act as a signpost pointing the way, finding aesthetic projects in forgotten places or creating them in new places. A series of discussions and debates made the city's residents aware that art does not exist without culture or culture without art. Furthermore, they demonstrated how closely the state of society and democracy are affected by culture and art together. Culture was deemed to play a crucial role in the general process of socialisation and education, and key importance was therefore attached to ecological education, including animal rights.

Predicted short- and long-term consequences of implementation of the ECOC 2016 projects

The short-term consequences of the ECOC for **Gdańsk** are foreseen mainly in terms of social changes and on the labour market. The local communities (residents of neighbourhoods) are expected to be strengthened, while the number of jobs should also rise along with the development of creative industries and tourist traffic. The long-term effects of the ECOC for Gdańsk are a complex issue. The key objective was to develop the mechanisms of social participation in the city's policy – in particular cultural policy – through research, consultations, identification of needs, and creating the conditions for public activation. The foundation of the Gdańsk 2016 metropolitan volunteer service was seen as offering numerous future benefits. The ECOC was expected to increase the sensitivity of Gdańsk's residents and Poles to diversity and the values of Kashubian culture, with helping coming to be regarded as a virtue, making it easier in future on an everyday basis to practise solidarity based upon cooperation and support. Culture was also anticipated to become more accessible. Establishing the metropolis was to make it possible to form a sense of identification with a large urban area, as well as increase opportunities for leisure activities. Regarding professionalisation of the culture sector, good practices were to be developed in management, with the practice of partnership, an extensive cultural information system and rational planning of the metropolis's cultural events producing a synergy effect.

The ECOC was supposed to restore the "sea" to the city by revitalising its waterways, canals and coastal areas, rejuvenating tourist traffic and raising the standard of services. The plan was for Gdańsk to gain a new position on Europe's touristic and cultural map. Major changes were promised in the use of the former shipyard areas, which would go from being degraded, industrial land to spaces devoted to culture, treated as an important cultural component of the New City district. The activation of these areas was to be supported by the Wikipolis and Alternativa projects, the European Solidarity Centre located in the area, Wyspa Institute of Art, artists' studios and initiatives designed to democratise the public space.

The long-term effects of ECOC **Katowice** were above all: community, culture and city. The aim was for Katowice's society/residents to form a positive opinion about their own city, allowing them to identify with it more strongly and to develop a sense of shared responsibility for the process of shaping it. The future city was to be created by the people associated with it, including the youngest and oldest generations, neighbourhood groups and previously excluded communities. The capacity for cooperation was to be passed on to the next generations of Katowicans and residents of the Silesian agglomeration. In terms of culture, the city anticipated improved cultural competencies, and in particular that Katowice would become a young cultural centre, open to visitors, including cultural operators and managers from throughout Europe. A major effect of the ECOC was expected to be discovery of the region by its inhabitants and tourists and increased interest in Silesian history and dialect. Katowice wanted to promote itself as a strong artistic and cultural hub in Central and Eastern Europe. In terms of urban changes, lively areas of public space were expected to emerge. It was hoped that the new city would be a friendly space for people with cognitive disorders and physical disabilities. Finally, Katowice was to transform into a competitive metropolis implementing modern, clean energy technologies and urban/transport solutions.

Lublin asked direct questions: "What comes after 2016?", "What will we be left with?" Its answer was that there needed to be an end to the process of constant discontinuities. The most important effect of the ECOC in Lublin was therefore to stimulate the belief in the value of cultural continuity. The hope was to get the city talking about the need for continuity of city-making process and historical transformations, and this led to an emphasis on such historical events as the Union of Lublin. Lublin was to play host to the modern "Towards the East" Workshop – a centre of eastern competencies, engagement in the Eastern Partnership, using art as a creative form of integration of Europeans of various cultures. Stability for Lublin meant creating a modern centre equipped with the tools for cultural work, bolstered by financial guarantees and underpinned by European partnership and experience of implementing large-scale artistic and social enterprises. For this reason, the first such institutions were created or planned, such as the "Culture of Knowledge" Workshop, the European Centre for Cultural Studies and the Cultural Observatory, delivering modern know-how for a well-educated team of cultural leaders and managers. Lublin was to be a city characterised by a good lifestyle, designed on a "human scale", giving residents a sense of belonging to a community of citizens. It was also be a "seeing city", a place where people remember the past, but also find a place for themselves without complexes in the present.

Łódź's main expectation was a change in image: from a post-industrial city to one of creative industries, with a particular emphasis on design, fashion, comics and film. The second anticipated outcome of the ECOC was that Łódź would be seen as a dynamic city with citizens engaged in culture and offering a high-quality, interdisciplinary range of culture. A further, very important result of being awarded the title would be an evolution in politicians' and decision makers' way of thinking about culture, going hand in hand with implementation of the modern premises of cultural policy and increased funds allocated to culture. The city aimed to counteract the dramatic process of depopulation by creating new workplaces as a consequence of development and construction of cultural institutions as well as the comprehensive revitalisation of the city. Łódź's general policy was thus characterised by good management. The city envisaged transferring the best practices from business to culture – in terms of administration, budget planning and evaluation. The intention was to create a brand of Łódź cultural managers, known for their success in preparing European-level festivals, attracting international visitors, nurturing competent domestic audiences and bringing top-ranking artists to the city.

The **Poznań** "storm" was supposed to guide the city's residents onto a new path of development based upon innovation, creativity and knowledge. The idea was to set up institutions and laboratories whose tasks and functions would extend beyond the short-term objective of ECOC 2016 to serve the city for many years, transforming it fundamentally. These included the "Konwersatorium" think tank, the Wielkopolska Creative Industry Chamber, the Microgrants system, school cultural coordinators and Inkub/Art, a typical business incubator working with and supporting the Chamber. Poznań also planned alterations to its urban planning. Konwersatorium operated in the form of thematic workshops, with the objective of developing solutions for city cultural policy and placing an emphasis on building Poznań's social capital. The Wielkopolska Creative Industry Chamber was supposed to bring together the major regional enterprises straddling industries and culture to develop good practices providing a model example for other communities and cities. The idea of Inkub/Art was to give young entrepreneurs working in culture a good start and to act as a kind of business school applying economic knowledge to culture. The new Poznań was supposed to be characterised by efficient use of the green spaces that comprise 27 percent of the city's area, revitalisation of the Old Town (including tower blocks), and urban transport and road infrastructure.

The long-term effects of the ECOC 2016 application envisaged by **Szczecin** were empowerment of residents, a radical improvement in access to culture, and greater significance of cultural and creative enterprises. Among Szczecin's main objectives was to encourage residents to participate in creating its cultural policy and setting out plans for the future, as well as to take active part in producing the ECOC programme and setting the city's strategic objectives and guidelines for culture. For the first time in Poland, they planned to test deliberative democracy and a participatory procedure for determining a city's cultural policy. Szczecin expected this means of budgetary planning to become the model for many Polish cities. In terms of access to culture, the city hoped to rejuvenate its districts and to strengthen creative enterprises on a local scale, which would contribute to dynamising the entire border region. Growth of small cultural businesses was expected to lead to increased competencies and administrative skills, bolstering Szczecin's role in the Common Cultural Space. Access to culture would be assured by reducing architectural barriers and creating modern accessibility in newly established cultural institutions. The organisers planned to create a culture cluster around Szczecin, bringing together companies from various sectors. A very important project was the so-called "Szczecin Charter", an international document proposing regulation and standardisation of the principles for dealing with material cultural heritage in cities in which population exchange has occurred.

Wrocław forecasted the outcome of the ECOC in the context of the city and the Lower Silesian voivodeship. In general, the team expected an increase in the level of social trust and residents' quality of life. Regarding Wrocław itself, they anticipated a continuation of their adopted line of uniting the city's residents with its difficult history and integration with a split identity. The main focus was on preserving the continuity of the culture of the Eastern borderlands with German influences, preserving the multicultural character of the capital of Lower Silesia. The ECOC's strategies of long-term effects provided a good fit to the earlier strategies for Wrocław and the voivodeship's cultural development. The city's name was played with to coin the phrase "Vrots-love", concentrating on the affinity its residents had with their home city. In the Lower Silesia region as a whole, comprehensive revalorisation and adaptation of built heritage was planned, along with work focusing on collaboration between cultural organisations and institutions and residents. Wrocław saw the organisation of large events (such as the European football championship in 2012) as an impetus stimulating its internal integration. This idea led the city to bid for other prestigious events whose logistics involve international promotion and brand creation.

Bibliography

Books and articles:

1. Augustyn A., 2012, *Polityka miejska w Polsce w świetle polityki spójności UE na lata 2014–2020*, "Problemy Rozwoju Miast", 9/2, pp. 7–15.
2. Bachtin M., 1982, *Problemy literatury i estetyki*, PWN, Warsaw.
3. Bagdadi S., 2003, *Museums and Theatre Networks in Italy: Determinants and Typology*, "International Journal of Arts Management", vol. 6, no 1, pp. 19–29.
4. Barber B., 2013, *If Mayors Ruled the World: Dysfunctional Nations, Rising Cities* Yale University Press, New Haven.
5. Bartlett R., 1994, *The Making of Europe: Conquest, Colonization and Cultural Change*, Princeton University Press, Princeton.
6. Bauer, M.W., Knill, CH., Pitschel, D., 2007, "Differential Europeanization in Eastern Europe: the Impact of Diverse EU Regulatory Governance Patterns", in: *Journal of European Integration*, vol. 29, no. 4, pp. 405–423.
7. Bauman Z., 1997, *Wśród nas, nieznajomych – czyli o obcych w (po) nowoczesnym mieście*, in: Zeidler-Janiszewska A. (ed.), *Pisanie miasta Czytanie miasta*, Series: Studia Kulturoznawcze, vol. 9, Poznan.
8. Bauman, Z., 2008, *The Art of Life*, Polity Press, Cambridge-Malden.
9. Benjamin W., 2005, *Pasaże*, Wydawnictwo Literackie, Krakow.
10. Beucker N., 2012, *Budowanie tożsamości miasta poprzez zastosowanie metod projektowych opartych na empatii*, in: Sluzer J. (eds.), *Stadtheimaten. Miejskie ojczyzny. Niemiecko – polskie punkty widzenia*, Jovis Dsikurs, Berlin.
11. Billert A., 2012, *Kultura i rozwój społeczny i przestrzenny miasta. Doświadczenia niemieckie*, in: Szultka S., Zbieranek P. (eds.), *Kultura – Polityka – Rozwój, Kultura-polityka-rozwój. O kulturze jako „dźwigni" rozwoju społecznego polskich metropolii i regionów*, Instytut Badań nad Gospodarką Rynkową, Gdansk.
12. Błaszczyk M., 2015, *Zanim kurtyna pójdzie w górę. Reprodukcja miejskiego spektaklu w kontekście Europejskiej Stolicy Kultury Wrocław 2016*, in: Błaszczyk M., Pluta J., (eds.), *Uczestnicy. Konsumenci. Mieszkańcy. Wrocławianie i ich miasto w oglądzie socjologicznym*, Wydawnictwo Naukowe Scholar, Warsaw.
13. Bogucka M., Samsonowicz H., 1986, *Dzieje miast i mieszczaństwa w Polsce przedrozbiorowej*, Ossolineum, Wroclaw–Warsaw–Krakow–Gdansk–Lodz.

14. Boix R., Rausell P. i Abeledo R., 2017, *The Calatrava model: reflections on resilience and urban plasticity*, "European Planning Studies", 25:1, pp. 29–47.

15. Borowiecki R., (ed.), 2004, *Perspektyw rozwoju sektora kultury w Polsce*, Oficyna ekonomiczna, Krakow.

16. Börzel, T.A., Risse T., 2000, "When Europe Hits Home: Europeanization and Domestic Change", *European Integration Online Papers* (EIoP), vol. 4, no. 15, pp. 1–20.

17. Bourdieu P., 1984, *Distinction: A Social Critique of the Judgement of Taste*, trans. Nice R., Harvard University Press, Cambridge-Malden.

18. Burgoński, P., 2012, "Europeizacja polskiej polityki równościowej i antydyskryminacyjnej", *Przegląd Europejski*, no. 2, pp. 145–167.

19. Buras, P., Pomorska K., 2008, "Europeizacja – nowe podejście analityczne w studiach nad polityka zagraniczną", *Stosunki Międzynarodowe*, no. 3–4, pp. 31–49.

20. Burszta W.J., Majewski, P., 2010, "Tożsamość kulturowa", *Kultura miejska w Polsce z perspektywy interdyscyplinarnych badań jakościowych*, Narodowe Centrum Kultury, Warsaw, pp. 19–44.

21. Caillois R., 2008, *Siła powieści*, trans. Swoboda T., Wydawnictwo UG, Gdansk.

22. Celiński A., 2013, *Miejskie polityki kulturalne*, Raport z badań, ResPublica Nowa, Warsaw.

23. Cerro Santamaría G. del, 2007, *Bilbao. Basque Pathways to Globalization*, Emerald Group Publishing, Amsterdam.

24. Chałasiński J., 1997, *Przeszłość i przyszłość inteligencji polskiej*, Świat Książki, Warsaw.

25. Currid E., 2007, *The Warhol Economy. How Fashion, Art, and Music Drive New York City*, Princeton University Press, Princeton/Oxford.

26. Czerwiński M., 1975, *Życie po miejsku*, Państwowy Instytut Wydawniczy, Warsaw.

27. Damrosz J., 1998, *Kultura polska w nowej sytuacji historycznej*, IK, Warsaw.

28. Davies N., 2005, *God's Playground. A History of Poland*, vol. 1, Oxford University Press, Oxford.

29. Fatyga B., 2014, *Wartości jako generatory żywej kultury*, Drozdowski R., Fatyga B., Filiciak M., Krajewski M., Szlendak T. (eds.) *Praktyki kulturalne Polaków*, Wydawnictwo Naukowe UMK, Torun.

30. Featherstone, K. Radaelli, C.M., 2003, *The Politics of Europeanisation*, Oxford University Press, Oxford.

31. Fiternicka-Gorzko M., Gorzko M., Czubara T., 2010, *Co z tą kulturą? Raport z badania eksploracyjnego stanu kultury w Szczecinie*, Wyd. Szczecin 2016, Szczecin.

32. Fiuk P., 2008, *Filharmonia w Szczecinie*, "Przestrzeń i Forma", no 10, p. 331.

33. Eisenstadt S., 2009, *Utopia i nowoczesność. Porównawcza analiza cywilizacji*, Oficyna Naukowa, Warsaw.

34. Fischer R. (ed.), 1997, *Arts Networking in Europe*, The Arts Council of England, London.

35. Featherstone K., Radaelli C. (eds.), 2003, *The Politics of Europeanisation*, Oxford University Press, Oxford.

36. Filar P., Kubicki P., 2012, *Podsumowanie*, in: Filar P., Kubicki P. (eds.), *Miasto w działaniu*, Instytut Obywatelski, Warsaw.

37. Florida R. 2002, *The Rise of the Creative Class*, Basic Books, New York.

38. Florida R., 2005, *Cities and the Creative Class,*, Routledge, New York/ London.

39. Foucault M., 1972, *The Archaeology of Knowledge*, trans. Sheridan A. M., Pantheon Books, New York.

40. Fukuyama F., 1992, *The End of History and the Last Man*, Avon Books, New York.

41. Gądecki J., Kubicki P., 2014, *Polityki miejskie*, "Politeja", no 1, pp. 135–156.

42. Gierat-Bieroń B., 2009, *Europejskie Miasto Kultury/Europejska Stolica Kultury 1985–2008*, Narodowe Centrum Kultury, Instytut Dziedzictwa, Krakow.

43. Gierat-Bieroń B., 2015, *Kierunki rozwoju polityki kulturalnej w Polsce po 1989 r. Koncepcje ministerialne (I)*, "Zarządzanie w kulturze", 16:3, pp. 205–221.

44. Gierat-Bieroń B., 2016, *Kierunki rozwoju polityki kulturalnej w Polsce po 1989 r. Koncepcje ministerialne (II)*, "Zarządzanie w kulturze", 17:2, pp. 91–107.

45. Gierat-Bieroń B., Galent M., 2005, *Wielka Brytania*, in: Gierat-Bieroń B., Kowalski K. (eds.), *Europejskie modele polityki kulturalnej*, Małopolska Szkoła Administracji Publicznej AEK, Instytut Europeistyki UJ, Krakow.

46. Golka M., 1989, *Transformacja systemowa a kultura w Polsce*, IK, Warsaw.

47. Gudrun P., 1999, *Networking culture. The role of European cultural networks*. Council of Europe Publishing, Strasburg.

48. Hannerz U., 1996, *Transnational Connections: Culture, People, Places*, Routledge, London.

49. Hilber M. L., Datko G., 2012, *Jak sprzedaje się duszę miasta*, in: Sluzer J. (ed.), *Stadtheimaten. Miejskie ojczyzny. Niemiecko – polskie punkty widzenia*, Jovis Dsikurs, Berlin.

50. Hausner J., 2013, *Kultura i polityka rozwoju*, Hausner J., Karwińska A., Purchla J. (eds.), *Kultura a rozwój*, Narodowe Centrum Kultury, Warsaw.

51. Hausner J., Karwińska J. A., Purchla J., 2013, *Kultura a rozwój*, Narodowe Centrum Kultury, Warsaw.

52. Ilczuk D., Misiag W., 2003, *Finansowanie i organizacja kultury w gospodarce rynkowej*, Instytut Badań nad Gospodarką Rynkową, Gdansk.

53. Jałowiecki B., Szczepański M., 2002, *Miasto i przestrzeń w perspektywie socjologicznej*, Wydawnictwo Naukowe Scholar, Warsaw.

54. Jedlicki J., 2002, *Jakiej cywilizacji Polacy potrzebują. Studia z dziejów idei i wyobraźni XIX wieku*, W.A.B., Warsaw.

55. Jurkiewicz-Eckert D., 2015, *Od Traktatu o Unii Europejskiej do Europejskiej Agendy dla Kultury – narodzony i rozwój polityki kulturalnej UE*, "Studia Europejskie", no 1 (73), pp. 65–89.

56. Kavaratzis M., Ashworth G., 2015, *Hijacking Culture: The Disconnection Between Place Culture and Place Brands*, "The Town Planning Review", vol. 86, no. 2, pp. 155–176.

57. Klaić, D., 2011, *Mobilność wyobraźni, Międzynarodowa współpraca kulturalna. Przewodnik*, NINA, Warsaw.

58. Kłosowski W., 2012, *Kultura jako czynnik rozwoju społecznego a polityki kulturalne polskich metropolii*, in: Szultka S., Zbieranek P. (eds.), *Kultura – polityka – rozwój. O kulturze jako „dźwigni" rozwoju społecznego polskich metropolii i regionów*, Instytut Badań nad Gospodarką Rynkowa, Gdansk.

59. Koolhaas R., 1994, *Delirious New York*, The Monacelli Press, New York.

60. Kostyrko T., Czerwiński M. (eds.), 1999, *Kultura polska w dekadzie przemian*, IK, Warsaw.

61. Kowalski K., 2013, *O istocie dziedzictwa europejskiego – rozważania*, Międzynarodowe Centrum Kultury, Krakow.

62. Kozak M., 2009, *Metropolia jako produkt turystyczny*, in: Jałowiecki B. (ed.), *Czy metropolia jest miastem*, Wydawnictwo Naukowe Scholar, Warsaw.

63. Krajewski M., 2014, *Kompetencje kulturalne Polaków*, in: Drozdowski R., Fatyga B., Filiciak M., Krajewski M., Szlendak T. (eds.), *Praktyki kulturalne Polaków*, Wydawnictwo Naukowe UMK, Torun.

64. Kubicki P., 2016, *Wynajdywanie miejskości. Polska kwestia miejska z perspektywy długiego trwania*, NOMOS, Krakow.

65. Kubicki P., 2012, *Efekt ESK,* "Kultura Enter. Miesięcznik wymiany idei", no 43.

66. Kubicki P., 2012, *Pomiędzy pamięcią a historią. Polskie miasta wobec wielokulturowego dziedzictwa,* "Pogranicze. Studia Społeczne" vol. XX, pp. 53–66.

67. Kubicki P., 2011, *Nowi mieszczanie – nowi aktorzy na miejskiej scenie,* "Przegląd Socjologiczny", vol. LX/2–3, pp. 203–227.

68. Kubicki P., 2010, *Miasto w sieci znaczeń. Kraków i jego tożsamości,* Księgarnia Akademicka, Krakow.

69. Kubicki P., 2010 *Nowi mieszczanie – nowa generacja. Wrocław – miasto odzyskane.* Zając J., (ed.), *Pokolenie – kategoria historyczna czy współczesna? Obraz przemian pokoleniowych w sztuce i społeczeństwie XX i XXI wieku,* Księgarnia Akademicka, Krakow.

70. Landry Ch., 2008, *The Creative City. A Tool Kit for Urban Innovators,* Routledge, London.

71. Landry Ch., 2006, *The Art of City-Making,* Sterling VA, London.

72. Luhmann, N., 1996, Social Systems, Stanford University Press, Stanford.

73. Leduff Ch., 2013, *Detroit: An American Autopsy,* Penguin, New York.

74. Leder A., 2014, *Prześniona rewolucja. Ćwiczenia z logiki historycznej,* Wydawnictwo Krytyki Politycznej, Warsaw.

75. Lewicka M., 2012, *Psychologia miejsca,* Wydawnictwo Naukowe Scholar, Warsaw.

76. Lewicki G., 2016 (ed.), *Miasta w nowym średniowieczu,* Series: Strategia miasta dla przyszłości, Biuro Festiwalowe IMPART 2016, Wroclaw.

77. Luhmann N., 1996, *Social Systems,* Stanford University Press, Stanford.

78. Mach Z., 1998, *Niechciane miasta. Migracja i tożsamość społeczna,* Universitas, Krakow.

79. Maffesoli M., 1996, *The Time of the Tribes. The Decline of Individualism in Mass Society,* trans. Smith D, Sage, London.

80. Majer A., 2014, *Odrodzenie miast,* Wydawnictwo Naukowe Scholar and Wydawnictwo Uniwersytetu Łódzkiego, Lodz-Warsaw.

81. Majer A., 2010, *Socjologia i przestrzeń miejska,* Wydawnictwo Naukowe PWN, Warsaw.

82. Nowak S., 1979, *System wartości społeczeństwa polskiego,* "Studia Socjologiczne", no 4, pp. 155–173.

83. Niedźwiedzki D., Kubicki P. (eds.), 2015, *Dylematy i kontrowersje wokół integracji europejskiej,* "Politeja", no 33.

84. Olsen J. P., 2002, *The Many Faces of Europeanization*, "Journal of Common Market Studies", no 40 (5), pp. 921–952.

85. Orzechowska-Wacławska J., 2015, *Rewitalizacja po baskijsku. Kulturowy kod „efektu Guggenheima"*, "Folia Sociologica. Acta Universitatis Lodziensis", no 54, pp. 109–125.

86. Orzechowska-Wacławska J., 2014, *Baskowie. Powstawanie współczesnego narodu*, Jagiellonian University Press, Krakow.

87. Orzechowska-Wacławska J., 2014, *Baskijskie polityki miejskie: konstruowanie nowej symboliki i nowego oblicza Bilbao*, "Politeja", no 27, pp. 209–227.

88. Plebańczyk K., 2002, *Prawne aspekty działalności kulturalnej w latach 90. – projekty reform ustrojowych*, "Zarządzanie w kulturze", vol, 3, pp. 37–45.

89. Pluta J., Żuk P. (eds.), 2006, *My wrocławianie. Społeczna przestrzeń miasta*, Wydawnictwo Dolnośląskie, Wroclaw.

90. Purchla J., 2013, *Dziedzictwo kulturowe*, in: Hausner J., Karwińska A., Purchla J. (eds.), *Kultura a rozwój*, Narodowe Centrum Kultury, Warsaw.

91. Purchla J., Rottermund A., 1999, *Projekt reformy ustroju publicznych instytucji kultury w Polsce*, "Rocznik Międzynarodowego Centrum Kultury", no 8, pp. 32–39.

92. Putnam R., 1993, *Making Democracy Work: Civic Traditions in Modern Italy*, Princeton University Press, Princeton.

93. Rewers E., 2005, *Post-polis. Wstęp do filozofii Ponowoczesnego miasta*, Universitas, Krakow.

94. Rewers E., 2010, *Wprowadzenie*, in: W. Rewers (ed.) *Miasto w sztuce – sztuka miasta*, Universitas, Krakow.

95. Rius-Ulldemolins J., Hernàndez G.-M., Torres M. i F., 2016, *Urban Development and Cultural Policy "White Elephants": Barcelona and Valencia*, "European Planning Studies", 24:1, pp 61–75.

96. Rybicka E., 2003, *Modernizowanie miasta. Zarys problematyki urbanistycznej w nowoczesnej literaturze polskiej*, Universitas, Krakow.

97. Rykwert J., 2013, *Pokusa miejsca. Przeszłość i przyszłość miast*, Międzynarodowe Centrum Kultury, Krakow.

98. Sassen S., 1991, *The Global City*, Princeton University Press, Princeton/ Oxford.

99. Sassen S., 1999, *Globalization and Its Discontents. Essays on the New Mobility of People and Money*, The New Press, New York.

100. Schuster J.M., 2007, *Informacja w polityce kulturalnej Infrastruktura informacyjna i badawcza*, Jagiellonian University Press, Krakow.

101. Senge, P.S. 1990, *The Fifth Discipline. The Art and Practice of the Learning Organization*, Century, London.

102. Sitek W., 1997, *Wrocławianie wobec wielkiej powodzi. Wspólnota i zagrożenie. Socjologiczny przyczynek do analizy krótkotrwałej wspólnoty*, Wydawnictwo Uniwersytetu Wrocławskiego, Wroclaw.

103. Sulzer J, 2012, *Miejskie ojczyzny – Ojczyzna Tożsamość Pamięć*, in: Sluzer J. (ed.), *Stadtheimaten. Miejskie ojczyzny. Niemiecko – polskie punkty widzenia*, Jovis Dsikurs, Berlin.

104. Sternal M., 2012, *Sieci współpracy kulturalnej – czym są, jak powstają i jak działają?*, in: *Pod lupą: Europejskie sieci współpracy kulturalnej w praktyce*, Punkt Kontaktowy ds. kultury, Instytut Adama Mickiewicza, Warsaw.

105. Styczyńska, N., 2016, "Does Europe Matter at All? European Issues in the Discourse of Polish Political Parties", in Gilles Rouet, Radovan Gura (eds), Les citoyens et l'intégration européenne, L'Harmattan, Paris.

106. Sweet, A.S. Sandholtz, W., 1998, *European Integration and Supranational Governance*, Oxford University Press, Oxford.

107. Szalewska K., 2012, *Pejzaż tekstowy. Czytanie miasta jako forma doświadczenia przeszłości we współczesnym eseju polskim*, Universitas, Krakow.

108. Szarota T., 1969, *Osadnictwo miejskie na Dolnym Śląsku w latach 1945– 1948*, Zakład Narodowy im. Ossolińskich, Wrocław-Warsaw- Krakow.

109. Szlendak T., 2014, *Formy aktywności kulturalnej*, in: Drozdowski R., Fatyga B., Filiciak M., Krajewski M., Szlendak T. (eds.), *Praktyki kulturalne Polaków*, Wydawnictwo Naukowe UMK, Torun.

110. Szultka S., P. Zbieranek, 2012, *Kultura-polityka-rozwój. O kulturze jako „dźwigni" rozwoju społecznego polskich metropolii i regionów*, Instytut Badań nad Gospodarką Rynkową, Gdansk.

111. Sztompka P. 2006, *Socjologia zmian społecznych*, Wyd. Znak, Krakow.

112. Sztompka P., 2000, *Trauma wielkiej zmiany. Społeczne skutki transformacji*, Instytut Studiów Politycznych PAN, Warsaw.

113. Joanna Szulborska-Łukaszewicz, J., 2009, *Polityka kulturalna w Krakowie*, Attyka, Krakow.

114. Touraine A., 2009, *Thinking Differently*, Polity Press, Cambridge–Malden.

115. Tomaszewski W., Riedel R., *Europeizacja w wymiarze tożsamościowym*, in: Pacześniak A., Riedel R. (eds.), 2014, *Europeizacja, mechanizmy, wymiary, efekty*, Wyd. Adam Marszałek, Torun.

116. Börzel T.A., 2009, *Networks in EU Multi-Level Governance: Concepts and Contributions*, "Journal of Public Policy", no. 2, pp. 135–151.

117. Tuan Yi- Fu, 1987, *Space and Place,* University of Minnesota Press, Minnesota.

118. Turowski J., 1988, *Model urbanizacji a problemy rozwoju małych miast,* "Studia Socjologiczne", no 3, pp. 200–211.

119. Turner V., 1974, *Dramas, Fields, and Metaphors: Symbolic Action in Human Society,* Cornell University Press, Ithaca–London.

120. Taylor Ch., 1989, *Sources of the Self: The Making of the Modern Identity,* Harvard University Press, Cambridge-Malden.

121. Urry J., 1990, *The Tourist Gaze,* Sage, London.

122. Krzysztof Wach, 2011, "Wymiary europeizacji i jej kontekst", in *Zeszyty Naukowe Uniwersytetu Ekonomicznego w Krakowie,* no. 852, pp. 29–43.

123. Wasilewski J., 2011, *Społeczeństwo polskie, społeczeństwo chłopskie,* "Studia Socjologiczne", no 3, pp. 353–368.

124. Wiktorska-Święcka A., 2014, *Europeizacja wartości demokratycznych w procesie kształtowania europejskiej tożsamości,* Paceśniak A., Riedel R. (eds.), *Europeizacja. Mechanizmy, wymiary, efekty,* Wyd. Adam Marszałek, Torun.

125. Waluch K., 2012, *Sieci współpracy kulturalnej w Europie,* Difin, Warsaw.

126. Zabaleta I., 1999, *The Basques in the International Press: Coverage by the New York Times (1950–1996),* Douglass W. A. (et al. eds.) *Basque Politics and Nationalism on the Eve of the Millennium,* University de Nevada Press, Reno.

127. Zukin S., 1995, *The Cultures of Cities,* Blackwell, Oxford.

Online sources:

1. Beltran A., *Calatrava ha cobrado más de 94 millones por la Ciudad de las Artes y las Ciencias,* "El País", http://ccaa.elpais.com/ccaa/2012/05/03/valencia/1336074084_564574.html (last accessed: Dec 5, 2019).

2. Deru J.P., *Powtórka z kultury. Sieci współpracy kulturalnej w Europie,* http://wiadomosci.ngo.pl/wiadomosc/672703.html (last accessed: Dec.10, 2019).

4. Deru J.P., *Development of Cultural Networks in Europe: Challenges and Trends,* http://www.culturecongress.eu/en/ngo/ngo_bestpractice_deru (last accessed: June 2019).

5. European Union, Regional Policy, *Cities of Tomorrow – Challenges, Visions, Ways Forward* (2011), https://ec.europa.eu/regional_policy/en/information/publications/reports/2011/cities-of-tomorrow-challenges-visions-ways-forward (last accessed: Dec 5, 2019).

6. Govan F.. *Valencia: the ghost city that's become a symbol of Spain's spending woes*, "The Telegraph", http://www.telegraph.co.uk/finance/financialcrisis/9573568/Valencia-the-ghost-city-thats-become-a-symbol-of-Spains-spending-woes.html (last accessed: Dec 5, 2019).

7. Interview with Robert Konieczny conducted by Monika Stelmach, *Na uroczystość włożyłem rolki*, http://www.dwutygodnik.com/artykul/6916-na-uroczystosc-wlozylem-rolki.html (last accessed: Dec 5, 2019).

8. *Leipzig Charter on Sustainable European Cities* 3, https://ec.europa.eu/regional_policy/archive/themes/urban/leipzig_charter.pdf (last accessed: Dec 5, 2019).

9. Tremlett G., *Architect Santiago Calatrava accused of 'bleeding Valencia dry'*, "The Guardian", https://www.theguardian.com/world/2012/may/08/architect-santiago-calatrava-valencia (last accessed: Dec 5, 2019)

10. VLC Valencia, *Estadísticas de turismo'09* and *Estadísticas de turismo 2015*; http://www.visitvalencia.com/es/Datos/IdiomaNeutral/PDF/estadisticas09.pdf and http://www.visitvalencia.com/es/estadisticas-turismo-valencia/#p=1 (last accessed: Dec 5, 2019)

11. http://katowice.wyborcza.pl/katowice/1,35063,19773082,katowice-niespotykana-dotad-frekwencja-w-muzeum-slaskim-i-nospr.html (last accessed Jan 31, 2017) and http://www.e-teatr.pl/pl/artykuly/219338,druk.html (last accessed: Dec 5, 2019)

12. http://radioszczecin.pl/4,117886,nowa-filharmonia-bije-rekordy (last accessed: Dec 5, 2019).

13. http://filharmonia.szczecin.pl/aktualnosci/202-Rekordowy_rok_Filharmonii (last accessed: Dec 5, 2019).

14. http://www.archsarp.pl/6545/muzeum-i-plac-centrum-dialogu-przelomy-w-szczecinie (last accessed: Dec 5, 2019).

15. http://www.radiowroclaw.pl/articles/view/56305/Narodowe-Forum-Muzyki-Podsumowanie-sezonu-2015-16 (last accessed: Dec 5, 2019).

Reports and EU Documents:

Report from the Commission to the European Parliament, the Council, the European Economic and Social Committee of the Regions. Post evaluation of the 2013 European Capitals of Culture (Košice and Marseille-Provence), Brussels, 2.3.2015 COM(2015) 74 final.

Ex-post evaluation of the 2013 European Capitals of Culture, 2014, Final Report for the European Commission DG Education and Culture, ECORYS, EU.

An international framework of good practice in research and delivery of the European Capital of Culture programme, 2013. Key recommendations from the European Capitals of Culture Policy Group (2009–2010), The European Capital of Culture Policy Group, Marseille Provence.

Garcia B., Cox T., 2013, European Capitals of Culture, Success Strategies and Long-time effects. Study, Policy Department. Structural and Cohesion Policies, European Union.

McCoshan A., Rampton J., Mozuraityte N., McAteer N., 2010, Ex-Post Evaluation of 2009 European Capital of Culture. Final Report to DG Education and Culture of the European Commission in the context of the Framework Contract for Evaluation Related Services and Support for Impact Assessment EAC/03/06, ECOTES, Birmingham.

Ex-post evaluation 2010. European Capitals of Culture, 2011, Final Report for the European Commission. DG Education and Culture, ECORYS, UE.

European Capitals of Culture: the road to success, from 1985 to 2010, 2009, European Commission, 2010, Office for Official Publications of the European Communities, Luxemburg.

European Commission, Communication on a European Agenda for Culture in a Globalizing World, Brussels, 10 May 2007, COM (2007), 242 final version.

Council conclusions of 24 May 2007 on the contribution of the cultural and creative sectors to the achievement of the Lisbon objectives, OJ C 311, 21.12.2007, p. 7–9.

Decision no 1622/2006/EC of the European Parliament and of the Council of 24 October 2006establishing a Community action for the European Capital of Culture event for the years 2007 to 2019. OJ L304, 1/11/2006.

Forum of European Networks of Cultural Centres, 1998, Council of Europe, Strasbourg.

Resolution of the Council and the Ministers of Culture Meeting within the Council of 14 November 1991 on European cultural networks, OJ C 314, 5.12.1991.

Reports and Applications:

1. *Coalition of the Cities*. Projekt współpracy w ramach program Europejskiej Stolicy Kultury 2016 Wrocław, n.d. (brochure).

2. *European Cities and Capitals of Culture*, 2004, Study prepared for European Commission, Part I, Part II, Pamler/RAE, Brussels.

3. *European Capital of Culture*, 2010, Essen for the Rühr, Book two, program ECOC.

4. *European Capital of Culture Lublin 2016*, 2011, Final Application form.

5. Gdańsk Application Form for title European Capital of Culture 2016, 2010, Gdansk.

6. *Impact 08: The Liverpool model. 2009*. European Capital of Culture Research Programme, Report by B. Garcia, R. Melville, T. Cox, University of Liverpool, Liverpool.

7. *Istambul 2010. European Capital of Culture*, 2010, Program, Istambuł.

8. *Lille 2004. Capitale Européenn de la Culture*. Program.

9. *Linz Welcome, Linz 2009. European Capital of Culture*, 2009, Program.

10. *Łódź. (Re) evolution of Imagination. European Capital of Culture 2016.* Application Form, Łódź.

11. Meyershough, J., *Monitoring Glasgow 1990*, 1991, Prepared by Glasgow City Council, Strathclyde Regional Council, Scottish Enterprise, Glasgow (pdf).

12. '*Poznań Cultural Storme*', European Capital of Culture 2016. Candidate, Poznan.

13. Spaces for Beauty, Wrocław Application form for a title of European Capital of Culture, 2011, Wrocław.

14. *Sibiu. European Capital of Culture 2007*, Program.

15. *Szczecin 2016. European Capital of Culture. Candidate*. 2010, Szczecin.

Internet sources:

http://filharmonia.szczecin.pl

http://www.nospr.org.pl

http://www.nfm.wroclaw.pl

http://www.bryla.pl

http://culture.pl

http://bilbao.bibel.pl/

http://www.nck.pl

Studies in European Integration, State and Society

Edited by Magdalena Góra, Zdzisław Mach and Katarzyna Zielińska

www.peterlang.com